American Book Company
The Standards Experts

MASTERING THE COMMON CORE
GRADE 7
ENGLISH LANGUAGE ARTS

Author: Zuzana Urbanek

Project Coordinator: Zuzana Urbanek

Reviewer: Ginger Howe

Executive Editor: Dr. Frank Pintozzi

American Book Company
PO Box 2638
Woodstock, GA 30188-1383
Toll Free: 1 (888) 264-5877   Phone: (770) 928-2834
Toll Free Fax: 1 (866) 827-3240
Website: www.americanbookcompany.com

ACKNOWLEDGEMENTS

The authors would like to gratefully acknowledge the technical contributions of Marsha Torrens and Becky Wright and the proofreading assistance of Susan Barrows.

We also wish to thank Mary Stoddard for her expertise in developing many of the graphics for this book.

© 2012 American Book Company
PO Box 2638
Woodstock, GA 30188-1318

ALL RIGHTS RESERVED

The text of this publication, or any part thereof, may not be reproduced or transmitted in any form or by any means, electronic or mechanical, including photocopying, recording, storage in an information retrieval system, or otherwise, without the prior written permission of the publisher.

Printed in the United States of America

01/12

Table of Contents

Copyright© American Book Company. DO NOT DUPLICATE. 1-888-264-5877.

Copyright © American Book Company. DO NOT DUPLICATE. 1-888-264-5877.

Copyright © American Book Company. DO NOT DUPLICATE. 1-888-264-5877.

Copyright© American Book Company. DO NOT DUPLICATE. 1-888-264-5877.

Preface

Mastering the Common Core in Grade 7 English Language Arts will help students who are learning or reviewing the Common Core State Standards. The materials in this book are based on the Common Core standards and the model content frameworks as published by the Partnership for Assessment of Readiness for College and Careers (PARCC) consortium.

This book contains several sections:

1) General information about the book

2) A literature unit (chapters 2 through 4) with a Literature Review practice chapter

3) An informational texts unit (chapters 5 and 6) with an Informational Texts Review practice chapter

4) Six additional chapters that review the concepts and skills and provide further practice

Standards are posted at the beginning of each chapter and at the beginning of each practice.

Teachers: See the "Answer Key and Teacher Resources for *Mastering the Common Core in Grade 7 English Language Arts*" to read tips for using this book and access additional material for classroom and one-on-one use.

We welcome comments and suggestions about the book. Please contact the authors at

American Book Company
PO Box 2638
Woodstock, GA 30188-1383

Toll Free: 1 (888) 264-5877
Phone: (770) 928-2834
Fax: (770) 928-7483
Website: www.americanbookcompany.com

Copyright © American Book Company. DO NOT DUPLICATE. 1-888-264-5877.

About the Author and Project Coordinator:

Zuzana Urbanek serves as ELA Curriculum Coordinator for American Book Company. She is a professional writer and editor with over twenty-five years of experience in education, business, and publishing. She has taught a variety of English courses at the college level and also has taught English as a foreign language abroad. Her master's degree is from Arizona State University.

About the Reviewer:

Ginger Howe has over twenty years of experience teaching middle school language arts and high school English. She has a bachelor's degree in Language Arts Education and a master's degree in Human Relations from the University of Oklahoma. She currently serves as the Secondary Language Arts and Reading Coordinator for Moore Public Schools in Oklahoma.

About the Executive Editor:

Dr. Frank J. Pintozzi is a former Professor of Education at Kennesaw State University. For over twenty-eight years, he has taught English and reading at the high school and college levels as well as in teacher preparation courses in language arts and social studies. In addition to writing and editing state standard-specific texts for high school exit and end-of-course exams, he has edited and written several college textbooks.

Copyright © American Book Company. DO NOT DUPLICATE. 1-888-264-5877.

Chapter 1
How to Write Constructed Responses

Welcome to *Mastering the Common Core in Grade 7 English Language Arts*! This book will help you review skills that will help you get ready for Common Core testing.

As you read this book, you will see practices with questions for you to answer. This is good practice for any future tests you take. Many of the questions are multiple choice; that means you need to choose an answer from the choices given.

Some questions, however, ask you to write your own answer in a blank. Other questions ask you to write a longer text on your own paper. You will be asked to read and write about different passages, both fiction and nonfiction texts. Items emphasize the important understandings you are expected to gain from reading. You will base your written responses on the reading passage.

The instructions for what to write will let you know what is expected of you. Be sure to read the constructed-response prompt carefully.

A **constructed response** is a paragraph or a short essay about a topic. A **prompt** is an introduction with a question you need to answer or an idea you need to address.

When you write responses for a test, trained readers will score your answers based on scoring rubrics. **Rubrics** are scales that describe different levels of performance. The trained readers follow scoring procedures that have been developed to ensure a high degree of objectivity and reliability. This chapter will help you get ready to answer those questions that ask you to write out your answers.

Copyright © American Book Company. DO NOT DUPLICATE. 1-888-264-5877.

Before we review writing a constructed response, let's take a look at the general scoring rubric for a constructed response.

	Rubric for 4-Point Scoring of Writing
4 pts	The response indicates that the student has a thorough understanding of the reading concept asked for in the task. The student has provided a response that is accurate, complete, and fulfills all the requirements of the task. Necessary support and/or examples are included, and the information is clearly text-based.
3 pts	The response indicates that the student has an understanding of the reading concept asked for in the task. The student has provided a response that is accurate and fulfills all the requirements of the task, but the required support and/or details are not complete or clearly text-based.
2 pts	The response indicates that the student has a partial understanding of the reading concept asked for in the task. The student has provided a response that includes information that is essentially correct and text-based, but the information is too general or too simplistic. Some of the support and/or examples and requirements of the task may be incomplete or omitted.
1 pt	The response indicates that the student has very limited understanding of the reading concept asked for in the task. The response is incomplete, may exhibit many flaws, and may not address all the requirements of the task.
0 pts	The response is inaccurate, confused, and/or irrelevant, or the student has failed to respond to the task.

You want to get the highest score you can when you write. Here are some ways to make sure you write the best responses.

WRITING CONSTRUCTED REPONSES

Here are some steps to keep in mind when you write short answers. These steps will help you write the best answers you can.

READ THE QUESTION CAREFULLY

First of all, read the prompt carefully. Make sure you understand what it is asking you to write about, and make sure your response is only about that topic. If you need help, ask your teacher.

WRITE CLEARLY

Answer each question clearly and completely. For example, if a question asks about why or how something happened, be sure to talk about the sequence of events as well as causes and effects. If it asks you to compare and contrast two people or events, be sure to talk about how they are alike or different.

Being clear also means that your writing must be grammatically correct. Use complete sentences, and be sure to check your spelling. Also look for and fix any other mistakes such as punctuation errors, missing words, and misplaced modifiers. If you find an error, erase it completely, or cross it out. Write what you actually mean directly above it or next to it.

Copyright © American Book Company. DO NOT DUPLICATE. 1-888-264-5877.

USE NEAT HANDWRITING

Make sure that people reading your answer can tell what it says. Write in a neat way that others can read.

Now read the following selection. Then study how a student replied to an extended-response question. Be sure your response has a beginning, a middle, and an end and that it provides an answer to the writing task with support based on the text. The sample response that follows this passage is a model response, and the test graders would likely assign the highest point value (4) to this response.

Excerpt from "The Offshore Pirate"

by F. Scott Fitzgerald

Half a dozen times they played at private dances at three thousand dollars a night, and it seemed as if these crystallized all his distaste for his mode of livelihood. They took place in clubs and houses that he couldn't have gone into in the daytime. After all, he was merely playing the role of the eternal monkey, a sort of sublimated chorus man. He was sick of the very smell of the theater, of powder and rouge and the chatter of the greenroom, and the patronizing approval of the boxes. He couldn't put his heart into it any more. The idea of a slow approach to the luxury of leisure drove him wild. He was, of course, progressing toward it, but, like a child, eating his ice cream so slowly that he couldn't taste it at all.

He wanted to have a lot of money and time and opportunity to read and play, and the sort of men and women round him that he could never have—the kind who, if they thought of him at all, would have considered him rather contemptible; in short he wanted all those things which he was beginning to lump under the general head of aristocracy, an aristocracy which it seemed almost any money could buy except money made as he was making it. He was twenty-five then, without family or education or any promise that he would succeed in a business career. He began speculating wildly, and within three weeks he had lost every cent he had saved.

Then the war came. He went to Plattsburg, and even there his profession followed him. A brigadier-general called him up to headquarters and told him he could serve his country better as a band leader—so he spent the war entertaining celebrities behind the line with a headquarters band. It was not so bad—except that when the infantry came limping back from the trenches he wanted to be one of them. The sweat and mud they wore seemed only one of those ineffable symbols of aristocracy that were forever eluding him.

Copyright © American Book Company. DO NOT DUPLICATE. 1-888-264-5877.

Chapter 1

The constructed-response question on the Common Core test might read as follows:

Writing Task

The character in this story is struggling. Find two examples of figurative language that the author uses to describe what he is going through. Explain what the examples mean, and describe how they help readers to know the character better.

What would your response be? Practice writing an essay that answers this prompt. Then look at the sample response, and study the scoring comments that follow it.

Model Student Response: 4-Point Score

   This part of "The Offshore Pirate" by F. Scott Fitzgerald is about a young man who does not like what he is doing. He looks at others and what they have, and he only sees what he doesn't have. He is jealous.

   The character wants luxury and leisure. He feels he is "progressing toward it, but, like a child, eating his ice cream so slowly that he couldn't taste it at all." This simile shows the frustration of the young man. Everyone knows or can imagine how annoying it is to not taste a treat due to eating so too slowly. Even if readers can't relate to why the man hates his work, they can still get the image and the feeling. The young man feels like a little kid who doesn't have the skills to get what he wants.

   Later in the passage, the man also wants what the soldiers have. It seems odd that he thinks their "sweat and mud they wore seemed only one of those ineffable symbols of aristocracy." But the sweat and mud they come back covered in represents what they all went through together. If you think about it what he really wants is to be a part of something and to accomplishing something.

   I think to the young man, both the ice cream example and the sweat and mud are symbols of belonging to something bigger that he feels he cannot have.

Score: 4 Points

This student read the prompt carefully and found the two requested examples of figurative language. In addition, the prompt asks how these examples allow readers to better know the main character. The student also provides an interpretation in the response to answer this part of the prompt. Notice how, in the response, the student provides the name of the story and author as well as writing out the examples of the figurative language. These are in quotation marks because they are direct quotations from the text.

Annotation (comments from scorers)

This response would receive 4 score points. It clearly responds to the prompt. Two examples of figurative language are explained (eating ice cream simile and sweat and mud symbol). The student goes on to tell how readers learn about the character from these examples (*He is jealous, The young man feels like a little kid who doesn't have the skills to get what he wants, what he*

Copyright © American Book Company. DO NOT DUPLICATE. 1-888-264-5877.

really wants is to be a part of something and to accomplishing something, and *both the ice cream example and the sweat and mud are symbols of belonging to something bigger that he feels he cannot have*). The response is well organized and coherent. Precise language and descriptions add clarity. Although there is a comma missing after *If you think about it*, there are no errors that hinder understanding.

Now read the next passage. Then study how a student replied to a constructed-response question. The sample response would likely earn three (3) points.

Loss and Gain

by Henry Wadsworth Longfellow

When I compare

What I have lost with what I have gained,

What I have missed with what attained,

Little room do I find for pride.

I am aware

How many days have been idly spent;

How like an arrow the good intent

Has fallen short or been turned aside.

But who shall dare

To measure loss and gain in this wise?

Defeat may be victory in disguise;

The lowest ebb is the turn of the tide.

The constructed-response question on the Common Core test might read as follows:

> **Writing Task**
>
> What is the narrator communicating in this poem? What conclusion does he reach in the end? Explain the meaning of the poem, using evidence from the text.

What would your response be? Practice writing an essay that answers this prompt. Then look at the sample response, and study the scoring comments that follow it.

Copyright © American Book Company. DO NOT DUPLICATE. 1-888-264-5877.

Model Student Response: 3-Point Score

> This person is sad. He is shamed of himself because he messed around when he shoud have been doing something with his life. He says "Little room do I find for pride" to show hes not proud of himself. He admits all that. But then he also says it might be for the best. Whos to say its not for the best. At the end he thinks it can turn around. Its like when people reach their lowest point so they get back up again. He has hope at the end.

Score: 3 Points

This response answers both questions in the prompt. The student supports the first answer about the narrator's message. However, the point about the narrator being sad and ashamed is supported by just one piece of evidence, which is scanty. The student then interprets the conclusion as meaning that the narrator has hope for the future. This is a reasonable interpretation, but there is nothing from the text used as evidence.

Annotation (comments from scorers)

The student's response is brief, less thorough, and less coherent than a 4-point response. More evidence from the text would ideally be used in the response. Also, there are several errors in spelling/usage (*shamed* should be *ashamed*, *shoud*), missing apostrophes (*hes*, *Whos*, *its*), and a slang construction (*Its like when*). However, the student does address and explain both what the poem means and the conclusion the narrator reaches in the end

Practice 1: Writing a Constructed Response

DIRECTIONS Both of the passages in this chapter are about characters who are unhappy with life at the moment. What idea do you think they would agree on? Compare the character in "The Offshore Pirate" to the narrator in "Loss and Gain." Decide something that the young man and the narrator would agree is true. Use evidence from the passages to support your answer.

Practice 2: Reviewing Responses of Others

DIRECTIONS Now that you have read the sample constructed responses, take a moment to notice which facts and details from the passages were used in some way when writing the responses. Use what you have learned to practice scoring the responses of others. Trade your papers with another student. For example, use the constructed responses you wrote for practice 1 in this chapter. Practice scoring each others' responses. Then discuss why you scored the responses as you did.

Copyright © American Book Company. DO NOT DUPLICATE. 1-888-264-5877.

Chapter 2
Reading Literature

This chapter covers the following seventh grade strand and standards:

Reading: Literature

Key Ideas and Details

1. Cite several pieces of textual evidence to support analysis of what the text says explicitly as well as inferences drawn from the text.

Craft and Structure

5. Analyze how a drama's or poem's form or structure (e.g., soliloquy, sonnet) contributes to its meaning.

Integration of Knowledge and Ideas

7. Compare and contrast a written story, drama, or poem to its audio, filmed, staged, or multimedia version, analyzing the effects of techniques unique to each medium (e.g., lighting, sound, color, or camera focus and angles in a film).

9. Compare and contrast a fictional portrayal of a time, place, or character and a historical account of the same period as a means of understanding how authors of fiction use or alter history.

Range of Reading and Level of Text Complexity

10. By the end of the year, read and comprehend literature, including stories, dramas, and poems, in the grades 6–8 text complexity band proficiently, with scaffolding as needed at the high end of the range.

Writing

Text Types and Purposes

1. Write arguments to support claims with clear reasons and relevant evidence.

2. Write informative/explanatory texts to examine a topic and convey ideas, concepts, and information through the selection, organization, and analysis of relevant content.

Production and Distribution of Writing

4. Produce clear and coherent writing in which the development, organization, and style are appropriate to task, purpose, and audience. (Grade-specific expectations for writing types are defined in standards 1–3 above.)

5. With some guidance and support from peers and adults, develop and strengthen writing as needed by planning, revising, editing, rewriting, or trying a new approach, focusing on how well purpose and audience have been addressed.

Research to Build and Present Knowledge

9. Draw evidence from literary or informational texts to support analysis, reflection, and research.

   a. Apply *grade 7 Reading standards* to literature (e.g., "Compare and contrast a fictional portrayal of a time, place, or character and a historical account of the same period as a means of understanding how authors of fiction use or alter history").

Speaking and Listening

Presentation of Knowledge and Ideas

4. Present claims and findings, emphasizing salient points in a focused, coherent manner with pertinent descriptions, facts, details, and examples; use appropriate eye contact, adequate volume, and clear pronunciation.

5. Include multimedia components and visual displays in presentations to clarify claims and findings and emphasize salient points.

Copyright © American Book Company. DO NOT DUPLICATE. 1-888-264-5877.

Chapter 2

In this chapter, we will explore some ideas that will help you read and understand literature. You will read about different kinds of literary works and look at how their structure affects their meaning. You will also see how to compare and contrast different kinds of works. Let's begin with a look at different types of literature.

LITERARY GENRES

There are different types of literature, which are called **genres**. A genre is a type of literature, and the works that fit into it all have a similar form. The major genres into which writing fits are nonfiction, fiction, poetry, and drama. Each of these has smaller genres under it. For example, one subgenre of fiction is science fiction. These stories all take place in the future or in outer space. Adventure stories could be either fiction or nonfiction. Here are some of the literary genres. As you study this table, notice how some subgenres might fit into more than one genre.

Literary Genres		Examples of works
Fiction is narrative writing, which means it tells a story. A writer creates fiction from the imagination. Fiction includes stories as short as one page all the way up to novels that are hundreds of pages in length.	**Example subgenres within fiction:** allegory, fable, fairy tale, fantasy, folktale, graphic novels, historical fiction, legend, mystery, myth, parody, realistic fiction, romance, satire, science fiction	"A Rose for Emily" by William Faulkner (mystery) *Invitation to the Game* by Monica Hughes (science fiction) *Greek Myths* by Geraldine McCaughrean (myth)
Nonfiction is writing that is factual. It is about real people and real events. It also includes functional texts such as directions and brochures.	**Example subgenres within nonfiction:** autobiographies, biographies, essays, historical accounts, informational articles, journals, opinion pieces, scientific explanations, speeches, technical manuals	*A Restless Spirit: The Story of Robert Frost* by Natalie S. Bober (biography) *Amistad: A Long Road to Freedom* by Walter Dean Myers (historical account)

Copyright © American Book Company. DO NOT DUPLICATE. 1-888-264-5877.

Literary Genres (continued)		Examples of works
Drama is a story (fiction or nonfiction) told through action and dialogue. It is a play that is meant to be acted out. It can be long, with many acts, or short with just one act. It can even be a skit that lasts just a few minutes. You can read a play and then go see it performed in the theater. A screenplay, which is used to make a movie, is also a form of drama. A teleplay is used to make a television show.	**Example subgenres within drama:** comedy, tragedy, farce, melodrama	*Romeo and Juliet* by William Shakespeare (tragedy) *Peggy, the Pint-Sized Pirate* by D. M. Bocaz-Larson (short comedy)
Poetry is different from prose because it is written in lines and stanzas (rather than in sentences and paragraphs using Standard English construction). It usually has rhythm, sometimes rhymes, and can convey deep emotion or vivid descriptions.	**Example subgenres within poetry:** ballad, blank verse, epic, odes, free verse, lyric, narrative, haiku, sonnet	*Paradise Lost* by John Milton (epic) "To Fanny" by John Keats (sonnet)

As you can see, there are many kinds of literature. For now, focus on the differences between the four genres (fiction, nonfiction, drama, poetry). We'll discuss a few more subgenres, as well as forms and structures of some works, later in this chapter.

EVIDENCE AND INFERENCES

You are sometimes asked to analyze what you read. *Analyze* means to examine closely. An important point to remember is to always **support your analysis with evidence**. Here is an example.

Read the following passage about the mongoose, Rikki-tikki-tavi, taken from Rudyard Kipling's *The Jungle Book*. Pay attention to character traits. Some are directly stated, and others are implied. Answer the questions that follow, and then read the explanations.

Copyright © American Book Company. DO NOT DUPLICATE. 1-888-264-5877.

It is the hardest thing in the world to frighten a mongoose, because he is eaten up from nose to tail with curiosity. The motto of all the mongoose family is "Run and find out," and Rikki-tikki was a true mongoose. He looked at the cotton wool, decided that it was not good to eat, ran all round the table, sat up and put his fur in order, scratched himself, and jumped on the small boy's shoulder.

"Don't be frightened, Teddy," said his father. "That's his way of making friends."

"Ouch! He's tickling under my chin," said Teddy.

Rikki-tikki looked down between the boy's collar and neck, snuffed at his ear, and climbed down to the floor, where he sat rubbing his nose.

"Good gracious," said Teddy's mother, "and that's a wild creature! I suppose he's so tame because we've been kind to him."

"All mongooses are like that," said her husband. "If Teddy doesn't pick him up by the tail, or try to put him in a cage, he'll run in and out of the house all day long. Let's give him something to eat."

What are three character traits that describe Rikki-tikki?

How would you answer? What evidence would you use to support your ideas? First, look at what the author tells you directly. He says a mongoose is "eaten up from nose to tail with curiosity." So, you can say Rikki is curious. You can use the author's own words as evidence to support that idea.

To figure out more, you might need to use **inference** skills. You will often need to make inferences to support your analysis of a text. An inference is an educated guess based on information given in a text, clues in the text, and previous experience and knowledge. You make inferences by "reading between the lines." When you make an inference, you are noticing relevant details and clues in a text and then combining those clues with what you already know. This allows you to figure out events in a story.

So, what can you tell about Rikki that the author doesn't tell you? Well, the author says that it is hard to frighten a mongoose. You might infer from this that Rikki is brave. The passage also says that he looks at the cotton wool and decides it is not good to eat. From this clue, you might say that he is smart. That's three traits.

Copyright © American Book Company. DO NOT DUPLICATE. 1-888-264-5877.

Activity

RL 1

Reread the excerpt from *The Jungle Book*. Think of two other inferences you can make about Rikki-tikki or about the family based on the passage. Write your inferences on the spaces provided. Then, discuss your inferences with a classmate or in a small group. What is the evidence for your inference? Is it something you found in the text or something you already knew?

Inference:

_____

Inference:

_____

HOW STRUCTURE AFFECTS MEANING

As you saw in the first section about genres, some written works share a certain **form or structure**. Understanding what genre or subgenre a text fits into can help you understand more about its meaning. In this section, you will read about two specific genres—drama and poetry—and how their structures affect meaning. First, let's review some facts about different kinds of drama and poetry.

DRAMA STRUCTURES

Drama is told in action and dialogue (conversation) between characters. Plays can be written in prose or poetry. They may be read as books, but they are intended to be acted out on the stage. Tragedies are often sad or serious, but the main thing that defines them is that the main character does not succeed in his or her goal. An example of a tragedy is *Tamburlaine the Great* by Christopher Marlowe.

Tragedies are more serious and sometimes sad. Comedies show the humor of the world and are usually funny. Drama can be in the form of skits, sketches, or plays that are one act or more. Reading drama is similar to reading fiction. The main difference is that, instead of narrative, you'll read stage directions. When reading drama, it is easy to keep up with dialogue since each line begins with the speaker's name. Try to picture yourself as the director of a movie, using the play as your script.

Copyright © American Book Company. DO NOT DUPLICATE. 1-888-264-5877.

Chapter 2

The text of a drama is different from other literary forms. There is a place for the characters' names as they take turns speaking. There are also stage directions, stage settings, and other unspoken elements written into it.

Act I

Scene III

Setting: A large lobby with glittering lights shining on a marble floor.

CAT: [*in a worried tone*] I hope we are not late for the show.

DOG: Listen. The music is just now starting. [*pats her paw kindly*] We're just in time.

[*The couple enters the brightly lit theater.*]

You can see how the instructions add to the action and dialogue of the story. Here are some of the structures of a play.

Stage directions are instructions for actors written into the text of a play. They are set off with parentheses ( ) or brackets [ ] and are written in italics. These directions are not read aloud but tell actors what actions to take. Sometimes the stage directions tell the actors what emotions they should be creating as they speak.

Acts and scenes divide the action of a play. The different acts signal major shifts in action. The most common division of acts is into five parts: introduction, conflict, climax, breakdown, and resolution. Scenes, on the other hand, are not exact in form between different plays. They often signal a simple change of location, time, or dialogue.

Dialogue is the conversation between two or more characters in a play. The author of a play (a playwright) writes the dialogue in a certain way. The author writes the name of a character each time the character speaks.

A **monologue** (one voice speaking) is a speech by a single actor. It can be made to another character, to himself or herself, or to the audience. This can provide character description and background information about the setting, conflict, and other characters. It is usually different from a soliloquy (see below), in which a character shares innermost thoughts and feelings with no one but the audience.

A **soliloquy** (suh-**lil**-uh-kwee) involves one character speaking to herself or himself. The actor speaks aloud about inner thoughts and feelings. Hamlet's "To be or not to be" speech is a famous example of a character letting the audience know what is going on with inner emotional reactions. Other examples include the character Tevye in the movie *Fiddler on the Roof* and characters in the TV show "The Practice."

Asides, also known as "stage whispers," are moments when an actor pretends to whisper information to another or to the audience while other characters on stage pretend not to hear. One example of asides is the short speeches made by the character Ferris Bueller in the movie *Ferris Bueller's Day Off.*

Copyright © American Book Company. DO NOT DUPLICATE. 1-888-264-5877.

POETRY STRUCTURES

Poetry is written with a focus on language rather than characters or facts, though it can include both of these. Unlike prose, poetry does not necessarily meet the conventions of Standard American English, such as punctuation and capitalization. Poets use literary devices to fill poems with emotion and meaning. Lyric poems focus on thought and emotion, while narrative poems tell a story. Here are some specific types of poems.

Some poems are written in **free verse**, which means the lines do not rhyme or have a set pattern. One example of a free-verse poem is Robert Louis Stevenson's "The Light-Keeper."

Other poems can be **rhymed**, which means certain lines and words in the poem make the same sounds. The rhyme scheme refers to which lines rhyme. Read these lines from Robert Frost's "Stars." Notice that the rhyme scheme is *abcb*. The *b* indicates the two lines that rhyme, which are lines 2 and 4.

> How countlessly they congregate
>
> O'er our tumultuous snow,
>
> Which flows in shapes as tall as trees
>
> When wintry winds do blow!—

Many poems have specific forms and patterns. Some of these are very strict. They may or may not rhyme. But the main characteristic of each is its structure.

Cinquains have a strict structure of five lines. Sometimes there is a rigid syllable structure as well, but this is not true for all cinquains. A cinquain usually looks like a triangle. Here is the basic structure of a cinquain, followed by an example poem:

Line 1: one word (usually a noun)

Line 2: two words (adjectives that describe line 1)

Line 3: three words (action verbs usually ending in -*ing* that describe line 1)

Line 4: four words (a phrase or sentence that relates to line 1)

Line 5: one word (either a synonym for line 1 or a word that sums the poem up)

> soccer
>
> fun sport
>
> kicking, running, scoring
>
> activity that requires stamina
>
> adrenaline

Copyright © American Book Company. DO NOT DUPLICATE. 1-888-264-5877.

A **sonnet** traditionally has fourteen lines of ten syllables each. Some sonnets vary from this, but they all have a specific rhyme scheme and number of syllables per line. Read this example.

Sonnet 18

by William Shakespeare

Shall I compare thee to a summer's day?

Thou art more lovely and more temperate.

Rough winds do shake the darling buds of May,

And summer's lease hath all too short a date.

Sometime too hot the eye of heaven shines,

And often is his gold complexion dimm'd;

And every fair from fair some time declines,

By chance, or nature's changing course, untrimm'd;

But thy eternal summer shall not fade

Nor lose possession of that fair thou ow'st;

Nor shall Death brag thou wand'rest in his shade,

When in eternal lines to time thou grow'st:

So long as men can breathe or eyes can see,

So long lives this, and this gives life to thee.

Haiku is poetry of three lines that originated in Japan. Each line has a specific number of syllables. The structure most used in American haiku has five syllables in the first line, seven in the second, and five in the third. Japanese haiku are traditionally about nature, but people today write haiku about many subjects. Here is an example of a haiku.

Freshly cut grasses

sharp and sweet scents wafting up

drying in the sun

Copyright © American Book Company. DO NOT DUPLICATE. 1-888-264-5877.

A **limerick** is a type of comical short poem, often with nonsense subject matter, that has a rhyme scheme of *aabba*. As an example, read this poem.

> Hickory dickory dock,
>
> The mouse ran up the clock.
>
> The clock struck one;
>
> The mouse ran down.
>
> Hickory dickory dock.

Lyric poems focus on thought and emotion, while **narrative** poems tell a story.

There are many other poetry forms. These examples give you a taste of the structures some of them take.

SATIRE

There are many subgenres of writing that can actually transcend genres. One example is satire. **Satire** uses humor and sarcasm to expose human folly and shortcomings. It can be light and amusing or dark and biting, and it is ultimately meant to bring about a change in the behaviors it points out. Satire transcends genres because it can be found in essays, stories, novels, plays, and so on. Some examples of satire include *Tartuffe*, a comedy play by Molière; *The Onion*, an Internet newspaper that features parodies of current news; and "A Modest Proposal," an essay by Jonathan Swift. Here is an example of satire used in a short poem. It is satirical because the poet makes fun of people who believe they are owed something simply for existing.

> ### A Man Said to the Universe
>
> by Stephen Crane
>
> A man said to the universe:
>
> "Sir, I exist!"
>
> "However," replied the universe,
>
> "The fact has not created in me
>
> A sense of obligation."

Writers have reasons for selecting certain forms and structures of writing. Their choice depends what they want to communicate. For instance, say an author wants to capture the brief moment of awe she experienced during a dazzling sunset. She might create a short poem that describes her sense of wonder. She uses the form of the short poem, rich with emotion and imagery, to help convey the brief experience she had.

Copyright © American Book Company. DO NOT DUPLICATE. 1-888-264-5877.

But **form and structure can shape meaning** as well. Say an author wants to write a play in the form of a basic Greek tragedy. By definition of that genre, much of his play's meaning (though not all of it) will be dictated by the form and structure of a Greek tragedy. So in his play, the central character *must* suffer some serious misfortune, perhaps even death. It will be a fate that is not entirely accidental. In some ways, the fate of main character will result from his own actions.

Practice 1: Genre, Structure, and Meaning

RL 1, 5

> **DIRECTIONS**   Read the passages, and then answer the questions that follow.

Fire and Ice

by Robert Frost

Some say the world will end in fire,

Some say in ice.

From what I've tasted of desire

I hold with those who favor fire.

But if it had to perish twice,

I think I know enough of hate

To say that for destruction ice

Is also great

And would suffice.

---

1   Which description explains why "Fire and Ice" can be identified as a poem?

   A   It has a plot that involves conflict and a solution.

   B   It uses imagery, rhyme, and a rhythmical pattern.

   C   It relates a true account of real people, places, and events.

   D   It tells a story about imaginary people, places, and events.

Copyright © American Book Company. DO NOT DUPLICATE. 1-888-264-5877.

2 "Fire and Ice" could have been written as a persuasive essay about how the world
   will end. Why did the author not write this as an essay? How does the poetic structure
   of this work affect its meaning?

_____

_____

_____

_____

Excerpt from *The Story of Nathan Hale: Dramatic Hours in Revolutionary History*

by Henry Fisk Carlton

CAST (in this excerpt)

CAPTAIN NATHAN HALE

CAPTAIN WILLIAM HULL

GENERAL WASHINGTON

WASHINGTON: Colonel Knowlton informs me that you and your company have been
assigned to cover the North Shore line of Long Island Sound.

HALE: Yes, sir!

WASHINGTON: Well, Captain Hale, I am seriously in need of exact information which
you may be able to secure.

HALE: What is that, sir?

WASHINGTON: Lord Howe's plans!

HALE: Yes, sir!

WASHINGTON: Can you get them?

HALE: I can try, sir.

WASHINGTON: You don't seem daunted by the magnitude of the undertaking.

HALE: It is an order, sir.

Copyright © American Book Company. DO NOT DUPLICATE. 1-888-264-5877.

WASHINGTON: Well, my boy, no man knows better than I the impossibility of some orders.

HALE: But, sir—

WASHINGTON: I hope, though, that this is not impossible. I have to have the information. The safety of my whole army depends upon it. I must know particularly where General Howe intends to strike next.

HALE: Yes, sir.

WASHINGTON: If he comes across the East River, we can protect ourselves and keep out of his way. But if he comes across Long Island Sound—do you realize what that may mean to us?

HALE: Yes, sir. He can cut off our retreat.

WASHINGTON: Exactly! So that's what I must know.

HALE: I'll find out for you, sir.

WASHINGTON: Good! Now, Captain, you may go about your task in any way you see fit. I suggest two or three alternatives. First, you may tempt one of the enemy or a Tory who has access to the British lines, with a sum of money. You may draw on me for whatever is necessary.

HALE: Yes, sir.

WASHINGTON: Or you might make a sally across the Sound, capture a prisoner or two, and secure bits of information.

HALE: Yes, sir.

WASHINGTON: Or, though I hate to suggest it, you might go yourself in disguise to the British lines, but that should be only in a last desperate effort.

HALE: I understand, sir.

WASHINGTON: Or if you could get in touch with certain persons on Long Island who have been of service to us before—let's see —there is a shoemaker in Jamaica—what is his name—oh, here it is—Simon Carter.

HALE: Simon Carter. Yes, sir.

WASHINGTON: If you can find any way to get in touch with him—

HALE: I'll find a way, sir.

WASHINGTON: The password is "Liberty" used twice in your first sentence to him.

HALE: Yes, sir.

WASHINGTON: I don't know what he can do for you, but he is trustworthy and he may have some information.

Copyright © American Book Company. DO NOT DUPLICATE. 1-888-264-5877.

HALE: I'll see him, sir.

WASHINGTON: Now, Captain, I don't want you to go yourself unless it is absolutely necessary. But I must have General Howe's plans as soon as possible.

HALE: Yes, sir. I understand. I'll see that you get them, sir.

WASHINGTON: Good! I believe you will, Captain. Good day.

HALE: Good day, sir.

[*Door closes.*]

HULL: [*coming in*] Well, Nathan, what news?

HALE: I've got a job.

HULL: On the staff?

HALE: No. I'm afraid it's more hazardous than that.

HULL: You're lucky! A hazardous job! Say, what I wouldn't give to be in your shoes! What is it? Are you at liberty to tell?

HALE: Of course I'll tell you, William. I'm to discover General Howe's plan of action.

HULL: [*whistles*] I should say you had drawn a hazardous assignment! I'd call it a labor of Hercules!

3 What can you tell about Hale from this excerpt?

   A He is willing to take risks for his country.

   B He wants a higher rank than he now has.

   C He is frightened by General Washington.

   D He wants to be as powerful as Hercules.

4 In this excerpt, Washington gives instructions, and Hale gives short responses. Why did the author structure the scene in this way? What does this tell you about the characters?

   _____

   _____

   _____

   _____

Copyright © American Book Company. DO NOT DUPLICATE. 1-888-264-5877.

Chapter 2

Read this line of dialogue spoken by Washington.

> *Or if you could get in touch with certain persons on Long Island who have been of service to us before—let's see—there is a shoemaker in Jamaica—what is his name—oh, here it is—*Simon Carter.

5   How does the author's use of dashes affect the meaning?

   A   It shows the character should speak without pausing at all.

   B   It is a way to depict an odd accent in Washington's voice.

   C   It shows hesitation as Washington tries to recall something.

   D   It provides places for the actors to follow stage directions.

6   The last stage direction calls for Hull to "whistle." How does this add to the meaning?

_____

_____

_____

_____

COMPARING AND CONTRASTING LITERATURE

You know how to compare (analyze similarities) and contrast (analyze differences). There are several ways to **compare and contrast literature**. In this section, you will compare and contrast similar subjects in fiction and nonfiction. Finally, you will see how to analyze adaptations of literary texts.

FICTION AND NONFICTION

Many works of fiction have real people, places, and events in them. You can read these works and see **how a fictional portrayal of a time, place, or character compares with the historical account**.

Historical fiction might feature made-up stories that take place during major historical events that really happened. Real history forms the backdrop for the plot. An example is *All the Broken Pieces* by Ann E. Burg. It is the story of Matt Pin, a fictional character, who is airlifted out of Vietnam during the war there. After being placed in a loving adoptive home, he must choose how the terrible memories of that time will shape his life. The book uses a real time in history as the setting but tells an invented story that might have happened, but didn't.

Other works might imagine a person who actually lived in a certain situation. Historical records might tell us a little about an event. But a fiction author can tell what happened in detail—even though it might not have happened exactly that way.

Page 20

Here is an example of a historical account and an excerpt from a work of fiction about the same subject. Read the passages and the questions and explanations that follow.

A Brief History of the Danes

The first humans settled in Denmark, a Scandinavian region in northern Europe, after the last Ice Age, around 10,000 BC. These early Danes were primarily hunters and fishermen. They wandered from place to place in search of food and shelter. Then around 4,000 BC, Danes began farming their land with crude tools. They created these from the same stone they used to fashion their weapons. With the advent of farming, Danes began settling into small colonies and towns. By 1,800 BC, Danish craftsmen were forging many of their goods from bronze. Iron was introduced around 500 BC. In the Iron Age, Danes first made contact with the mighty Romans. They exchanged their goods for the Mediterranean luxuries of the Roman Empire. When the Roman Empire collapsed in the fifth century, the Danes continued to trade with the eastern half of that territory. This was called the Byzantine Empire. Like all of Europe in the sixth century, much of the Danish population was ravaged by a catastrophic outbreak of the plague.

In the seventh century, European countries began seeking to acquire more territory and expand their borders. It was a period of territorial and political unrest. This resulted in a number of loosely joined kingdoms under English control. They included Northumbria, Mercia, Wessex, East Anglia, Sussex, and a few others. For another century or so, the balance of power in England shifted from one kingdom to another, most notably between Mercia and Northumbria. By the middle of the ninth century, England was divided into three major kingdoms—but peace did not last for long. In 865, the Danes invaded England. In the wake of the nine-year conflict, after much loss of life, only the southernmost kingdom of Wessex, ruled by King Alfred, remained under English control. But under King Alfred and his successors, England fought back and gradually regained territory at the expense of the Danes.

Copyright © American Book Company. DO NOT DUPLICATE. 1-888-264-5877.

Chapter 2

In this story, the hero is a young Saxon thane (a baron who owns land), who takes part in all the battles fought by King Alfred.

Excerpt from *The Dragon and the Raven*

by George Alfred Henty

"The news is bad, Edmund. The Danes are ever receiving reinforcements from Mercia, and scarce a day passes but fresh bands arrive at Thetford, and I fear that ere long East Anglia, like Northumbria, will fall into their clutches. Nay, unless we soon make head against them they will come to occupy all the island, just as did our forefathers."

"That were shame indeed," Edmund exclaimed. "We know that the people conquered by our ancestors were unwarlike and cowardly; but it would be shame indeed were we Saxons so to be overcome by the Danes, seeing moreover that we have the help of God, being Christians, while the Danes are pagans and idolaters."

"Nevertheless, my son, for the last five years these heathen have been masters of Northumbria, have wasted the whole country, and have plundered and destroyed the churches and monasteries. At present they have but made a beginning here in East Anglia; but if they continue to flock in they will soon overrun the whole country, instead of having, as at present, a mere foothold near the rivers except for those who have come down to Thetford. We have been among the first sufferers, seeing that our lands lie  round Thetford, and hitherto I have hoped that there would be a general rising against these invaders; but the king is indolent and unwarlike, and I see that he will not arouse himself and call his ealdormen and thanes together for a united effort until it is too late.

"Already from the north the Danes are flocking down into Mercia, and although the advent of the West Saxons to the aid of the King of Mercia forced them to retreat for a while, I doubt not that they will soon pour down again."

"'Tis a pity, father, that the Saxons are not all under one leading. Then we might surely defend England against the Danes. If the people did but rise and fall upon each band of Northmen as they arrived, they would get no footing among us."

"Yes," the father replied, "it is the unhappy divisions between the Saxon kingdoms which have enabled the Danes to get so firm a footing in the land. Our only hope now lies in the West Saxons. Until lately they were at feud with Mercia. But the royal families are now related by marriage, seeing that the King of Mercia is wedded to a West Saxon princess, and that Alfred, the West Saxon king's brother and heir to the throne, has lately espoused one of the royal blood of Mercia. The fact that they marched at the call of the King of Mercia and drove the Danes from Nottingham shows that the West Saxon princes are alive to the common danger of the country. If they are but joined heartily by our people

Copyright © American Book Company. DO NOT DUPLICATE. 1-888-264-5877.

of East Anglia and the Mercians, they may yet succeed in checking the progress of these heathen. And now, Edmund, as we see no hope of any general effort to drive the Danes off our coasts, 'tis useless for us to lurk here longer. I propose tomorrow, then, to journey north into Lincolnshire, to the Abbey of Croyland, where, as you know, my brother Theodore is the abbot; there we can rest in peace for a time, and watch the progress of events."

[…]

While they had been thus talking Egbert had been broiling the eels and wild ducks over the fire. He was a freeman, and a distant relation of Edmund's father, Eldred, who was an ealdorman in West Norfolk, his lands lying beyond Thetford, and upon whom, therefore, the first brunt of the Danish invasion from Mercia had fallen.

In the excerpt from *The Dragon and the Raven*, what parts are based on history?

From your reading of the historical account, you can see that the Danes did invade England, and the Saxons fought them for power. The place names are real, so the setting is based in reality. Many of the people mentioned lived too. This includes the Danes and Saxons in general and specific people like King Alfred. The characters in this scene, Edmund, his father, and Egbert, are invented and given roles to play.

What major differences are there between the article "A Brief History of the Danes" and the novel *The Dragon and the Raven*?

What do you see as the main contrasts? The first one, as mentioned, is that there are made-up characters in the novel. Their fictional involvement helps explain the history in a more personal way than a dry factual account might. This brings up another difference. The book has a hero—Edmund—and he is a Saxon. So, the story is told from a Saxon perspective. The historical account gives a more balanced, neutral recounting of the events. Another difference is the use of dialogue. The characters talk to each other in the novel. There is no conversation in the historical account. The history passage, however, offers more details, dates, and other facts that help you learn about the actual events. Unlike the factual writing in the nonfiction account, the author of the novel uses many literary devices. These include imagery, figurative language, and vivid descriptions. (This is not to say that nonfiction writers *never* use these devices, but they are more common in fiction.) You will read more about these in chapter 4.

Copyright © American Book Company. DO NOT DUPLICATE. 1-888-264-5877.

Chapter 2

Practice 2: Fiction and Nonfiction

RL 1, 9, 10

> **DIRECTIONS** Review the nonfiction and fiction passages in the section above. Then answer the questions below.

1   Which fact that is given in "A Brief History of the Danes" would the author of *The Dragon and the Raven* be least likely to include?

   A   The kingdoms of England were enjoying peace before the Danes invaded.

   B   The Danes were devastated by the plague like everyone else in Europe.

   C   The Danes started out as an aggressive tribe and remained true to their roots.

   D   The remaining kingdom of England eventually triumphed over the Danes.

2   In *The Dragon and the Raven*, the characters talk about past invasions. What attitude do they show about their country that "A Brief History of the Danes" does not reveal?

   A   They would rather follow the Danes than continue suffering in poverty.

   B   They are disappointed about how many times England has been conquered.

   C   They want to make sure that no other people ever invade England again.

   D   They are proud of their ancestors and want to uphold the example they set.

3   Find an example of language in *The Dragon and the Raven* that shows how the characters feel about the Danes invading England. Give the wording, and explain what emotions it reveals.

_____

_____

_____

_____

_____

Writing Task

Using the texts, "A Brief History of the Danes" and *The Dragon and the Raven*, as examples, explain why an author would write historical fiction. What do readers gain from it that they do not get from nonfiction accounts? Remember to use evidence from the example texts to support your ideas.

Copyright © American Book Company. DO NOT DUPLICATE. 1-888-264-5877.

Copyright © American Book Company. DO NOT DUPLICATE. 1-888-264-5877.

Activity

RL 1, 9, 10, **SL** 4, 5

Read a fiction story or book that takes place in the Old West (some suggestions are listed below). Then research the actual time and place in which the story is set. You can find such information in a book about the Old West or on websites. Write an essay that compares and contrasts the facts from your nonfiction research with the way the setting is portrayed in the story you read. How important is the setting? Are there also any people in the story who actually lived at the time? Be sure to use evidence from the texts to support your ideas. Present your findings to the class. Include multimedia to help listeners understand.

Suggested Reading

Western fiction by Louis L'Amour

Western fiction by Janette Oke

Old Ramon by Jack Schaefer

Pioneers Go West by George R. Stewart

The House of Winslow series by Gilbert Morris

A Tale of the Western Plains by George Alfred Henty

ADAPTATIONS

An **adaptation** is a version of a work that is produced in another medium. For example, the novel *Harry Potter and the Deathly Hallows* was adapted to film. Two movies were made to tell the story from this book.

Long and short stories, plays, and poems all can be adapted. There are many ways to make adaptations. A literary work can become a play, a movie, or a video game. It might even be adapted to another literary genre.

For example, you might have seen a movie that was based on a comic book. Many comic book heroes like Batman, Superman, the Fantastic Four, and the X-Men have been brought to the big screen. When a written play is acted out on stage, that is also an adaptation. Sometimes a play is adapted with songs to become a musical. The possibilities are almost endless!

You will be asked to **compare and contrast literary works and their adaptations**. When you do this, you will look for the effects of the new medium on the original work. You might read a play that is set in ancient times. But your school or a local theater might put on the play and make it happen in modern times. What you need to figure out is why. Was it because they didn't have the right costumes? Or was it to help the audience relate more to the story?

You also need to look at any new elements that are added for each medium. You will read in chapter 3 about the elements of literature, like plot, characters, and setting. These can be parts of other media as well. But think about what gets added that is not present in the written word—elements like sound, color, lighting, camera angles, and so on.

Here is an example of an original work and an adaptation.

Excerpt from "Song of Hiawatha"

by Henry Wadsworth Longfellow

Forth upon the Gitche Gumee,

On the shining Big-Sea-Water,

With his fishing-line of cedar,

Of the twisted bark of cedar,

Forth to catch the sturgeon Nahma

Mishne-Nahma, King of Fishes,

In his birch-canoe exulting

All alone went Hiawatha.

Through the clear, transparent water

He could see the fishes swimming

Far down in the depths below him;

See the yellow perch, the Sahwa,

Like a sunbeam in the water,

See the Shawgashee, the craw-fish,

Like a spider on the bottom,

On the white and sandy bottom.

At the stern sat Hiawatha,

With his fishing-line of cedar;

In his plumes the breeze of morning

Played as in the hemlock branches;

On the bows, with tail erected,

Sat the squirrel, Adjidaumo;

In his fur the breeze of morning

Played as in the prairie grasses.

On the white sand of the bottom

Lay the monster Mishe-Nahma,

Lay the sturgeon, King of Fishes;

Through his gills he breathed the water,

With his fins he fanned and winnowed,

With his tail he swept the sand-floor.

There he lay in all his armor;

On each side a shield to guard him,

Plates of bone upon his forehead,

Down his sides and back and shoulders

Plates of bone with spines projecting!

Painted was he with his war-paints,

Stripes of yellow, red, and azure,

Spots of brown and spots of sable;

And he lay there on the bottom,

Fanning with his fins of purple,

He the terror of the fishes,

The destroyer of the salmon,

The devourer of the herring.

Copyright © American Book Company. DO NOT DUPLICATE. 1-888-264-5877.

"Take my bait!" cried Hiawatha,

Down into the depths beneath him,

"Take my bait, O Sturgeon, Nahma!

Come up from below the water,

Let us see which is the stronger!"

And he dropped his line of cedar

Through the clear, transparent water,

Waited vainly for an answer,

Long sat waiting for an answer,

And repeating loud and louder,

"Take my bait, O King of Fishes!"

Quiet lay the sturgeon, Nahma,

Fanning slowly in the water,

Looking up at Hiawatha,

Listening to his call and clamor,

His unnecessary tumult,

Till he wearied of the shouting;

And he said to the Kenozha,

To the pike, the Maskenozha,

"Take the bait of this rude fellow,

Break the line of Hiawatha!"

Copyright © American Book Company. DO NOT DUPLICATE. 1-888-264-5877.

Chapter 2

Page from a graphic novel adaptation of "Song of Hiawatha"

What do you notice first as you compare these two versions? The original poem tells in detail this part of Hiawatha's adventure. It has a specific beat that mimics the rhythm of some Native American music. Notice how some of that rhythm is lost in the graphic novel version. The words are spaced differently and used in the structure that is specific to graphic novels. The illustration frames and speech balloons break up the rhythm. In fact, many lines from the

Page 28

Copyright © American Book Company. DO NOT DUPLICATE. 1-888-264-5877.

original are left out of the graphic version. Why do you think they are not included? Most likely, it is due to space restrictions. Look at which lines are left out, and evaluate how this affects the meaning of the tale.

On the other hand, many aspects are added in the graphic version. The most obvious one is the drawings. How do these help you understand the story in the poem? What looks different than how you imagined it when you read the original poem? What else do you see that is unique to the graphic novel adaptation of this poem?

Now, think about an audio recording of "The Song of Hiawatha." If you listened to it, you would not see pictures, as you do with the graphic novel. However, you would hear the speaker's interpretation of events, with softer portions in calm times and excitement during the height of the adventure. What if the poem were adapted to a stage play? What might be different then? Every medium has its own techniques and formats that bring out something different in an adapted work.

The same is true in filmed adaptations. Have you seen movies that are based on books? Some recent ones include the Twilight series based on the books by Stephenie Meyer, the Chronicles of Narnia books by C. S. Lewis, the Harry Potter series by J. K. Rowling, and an assortment of superhero films adapted from comic books and graphic novels. If you saw some of these, had you read any of the books before seeing the movies? If so, what differences did you see in how they were adapted to film? How did the choices about setting, lighting, camera angles, focus, and so on affect the portrayal of the story? Were any portions of the book entirely left out of the film? Or were there even things that happened in the movie that didn't occur in the book?

An author creates a world that you interpret as you read the words in a book. For example, you might read a sentence like this in a mystery novel: "The light at the end of the tunnel was faint but unmistakable. Someone was down there." What does that light look like in your imagination? You have a specific way of picturing it. Say that you then see a film adaptation of the story. When this scene arrives, the light glows in a strange green color. This is an interpretation that the creators of the movie have made. It is the way they pictured the scene. The author does not specify a color.

Another example is when a character is described as frightening or imposing. A camera angle that can help create this idea is one that shows the character from below, as though you are looking up at him or her. This helps the character look bigger and more menacing.

Many things can change when adaptations are made. The key is to analyze how the unique elements of each medium affect the story.

Copyright © American Book Company. DO NOT DUPLICATE. 1-888-264-5877.

Practice 3: Adaptations

RL 7, W 1, 2, 4, 5, 9.a

<table>
<tr><td colspan="2">Writing Task

Choose one of the pairs of works below, which all include a book and its various film adaptations. Ask your teacher for suggestions about which one you should choose. Be sure to get permission to watch any movies that are rated PG or PG-13. First, read the book (or play), paying attention to the plot, setting, characters, and message in the story. Then watch the movie adapted from it. Write an analysis of how film techniques (color, lighting, camera angles, and so on) affected the story.</td></tr>
<tr><td>Book</td><td>Film adaptation(s)</td></tr>
<tr><td>A Christmas Carol by Charles Dickens</td><td>A Christmas Carol (1984) starring George C. Scott, Frank Finlay

A Christmas Carol (1999) starring Patrick Stewart, Richard E. Grant

A Christmas Carol (2009) animated film</td></tr>
<tr><td>Alice's Adventures in Wonderland by Lewis Carroll</td><td>Alice in Wonderland (1951) animated film

Alice in Wonderland (1999) starring Tina Majorino, Whoopi Goldberg

Alice in Wonderland (2010) starring Mia Wasikowska, Johnny Depp</td></tr>
<tr><td>Holes by Louis Sachar</td><td>Holes (2003) starring Sigourney Weaver, Shia LeBeouf</td></tr>
<tr><td>I Am Number Four by Pittacus Lore</td><td>I Am Number Four (2011) staring Alex Pettyfer, Timothy Olyphant</td></tr>
<tr><td>Little Women by Louisa May Alcott</td><td>Little Women (1994) starring Trini Alvarado, Winona Ryder</td></tr>
<tr><td>Treasure Island by Robert Louis Stevenson</td><td>Treasure Island (1950) starring Bobby Driscoll, Robert Newton

Treasure Island (1990) starring Charlton Heston, Christian Bale</td></tr>
</table>

Copyright © American Book Company. DO NOT DUPLICATE. 1-888-264-5877.

CHAPTER 2 SUMMARY

Genres are types of literature with a similar form. The main genres include **fiction**, **nonfiction**, **drama**, and **poetry**. Each has many subgenres.

As you analyze what you read, remember to always **support your analysis with evidence**.

To fully understand a text, you might need to use **inference** skills to read between the lines.

Some written works share a certain **form or structure**. For example, **drama** includes stage directions, dialogue, soliloquy, and so on. **Poetry** can take on many structures including sonnet, haiku, and limerick. The choice of **form and structure can shape meaning** in the writing.

There are several ways to **compare and contrast literature**.

You can read fiction and nonfiction works about the same subject and see **how a fictional portrayal of a time, place, or character compares with the historical account**.

You also can **compare and contrast literary works and their adaptations** in other media, such as audio, live performance, or film.

Copyright © American Book Company. DO NOT DUPLICATE. 1-888-264-5877.

For more practice with this chapter's material, see the Literature Review on page 61.

Copyright © American Book Company. DO NOT DUPLICATE. 1-888-264-5877.

Chapter 3
Literary Elements

This chapter covers the following seventh grade strand and standards:

Reading: Literature

Key Ideas and Details

1. Cite several pieces of textual evidence to support analysis of what the text says explicitly as well as inferences drawn from the text.

2. Determine a theme or central idea of a text and analyze its development over the course of the text; provide an objective summary of the text.

3. Analyze how particular elements of a story or drama interact (e.g., how setting shapes the characters or plot).

6. Analyze how an author develops and contrasts the points of view of different characters or narrators in a text.

Range of Reading and Level of Text Complexity

10. By the end of the year, read and comprehend literature, including stories, dramas, and poems, in the grades 6–8 text complexity band proficiently, with scaffolding as needed at the high end of the range.

Literary elements are the building blocks of writing. Like the walls of a house, these elements provide the structures that authors use to create a work of literature. Writers introduce you to interesting characters. While getting to know these characters, you follow the plot (sequence of events) that shapes each story you read. Through your reading adventures, you come to understand certain themes (underlying messages) that are a part of the literature you explore. In this chapter, you will look at the literary elements that authors use in their writing.

Elements like plot, theme, and characterization work together to create a meaningful story. For instance, an author might develop a story revolving around three contrasting sisters who are raised in a small southern town during the 1950s. They rally together during a crisis that threatens to tear their family apart. The author tightly intertwines the plot, characters, and setting to draw out meaning about southern culture and family bonds. As you read, keep in mind that all literary elements have impact on meaning.

CHARACTERS

The author creates **characters** to appear in a literary work. They must reveal their ideas and feelings to each other and to the reader. A character can be a person, animal, or object. The way that characters in a story interact (behave) with each other is a big part of telling the story. Through their words and actions, the story comes alive for readers. Sometimes, authors come right out and say what a character is like. Other times, authors reveal characters to readers through narration, dialogue, and actions.

Copyright © American Book Company. DO NOT DUPLICATE. 1-888-264-5877.

- **Description** allows an author to tell how characters look, dress, how old they are, and so on. This is just as you might describe a friend to someone. In her book, *Little Women*, Louisa May Alcott includes a paragraph in the first chapter that describes the main characters. She prefaces this introduction with "As young readers like to know 'how people look,' we will take this moment to give them a little sketch of the four sisters ..."

- **Narration** is the telling of the story through a speaker. The speaker could be one of the characters or could be an unknown observer. The speaker will tell how other characters feel or think about another character or will describe how they act toward that character. In *The Red Badge of Courage*, there is an unknown narrator who tells the story through the eyes of a young soldier.

- **Dialogue** is conversation between two or more people. People in literature speak to each other as people in your class do. Mark Twain, in *Adventures of Huckleberry Finn*, shows the character traits of Huck and Jim in the talks they share while they float down the Mississippi River.

- **Actions** of a character sometimes speak louder than words to show the character's true self. How characters deal with problems also says a lot about them. Do the characters run from difficulty, or do they work through problems? The main characters in O. Henry's "The Gift of the Magi" show their love for each other by placing the happiness of the other before their own. How a character behaves toward others reveals character traits.

POINT OF VIEW

Point of view is the perspective from which a story is told. This depends on the **narrator** who tells the story. A story written in **first-person point of view** is told from the perspective of one of the characters. The narrator uses the pronouns *I*, *me*, and *we* to describe the plot. The first-person narrator can be a main character in the story or a minor one.

> **Example:** I suppose the general superstition about midnight was increased by my recent experiences. I waited with a sick feeling of suspense.
>
> – Bram Stoker, *Dracula*

A story in **third-person point of view** is told by an unnamed observer who stands back from the story. The narrator describes characters as *he*, *she*, or *they*.

> **Example:** She looked back at him for some time with a heated face, in which there hung a red shadow of anger.
>
> – G. K. Chesterton, *The Head of Caesar*

Third-person point of view can be **limited**, which means the narrator tells the story from the viewpoint of one character. Readers find out only what that character sees, hears, feels, and thinks. Or, it can also be **omniscient** (om-**nish**-uhnt), meaning the narrator tells about the

Copyright © American Book Company. DO NOT DUPLICATE. 1-888-264-5877.

experiences and thoughts of all the characters in the story. Finally, it can even be **objective**, meaning a narrator tells the story without describing any character's thoughts, opinions, or feelings.

Point of view is crucial to the story. You know that an author writes for a specific purpose, but he or she also chooses the point of view to get the most effect out of the story. Point of view affects the story's interpretation as well as the theme. Think about your favorite hero stories. How different would they be if the stories were told from the evil villain's point of view?

Practice 1: Characters and Point of View

RL 1, 6

DIRECTIONS	Read the passage, and answer the questions.

Excerpt from *A Christmas Carol*

by Charles Dickens

"A merry Christmas, uncle! God save you!" cried a cheerful voice. It was the voice of Scrooge's nephew, who came upon him so quickly that this was the first intimation he had of his approach.

"Bah!" said Scrooge. "Humbug!"

He had so heated himself with rapid walking in the fog and frost, this nephew of Scrooge's, that he was all in a glow; his face was ruddy and handsome, his eyes sparkled, and his breath smoked again.

"Christmas a humbug, uncle!" said Scrooge's nephew. "You don't mean that, I am sure?"

"I do," said Scrooge. "Merry Christmas! What right have you to be merry? What reason have you to be merry? You're poor enough."

"Come, then," returned the nephew gaily. "What right have you to be dismal? What reason have you to be morose? You're rich enough."

Scrooge, having no better answer ready on the spur of the moment, said "Bah!" again; and followed it up with "Humbug."

"Don't be cross, uncle!" said the nephew.

Copyright © American Book Company. DO NOT DUPLICATE. 1-888-264-5877.

Chapter 3

> "What else can I be," returned the uncle, "when I live in such a world of fools as this? Merry Christmas! Out upon merry Christmas! What's Christmas time to you but a time for paying bills without money; a time for finding yourself a year older, but not an hour richer; a time for balancing your books and having every item in 'em through a round dozen of months presented dead against you? If I could work my will," said Scrooge indignantly, "every idiot who goes about with 'Merry Christmas' on his lips, should be boiled with his own pudding, and buried with a stake of holly through his heart. He should!"
>
> "Uncle!" pleaded the nephew.
>
> "Nephew!" returned the uncle, sternly, "keep Christmas in your own way, and let me keep it in mine."
>
> "Keep it!" repeated Scrooge's nephew. "But you don't keep it."

1   Based on Scrooge's character, what tone of voice does he most likely use when repeating his nephew's cry of "Merry Christmas"?

   A   Sarcastic

   B   Sincere

   C   Ashamed

   D   Emphatic

2   Why is Scrooge's nephew in such a hurry?

   A   He is overwhelmed with affection for his uncle.

   B   His uncle has given him many chores to complete.

   C   He is excited that Christmas morning has arrived.

   D   Worrying about his poverty has made him frantic.

3   By exclaiming "Bah!" and "Humbug!" what does Scrooge imply? Be sure to support your conclusion with evidence.

   _____

   _____

   _____

   _____

Copyright © American Book Company. DO NOT DUPLICATE. 1-888-264-5877.

4   Scrooge and his nephew get into an argument about money. What important
    difference in point of view do they have?

    A   Scrooge presumes that poor people can't be happy, and his nephew says that rich
    Scrooge should be very happy in that case.

    B   Scrooge is worried about business, and his nephew thinks that the Christmas hol-
    iday is no time to think of such concerns.

    C   Scrooge thinks that his nephew should be spending more time making money for
    his family and less time celebrating.

    D   Scrooge finds it hard to believe so many people are poor, but his nephew thinks
    that someone so rich should realize this.

5   How would this passage most likely change if it was written from Scrooge's point of
    view?

_____

_____

_____

_____

_____

_____

PLOT

The **plot** is the pattern of events in a story, including how the story works out. It refers to all the related events that move from the story's beginning to its end.

In a story, the **exposition**, or **introduction**, sets the stage for the events to come. It usually gives details about the setting and characters. In *Because of Winn-Dixie*, the first sentence tells us the narrator and point of view: "My name is India Opal Buloni …" In the first few chapters, the reader learns about the main character and the dog she finds.

As the plot of a story unfolds, problems, or **conflicts**, occur between opposing forces. (You will read more about conflicts in the next section.) We see **rising action** as these various conflicts complicate the lives of the characters. For example, one conflict in *Because of Winn-Dixie* is shown in the strained relationship Opal has with her father.

The highest point of action in a story is called the **climax**. This turning point is usually filled with suspense, as readers want to find out what will happen next as the story reaches a peak. In *Because of Winn-Dixie*, the climax occurs when Opal has a party and forgets Winn-Dixie is outside when a thunderstorm blows in. After the highest point of action, most stories begin to move toward the end. This is called **falling action**. Major conflicts begin to be solved, and other details of the story are wrapped up.

Copyright © American Book Company. DO NOT DUPLICATE. 1-888-264-5877.

The **resolution**, or **denouement** (day-noo-**mahn**), is the outcome of a story. Conflict is resolved, and loose ends may be tied up. Some stories, of course, leave questions unanswered. By the end of *Because of Winn-Dixie*, Opal has grown and learned much, thanks to her new friend, Winn-Dixie.

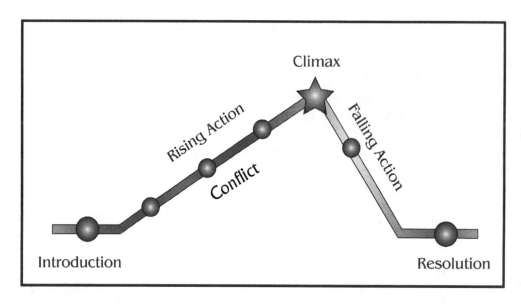

A story might contain additional events that advance the plot. A **flashback** is a scene or event that happened before the beginning of a story. It can be a memory, a dream, or a simple retelling of past events by one of the characters. For instance, the entire story in *Moby-Dick* is actually a flashback—a tale told later by the sole survivor, Ishmael.

Foreshadowing is a way for an author to provide clues about future events in the plot. For example, a dark, stormy night or a sudden windstorm often foreshadows that something sinister is about to happen.

THEME

Identifying the **theme** is an important part of understanding literature. The theme is the underlying meaning or message of a work of literature. It is the idea about life that is revealed through some aspect of the story. When you are looking for a literary theme, you might consider how the main character changes or learns an important lesson in the course of the story. Other important ideas to consider are the title and important passages in the work.

Generally, the theme is not stated directly, but must be inferred, or figured out, by the reader. Sometimes in a work of literature, there are ideas that are important but not large enough to be considered a theme. You can think of these ideas as topics. It is important that you are able to distinguish a theme, which is the underlying meaning that a work of literature reveals, from a central idea, which is simply a subject that the work addresses in some way. Read this example.

Copyright © American Book Company. DO NOT DUPLICATE. 1-888-264-5877.

The Dog and the Shadow

from Aesop's fables

It happened that a dog got a piece of meat and was carrying it home in his mouth to eat it in peace. Now, on his way home, he had to cross a plank lying across a running brook. As he crossed, he looked down and saw his own shadow reflected in the water beneath. Thinking it was another dog with another piece of meat, he made up his mind to get that dog's meat also. So he snapped at the dog in the water, but as he opened his mouth, the piece of meat fell out. It fell into the water and was never seen again.

The theme, or lesson, of this fable is this: when you are greedy, you can lose everything. The central idea, on the other hand, might be the simple fact that dogs will try to accumulate all the food they can.

THEME AND CENTRAL IDEA

Theme is not specific to one kind of writing or even to one subject. For instance, a poet may write a poem exploring the emotional devastation of war while a historian may write a research paper exploring the economic devastation of war. How a theme or a message is treated depends on the subject and the person handling it. Let's look at how two different writers work with a similar **theme and central idea** in two different types of writing.

Author #1: Edgar Allan Poe

Type of writing: Fiction

Subject: Literature

Theme: Money and power cannot help someone escape a dreaded disease

The "Red Death" had long devastated the country. No pestilence had ever been so fatal, or so hideous. Blood was its Avatar and its seal—the redness and the horror of blood. There were sharp pains, and sudden dizziness, and then profuse bleeding at the pores, with dissolution. The scarlet stains upon the body and especially upon the face of the victim were the pest ban which shut him out from the aid and from the sympathy of his fellow-men. And the whole seizure, progress, and termination of the disease, were the incidents of half an hour.

– from "The Masque of the Red Death" by Edgar Allan Poe

[In the rest of the story, rich Prince Prospero isolates himself and his court in his palace. He hopes to escape the fate of the rest of the land. But someone dressed as the Red Death comes to the party. The Prince is shocked and makes him remove his mask. It turns out to be death. Through symbolism, the story shows that one cannot use money or power to escape disease.]

Copyright © American Book Company. DO NOT DUPLICATE. 1-888-264-5877.

Author #2: A scientist

Type of writing: Nonfiction

Subject: Science

Central Idea: Disease

 Tuberculosis is an infection of the lungs. It can be transmitted from one person to another when an infected person sneezes, coughs, or even speaks. People with tuberculosis often have a bloody cough, fever, and listlessness. Tuberculosis can be prevented by vaccines and treated by antibiotics.

Notice the differences between these two texts. Poe writes about disease using emotional words like "hideous" and "sympathy." He shows the fear and horror that goes along with the infectious disease. By contrast, the scientist's description of a similar disease, tuberculosis, is more clinical. It describes the facts of the disease: what it is, how it is transmitted, what the symptoms are, and how it is treated. It does not show emotion, because that is not the purpose of a scientific article. While literature tends to use vivid description and imagination, science relies on fact. Therefore, a similar theme and central idea are treated differently in these types of writing.

SUMMARIZING

To **summarize** means to come up with your own words for a condensed version of a passage. This can be a helpful way to remember points. This is another skill you already know how to use. When describing a story to your friends, you mention the main character, key events, and details you liked or didn't like. When reading, try jotting down a summary of each paragraph in a longer passage. This will help you organize its contents in your mind and provide a guide to finding answers to questions.

Copyright © American Book Company. DO NOT DUPLICATE. 1-888-264-5877.

For the following passage, write a summary of about forty to sixty words.

Excerpt from *The Negro*

by W. E. B. Du Bois

Africa is at once the most romantic and the most tragic of continents. Its very names reveal its mystery and wide-reaching influence. It is the "Ethiopia" of the Greek, the "Kush" and "Punt" of the Egyptian, and the Arabian "Land of the Blacks." To modern Europe it is the "Dark Continent" and "Land of Contrasts." In literature it is the seat of the Sphinx and the lotus eaters, the home of the dwarfs, gnomes, and pixies, and the refuge of the gods. In commerce it is the slave mart and the source of ivory, ebony, rubber, gold, and diamonds. What other continent can rival in interest this Ancient of Days?

There are those who would write universal history and leave out Africa. But how can one leave out the land of Egypt and Carthage? …Yet it is true that the history of Africa is unusual, and its strangeness is due in no small degree to the physical peculiarities of the continent.

With three times the area of Europe, it has a coast line a fifth shorter. Like Europe it is a peninsula of Asia, curving southwestward around the Indian Sea. It has few gulfs, bays, capes, or islands. Even the rivers, though large and long, are not means of communication with the outer world.

How would you summarize this passage? Practice on your own, then come back and look at the example summary below.

Example summary of excerpt from *The Negro*
by W. E. B. Du Bois

Africa has a complex history. It has produced empires, art, resources, and religion, but it also faced slavery. Strangely, some historians don't bother including Africa. Maybe they have misconceptions because Africa's geography isolated it from much of the world for so long.

W. E. B. Du Bois

HOW LITERARY ELEMENTS WORK TOGETHER

All of the **elements work together** in a story or a drama. The setting can affect the characters and the plot. The characters in the story also affect the plot. There are many layers of interaction.

When you read, notice that plot events often explain the way a character has acted in the past or behaves now. Say that a main character is fearful of traveling by plane. A flashback might reveal details that this character's best friend was lost in a plane crash.

Copyright © American Book Company. DO NOT DUPLICATE. 1-888-264-5877.

Chapter 3

Read this passage, and then study the questions and explanations after it.

Excerpt from *Adventures of Tom Sawyer*

by Mark Twain

About noon the next day the boys arrived at the dead tree: they had come for their tools. Tom was impatient to go to the haunted house; Huck was measurably so, also but suddenly said:

"Looky here, Tom, do you know what day it is?"

Tom mentally ran over the days of the week, and then quickly lifted his eyes with a startled look in them.

"My! I never once thought of it, Huck!"

"Well, I didn't neither, but all at once it popped on to me that it was Friday."

"Blame it, a body can't be too careful, Huck. We might a got into an awful scrape, tackling such a thing on a Friday."

"Might! Better say we would! There's some lucky days, maybe, but Friday ain't."

"Any fool knows that. I don't reckon you was the first that found it out, Huck."

"Well, I never said I was, did I? And Friday ain't all, neither. I had a rotten bad dream last night, dreamt about rats."

"No! Sure sign of trouble. Did they fight?"

"No."

"Well, that's good, Huck. When they don't fight it's only a sign that there's trouble around, you know. All we got to do is to look mighty sharp and keep out of it. We'll drop this thing for today, and play. Do you know Robin Hood, Huck?"

"No. Who's Robin Hood?"

"Why, he was one of the greatest men that was ever in England—and the best. He was a robber."

"Cracky, I wisht I was. Who did he rob?"

"Only sheriffs and bishops and rich people and kings, and such like. But he never bothered the poor. He loved 'em. He always divided up with 'em perfectly square."

Copyright © American Book Company. DO NOT DUPLICATE. 1-888-264-5877.

How do the setting, plot, and characters interact in this passage?

At the beginning of the excerpt, the boys are planning to go to a haunted house. They meet at a dead tree, so we can tell they are outside, most likely in or near the woods. It seems like an isolated and possibly scary place. But they have been there before, since the passage tells they have come to pick up their tools. They come up with an excuse not to visit the haunted house. This tells you that they are probably more scared than excited about the adventure. They decide instead to take advantage of their surroundings—the woods—and play Robin Hood. This folk hero and his band of thieves "robbed from the rich and gave to the poor," as Tom explains to Huck. This tells you that Tom has read more than Huck, since he knows all about Robin Hood.

What does the boys' conversation show you about their lives?

The way the boys speak, in a southern dialect, gives you an idea about where they live. Their activities tell you a little about their age. As they talk about Friday being an unlucky day, you can tell that they are superstitious (believing that certain things cause good or bad fortune). When Tom talks about Robin Hood, he clearly admires him for stealing from the rich and giving to the poor. This tells you that Tom and Huck most likely are poor themselves.

Practice 2: Literary Elements

RL 1, 2, 3, 6, 10

> **DIRECTIONS**   **Read the following passages, and answer the questions.**

The Town Mouse and the Country Mouse

by Aesop

1   Once upon a time, a Town Mouse went on a visit to his cousin in the country. This Country Mouse was rough and ready, but he loved his town friend and made him heartily welcome. Beans and bacon, cheese and bread were all he had to offer, but he offered them freely.

2   The Town Mouse rather turned up his long nose at this country fare and said: "I cannot understand, Cousin, how you can put up with such poor food as this. But, of course, you cannot expect anything better in the country. Come with me, and I will show you how to live. When you have been in town a week, you will wonder how you could ever have stood a country life."

Copyright © American Book Company. DO NOT DUPLICATE. 1-888-264-5877.

3   No sooner said than done, the two mice set off for the town and arrived at the Town Mouse's residence late at night. "You will want some refreshment after our long journey," said the polite Town Mouse, and took his friend into the grand dining room. There they found the remains of a fine feast, and soon the two mice were eating up roasts and ham, cakes and jellies, and all that was nice. Suddenly, they heard growling and barking. "What is that?" said the Country Mouse. "It is only the dogs of the house," answered the other. "Only!" said the Country Mouse. "I do not like that music at my dinner." Just at that moment the door flew open, in ran two terriers, and the two mice had to scamper down and run off.

4   "Good-bye, Cousin," said the Country Mouse, "What! Going so soon?" said the other.

5   "Yes," he replied…

6   "Better beans and bacon in peace than roasts and cakes in fear."

1   Choose the summary that best describes the plot of this fable.

A   Town Mouse goes to visit his country cousin and invites the Country Mouse to the city. The Country Mouse visits the city and hastily returns to his country home, disturbed by all of the sights, sounds, and dangers of the fast-paced city life.

B   A Country Mouse goes to visit his town cousin and invites the Town Mouse to the country. The Town Mouse visits the country and returns hastily to his city home, disturbed by all of the slow-paced events of the country.

C   A Town Mouse goes to visit his country cousin and invites the Country Mouse to the city. The Country Mouse visits the city, finds himself intrigued by the fast life, and decides to remain in the city.

D   A Country Mouse goes to visit his town cousin and invites the Town Mouse to the country. The Town Mouse visits the country, finds himself intrigued by the slow-paced events of the country, and decides to remain in the country.

2   What is the climax of this story?

_____

_____

_____

Copyright © American Book Company. DO NOT DUPLICATE. 1-888-264-5877.

Read this line from Paragraph 2.

Come with me, and I will show you how to live.

3   What is this an example of?

    A   Resolution

    B   Characterization

    C   Flashback

    D   Foreshadowing

4   Which statement best describes the theme of this passage?

    A   The grass is not always greener on the other side of the fence.

    B   If you are unhappy with your life, move to another place.

    C   Sometimes, the early bird does not get the worm.

    D   Don't count your chickens before they hatch.

Excerpt from "Tough Times on the Farm"

by Dennis Martin

I was raised in a small town on the shores of Lake Erie. The big water was only three blocks away from my house, and as a young boy I spent much of my time fishing from its shore with my two friends, Sparky and Dave. When I wasn't fishing, I was busy working. Life in the city brought many opportunities for a young boy to make money. First, there was my paper route. I would fold the papers in thirds, tuck in the ends real tight, load them in the basket on the front of my bike, and throw them on the porches of all my customers. Not only did I get paid every week, but during the holiday season, I would always receive nice tips from the homeowners. With the changing of the seasons came more means of making money for a boy of industrious inclinations. In the winter, I would shovel the snow off the walks for all the elderly people. In the spring and summer, I would cut their grass, and in the fall I would rake their leaves and clear their lawns of the ubiquitous buckeyes. Life was good, and I always had money to spend.

---

5   What point of view does this passage use? How can you tell?

_____

_____

_____

6   Based on the passage, what can you tell about the narrator?

    A   He is a troublemaker.

    B   He works very hard.

    C   He doesn't go to school.

    D   He has no friends.

Copyright © American Book Company. DO NOT DUPLICATE. 1-888-264-5877.

7   What is most likely the theme of this passage?

    A   Enjoy childhood, as you will work a long time in adulthood.

    B   With every passing year, there is more and more to do.

    C   In small towns, work always tends to be seasonal.

    D   If you work hard, you will reap many rewards.

8   What effect does the setting have on this story?

_____

_____

CHAPTER 3 SUMMARY

Literary elements are the building blocks of writing.

Characters are people, animals, or objects that perform the actions in a story. Authors reveal characters through **description**, **narration**, **dialogue**, and **actions**.

Point of view is the perspective of the **narrator** who tells the story. **First-person point of view** means a character in the story tells it, while **third-person point of view** means it is told by an unnamed observer. Third-person point of view can be **limited** (readers learn most about one character), **omniscient** (readers know everything about all the characters) or **objective** (readers see what happens but do not learn about thoughts and feelings).

The **plot** is the pattern of events in a story and includes the following stages:

- **Exposition or introduction**
- **Conflicts**
- **Rising action**
- **Climax**
- **Falling action**
- **Resolution or denouement**

A **flashback** shows an event in the past that affects the plot or characters. **Foreshadowing** is a reference that suggests a future event.

The **theme** is the underlying meaning or message of a work of literature. Different types of writing can have similar **themes and central ideas** about a topic.

Summarize means using your own words for a condensed version of a passage.

Elements work together in a story or drama so that each has an effect on the others. The various elements also work together to give shape and meaning to the story.

For more practice with this chapter's material, see the Literature Review on page 61.

Copyright © American Book Company. DO NOT DUPLICATE. 1-888-264-5877.

Chapter 4
Literary Devices

This chapter covers the following seventh grade strand and standards:

Reading: Literature

Key Ideas and Details

1. Cite several pieces of textual evidence to support analysis of what the text says explicitly as well as inferences drawn from the text.

Craft and Structure

4. Determine the meaning of words and phrases as they are used in a text, including figurative and connotative meanings; analyze the impact of rhymes and other repetitions of sounds (e.g., alliteration) on a specific verse or stanza of a poem or section of a story or drama.

Range of Reading and Level of Text Complexity

10. By the end of the year, read and comprehend literature, including stories, dramas, and poems, in the grades 6–8 text complexity band proficiently, with scaffolding as needed at the high end of the range.

LITERARY DEVICES

In this section, you will read about the ways in which authors make writing interesting and memorable. This includes the use of figurative language and sound devices. These **literary devices** help to shape the literature that you read.

All writing has words, but the way authors use words makes each story, novel, play, and poem unique. As you saw in chapter 2, all literature has certain devices that must be present. But authors can choose from among elements they can include.

FIGURATIVE LANGUAGE

Have you ever heard a statement similar to one of these?

You could have knocked me over with a feather!

My brother eats like a pig.

She has a heart of gold.

Charlie is a beast on the soccer field!

Copyright © American Book Company. DO NOT DUPLICATE. 1-888-264-5877.

These are all examples of **figurative language**. In literature, writers use figurative language to liven up their writing. Often, one thing is described in terms of something else. To do this, authors use creative comparisons. Figurative language is most often used to convey meaning, mood, and images in a passage. Now, let's look at some of the types of figurative language you might find in literature.

Types of Figurative Language	
Device	**Definition**
Allusion	An **allusion** is a reference to a well-known place, literary or art work, famous person, or historical event. Today, these references are often related to pop culture. Allusions are dependent on the reader being familiar with the work or item mentioned. **Example:** If you tell your friends that your cousin reminds you of Bart Simpson, they would have a definite picture of that boy's personality!
Analogy	An **analogy** is a comparison of two unlike things that uses imagery to help understand a concept. **Example:** "Life is like a box of chocolates: you never know what you're going to get." – Forrest Gump
Hyperbole	**Hyperbole** is the use of overstatement or exaggeration. It is a special type of figurative language that allows writers to infuse shades of meaning into their descriptions of characters and plots. Many hyperboles can be funny. **Example:** "I have seen this river so wide it only had one bank." – Mark Twain
Imagery	**Imagery** is language that appeals to the senses. Most images are visual; they appeal to the sense of sight, creating pictures that readers can see in their minds. Other images appeal to the senses of touch, taste, hearing, or smell. **Example:** Joey awoke to the aroma of blueberry pancakes and bacon. He could hear the "sizzle pop" sound of the bacon frying in Grandma's iron skillet. Opening his eyes, he saw the floral pattern of the wallpaper that trimmed the tops of Grandma's guest-bedroom walls.

Copyright © American Book Company. DO NOT DUPLICATE. 1-888-264-5877.

Irony	Irony is a contrast between expectation and reality. There are three common types of irony.

- **Verbal irony** involves a contrast between what is said or written and what is meant.

Example: After a day of mischief, little Juan was tired. With a smile, his mother put him down for a nap, cooing sweetly, "Now, you can rest, *my little angel*."

- **Situational irony** occurs when what happens is very different from what is expected to happen.

Example: In Aesop's fable "The Tortoise and the Hare," a slow-moving tortoise *wins a race of speed* against a much-speedier hare.

- **Dramatic irony** occurs when the audience or the reader knows something a character does not know.

Example: In reading a tragic novel in which a character is gravely ill and going to die, the reader might learn of the character's fate *before* the character does.

Metaphor	A **metaphor** is an imaginative comparison between two unlike things in which one thing is said to be another thing. Metaphors, unlike similes, do not use words such as *like*, *as*, *than*, or *resembles*, to express comparisons. **Example:** The roar of the engines was thunder, and the sparks flying on the speedway were its partner, lightning.
Personification	**Personification** is a figure of speech in which a nonhuman thing or quality is given human characteristics. Often, the use of personified objects in literature conjures up vivid mental images that readers can picture. **Example:** The numbers danced off the page of my algebra test.

Copyright © American Book Company. DO NOT DUPLICATE. 1-888-264-5877.

Pun	A **pun** is a way of using words so that their meaning can be taken in different ways, which makes what is said humorous. A pun is often referred to as a *play on words*.
	Example: Notice the word play in the following excerpt from *Alice's Adventures in Wonderland*, by Lewis Carroll.
	"And how many hours a day did you do lessons?" said Alice, in a hurry to change the subject. "Ten hours the first day," said the Mock Turtle, "nine the next, and so on." "What a curious plan!" exclaimed Alice. "That's the reason they're called lessons," the Gryphon remarked: "because they lessen from day to day."
	The pun involves the similar sounds but vastly different meanings of the words *lessons* and *lessen*.
Simile	A **simile** makes a comparison between two unlike things, using a word such as *like, as, than,* or *resembles*. Writers commonly use similes to express their ideas in a precise or imaginative manner.
	Example: He is crazy like a fox.
Symbolism	A **symbol** is a person, place, thing, or event that has its own meaning but also stands for something beyond itself. Symbols are used in everyday life.
Helen Keller	**Example:** Many examples of symbolism appear in *The Miracle Worker* by William Gibson. It is a play about how Anne Sullivan taught sign language to Helen Keller. One symbol is a rag doll that Helen carries. She tries to put buttons where the doll's eyes should be. The doll represents Helen in a way, and her action symbolizes her desire to connect with the outside world.

Writers also give precise and imaginative expression to the ideas they wish to convey. They choose words with just the right **connotations**. For example, the words *odor* and *aroma* can both mean "smell." However, if you told a chef that her dinner had an interesting aroma, she would probably thank you. But if you told her that her dinner had an interesting odor, she would probably be offended. Both of these words denote, or mean, "smell." But the connotation of aroma is positive while that of odor can be negative. (For more about denotation and connotation, see chapter 7.)

Copyright © American Book Company. DO NOT DUPLICATE. 1-888-264-5877.

Example: Both the words *reliable* and *accountable* are denoted as *responsible*. However, without understanding their connotations, these words can be misused. Read the following sentences:

1   I can trust Janine to look after my pet iguana because she is such an *accountable* girl.

2   Jessie, who carelessly had overturned the pitcher, was held *reliable* for the damage.

In sentence 1, the word *accountable* seems awkward because of its connotation as *blameworthy* rather than *dependable*. In sentence 2, the word *reliable* seems awkward because of its connotation as *trustworthy* rather than *blameworthy*.

Now read the following selection from Geoffrey Chaucer's *Canterbury Tales*. Notice how the denotations and connotations of his words enrich the description of Chanticleer, the proud rooster:

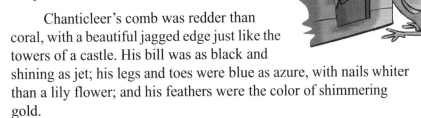

> Chanticleer's comb was redder than coral, with a beautiful jagged edge just like the towers of a castle. His bill was as black and shining as jet; his legs and toes were blue as azure, with nails whiter than a lily flower; and his feathers were the color of shimmering gold.

Chaucer uses words like *coral*, *shining*, *towers*, and *shimmering gold* because of their strong connotations. Taken together, these lead to an emotional response: they bring up the image or feeling of majesty, beauty, and magnificence.

How words relate in context can greatly affect the meaning and mood in writing.

Practice 1: Figurative Language

RL 1, 4, 10

> **DIRECTIONS**   **Read and answer the questions.**

1   Which of the following is an example of situational irony in the fairy tale "Cinderella"?

   A   The mean stepsisters never work and are mad at Cinderella for ruining their dresses.

   B   Cinderella is treated like a servant but is chosen by the prince over her pampered stepsisters.

   C   The evil stepmother tries to get the prince to notice her daughters because she wants to be rich.

   D   The king has a ball so the prince can choose a wife from many eligible young ladies.

Copyright © American Book Company. DO NOT DUPLICATE. 1-888-264-5877.

2   If a friend told you her father reminds her of Ebenezer Scrooge, what would this allusion say about his personality?

   A   He loves children.

   B   He enjoys cooking.

   C   He is stingy with money.

   D   He gets haunted by ghosts.

3   In *Romeo and Juliet,* when Mercutio is about to die of a stab wound, he says, "Ask for me tomorrow and you shall find me a grave man." Explain what makes this a pun.

_____

_____

_____

_____

Read each passage, and then answer the questions that follow.

Colin had been nervous all day. He had been practicing his oral history report for three weeks, yet he felt unprepared. He shuddered to think how he would feel standing in front of his classmates trying to remember details about the Trail of Tears. Colin was so nervous about his speech that he had forgotten to write his name on his spelling quiz and made careless mistakes on his math test.

Now, as he sat at the lunch table, knowing the speech would be next period during social studies, Colin felt just like a newly hatched chick—he wanted to crawl right back into his shell. He slowly ate his lunch, lost in thought, going over the speech in his head. So consumed by worries about the coming speech, Colin forgot to grab a napkin and wipe his mouth after lunch. Unknowingly, he left the cafeteria and headed to social studies class with a milk moustache.

Finally, it was Colin's turn to speak. He got up and walked slowly to the front of the classroom, turning to face the other students. A soft ripple of giggles made their way to him, starting with a small point-and-sniggle from Amy Tinsley in the back. When Mrs. Boles looked up from her notes to see what the children found so amusing, she had to hold back her own giggle. "Colin, dear," she said in her gentle way, "you are wearing a milk moustache."

4   How does the use of irony affect this story?

   A   The readers understand that Colin is nervous about his report.

   B   The readers are first to know that Colin has a milk moustache.

   C   The readers find out that Colin's teacher is named Mrs. Boles.

   D   The readers know that the subject of Colin's report is the Trail of Tears.

Copyright © American Book Company. DO NOT DUPLICATE. 1-888-264-5877.

5 By comparing Colin to a "newly hatched chick," what does the author tells us about Colin's speaking experience?

    A He has only made one speech, but he's happy to make another.

    B He has given speeches many times.

    C He loves to give speeches, especially on the Trail of Tears.

    D He has not made many speeches before.

Excerpt from "Life"

by Emily Dickinson

He ate and drank the precious words,

His spirit grew robust;

He knew no more that he was poor,

Nor that his frame was dust.

He danced along the dingy days,

And this bequest of wings

Was but a book. What liberty

A loosened spirit brings!

---

6 The main character "danced along the dingy days." What does the author mean by this?

    A He was employed in the cleaning business.

    B The book he was reading was about dancing.

    C Boring days went by quickly thanks to reading.

    D His life passed him by because he was preoccupied.

7 The poem says "this bequest [gift] of wings / Was but a book. What liberty / A loosened spirit brings!" What point is the author making about reading? Use the rest of the poem to support your idea.

_____

_____

_____

_____

Copyright © American Book Company. DO NOT DUPLICATE. 1-888-264-5877.

Sitting propped up by pillows in his bed, Kunal looked around his room. He saw his new computer system, complete with the latest technology and gadgets. It sat there on the desk that had been a surprise from his older brother who was away at college. On his right was the flat-screen television that his parents had bought for him. The corkboard beside the TV had little space left; it was crowded by funny pictures and get-well cards from friends and family. Kunal could not help but think of himself as incredibly lucky and loved, despite the heavy cast on his broken leg. He would have lots of time to use his computer and watch his TV now that he could no longer compete. He wouldn't be traveling to all the state and regional tournaments with the team. He had played basketball as long as he could remember, always perfecting his game. And now that he was so close, he might never get the scholarship he was hoping for. It would have made sense had he broken his leg playing. But he was in this cast because of taking a clumsy step off a curb!

8   Which type of imagery is used mostly in the following passage? Give at least two examples of which sense the author appeals to most.

_____

_____

_____

_____

9   What object could most be considered a symbol for Kunal not being able to play basketball?

   A   The cast on his leg

   B   The computer

   C   His new television

   D   His room

Copyright © American Book Company. DO NOT DUPLICATE. 1-888-264-5877.

Frederick Douglass was a slave who gained his freedom and became a famous abolitionist (a person who believes there should be no slavery and often fights for this cause), speaker, author, and publisher.

Excerpt from *My Bondage and My Freedom*

by Frederick Douglass

Frederick Douglass

"Make a noise," "make a noise," and "bear a hand" are the words usually addressed to the slaves when there is silence among them. This may account for the almost constant singing heard in the Southern states. There was, generally, more or less singing among the teamsters, as it was one means of letting the overseer know where they were, and that they were moving on with the work. But, on allowance day, those who visited the great house farm were peculiarly excited and noisy. While on their way, they would make the dense old woods, for miles around, reverberate with their wild notes. These were not always merry because they were wild. On the contrary, they were mostly of a plaintive cast, and told a tale of grief and sorrow. In the most boisterous outbursts of rapturous sentiment, there was ever a tinge of deep melancholy. I have never heard any songs like those anywhere since I left slavery, except when in Ireland. There I heard the same *wailing notes*, and was much affected by them. It was during the famine of 1845-6.

10 What does the author say that their singing symbolized for the slaves?

    A Yearning   **B** Happiness   **C** Freedom   **D** Melancholy

SOUND DEVICES

Have you ever had to recite a poem? Some forms of literature, such as poetry, are written to be read aloud. In these cases, **sound devices** help to shape the writing of these literary forms. Writers use the following sound devices to give creativity and style to their writing. As with other literary devices, sound devices are used to convey meaning, mood, and imagery.

Copyright © American Book Company. DO NOT DUPLICATE. 1-888-264-5877.

Alliteration is the repetition of the same or very similar consonant sounds at the beginning of words. Alliteration helps emphasize words. It is used most often in poetry.

Example: The whisper of the wind-blown willows (repeats the "w" sound)

Onomatopoeia refers to words that sound like what they are describing. Onomatopoeia helps to create the sound imagery of poetry.

Examples: *meow, buzz, tick-tock, boom*

Rhyme is the repetition of accented vowel sounds and all sounds following them in words placed close together in a poem.

Example: The cat in the hat sat on the mat. (*Cat, hat, sat,* and *mat* all rhyme.)

Two types of rhyme are internal rhyme and end rhyme.

- **Internal rhyme** means that words within a line rhyme.

Example: We fight with all our might to win by ten tonight!

Fight, might, and *tonight* all rhyme.

- **End rhyme** occurs at the end of lines.

Example:

> Here a star, and there a star,
>
> Some lose their way.
>
> Here a mist, and there a mist,
>
> Afterwards – day!
>
> – Emily Dickinson

In this poem, lines 2 and 4 use end rhyme.

The pattern of end rhyme in a poem is called a **rhyme scheme**. Readers use separate letters of the alphabet to identify each new sound in a poem's rhyme scheme. For example, the following quatrain (a poem or stanza consisting of four lines) has an *abab* rhyme scheme:

> Thou art my life, my love, my heart (*a*)
>
> The very eyes of me (*b*)
>
> And hast command of every part (*a*)
>
> To live and die for thee. (*b*)
>
> – from "To Athena Who May Command Him Any Thing" by Robert Herrick

Copyright © American Book Company. DO NOT DUPLICATE. 1-888-264-5877.

RHYTHM

Just like in music, **rhythm** refers to the beat and pace of written words. This is achieved by stressing certain syllables. Especially in poetry (in which meter is used to measure syllables), rhythm becomes important in the overall structure of the writing. Depending on how sounds are arranged, rhythm can be fast or slow, choppy or smooth, pleasant or harsh. Rhythm in prose (stories and novels) comes from repetitions of sounds and pauses.

Notice the rhythm of the excerpt from "The Song of Hiawatha" by Henry Wadsworth Longfellow.

> By the shore of Gitchie Gumee,
>
> By the shining Big-Sea-Water,
>
> At the doorway of his wigwam,
>
> In the pleasant Summer morning,
>
> Hiawatha stood and waited.

The rhythm is repetitive, with the stress on the same syllables in each line. So it sounds almost like a Native American chant.

Practice 2: Sound Devices

RL 1, 4, 10

DIRECTIONS	Read the passage, and then answer the questions that follow.

Excerpt from "The Raven"

by Edgar Allan Poe

Once upon a midnight dreary, while I pondered, weak and weary,

Over many a quaint and curious volume of forgotten <u>lore</u>,

While I nodded, nearly napping, suddenly there came a tapping,

As of some one gently rapping, rapping at my chamber <u>door</u>.

"'Tis some visitor," I muttered, "tapping at my chamber <u>door</u>—

Only this, and nothing <u>more</u>."

Copyright © American Book Company. DO NOT DUPLICATE. 1-888-264-5877.

Chapter 4

1 In this poem, what literary sound device is used in the underlined words?

   A Alliteration   **C** End rhyme

   B Onomatopoeia   **D** Internal rhyme

2 Which literary sound device is used in the phrase "while I pondered, weak and weary"?

_____

3 The rhythm of the poem is steady until the last line. Why does it most likely change then?

   A It trails off to show the reader that the narrator of the poem has left the room.

   B It ends abruptly to give an eerie, suspenseful feeling about what comes next.

   C It gets faster as the narrator becomes more frightened, and his heart beats faster.

   D It slows down to show that it is late at night, and the house is very quiet.

Excerpt from "Life"

by Emily Dickinson

Glee! The great storm is over!

Four have recovered the land;

Forty gone down together

Into the boiling sand.

---

4 Which of the following represents the rhyme scheme of this poem?

   A abcc

   B abcb

   C abaa

   D abbc

Copyright © American Book Company. DO NOT DUPLICATE. 1-888-264-5877.

CHAPTER 4 SUMMARY

Authors use **literary devices** to shape the literature they write.

They use **figurative language** to liven up their writing through precise and imaginative expressions, including the following:

- **Allusion**
- **Analogy**
- **Hyperbole**
- **Imagery**
- **Irony**
  - ■ **Verbal irony**
  - ■ **Situational irony**
  - ■ **Dramatic irony**
- **Metaphor**
- **Personification**
- **Pun**
- **Simile**
- **Symbolism**

Writers also express themselves with precision and imagination by choosing words with just the right **connotations**.

Especially in works meant to be read aloud, writers use **sound devices** to add creativity and style. Sound devices include the following:

- **Alliteration**
- **Onomatopoeia**
- **Rhyme**
  - ■ **Internal rhyme**
  - ■ **End rhyme**
  - ■ **Rhyme scheme**
- **Rhythm**

For more practice with this chapter's material, see the Literature Review on page 61.

Copyright © American Book Company. DO NOT DUPLICATE. 1-888-264-5877.

Copyright © American Book Company. DO NOT DUPLICATE. 1-888-264-5877.

Literature Review

This chapter covers the following seventh grade strand and standards.

RL 1–7, 9–10, W 1–4, 7–9, SL 1–6, L 1–6

This review will give you more practice with the skills you read about in chapters 2, 3, and 4. Read the passages, and answer the questions that follow. Then, you will write about what you read.

Practice 1: Analyzing Passages

RL 1, 2, 3, 4, 6, 9, 10, W 1, 2, 4, 9, 10, L 4.a

DIRECTIONS **Read the passages, and answer the questions that follow.**

Early Years of the New York City Police

The New York City Police Department was established in 1844, when the city had some 320,000 residents. A police force of about 900 officers was formed, replacing the old night watch, marshals, and constables. The NYPD was reorganized in 1845 into three districts. Each had its own station house, court, magistrates, and clerks. The force was closely modeled on the military-style police of London. In 1857, state legislators in Albany made further changes. They felt New York City government was getting too strong. The state created a new Metropolitan police and abolished the existing Municipal police, but not without a fight. The Municipals refused to break up for several months, and the two forces clashed repeatedly. It was a heyday for crime, as the "Mets" would have their arrests interrupted by the Municipals. Finally, the courts upheld the state's decision, and the Municipals were disbanded.

Copyright © American Book Company. DO NOT DUPLICATE. 1-888-264-5877.

Over the next few years, the police were involved in large-scale riots. This included the 1863 Draft Riots and the Tompkins Square Riot involving thousands of unemployed workers. There were also clashes in poor immigrant neighborhoods, and officers were accused of police brutality. The newspapers covered numerous cases like these. Soon there was public resentment of the NYPD.

In the 1870s, the political machine Tammany Hall began to take over the police. There was widespread corruption. Many officers took bribes from local businesses. In exchange for money, they would overlook illegal practices. They also turned a blind eye to fraud at polling places, allowing corrupt officials to take or remain in office. In 1894, the Lexow Committee investigated and gave a scathing report. It recommended major reform. In 1895, Theodore Roosevelt (later the twenty-sixth president) was appointed police commissioner. Roosevelt hired new officers who were not tied politically. He also recruited from ethnic minorities and even hired the first woman.

By the early 1900s, the NYPD was far more professional and modern. Reports of police misconduct dropped notably. Roosevelt established new units like a bomb squad and emergency service. He also brought in firearms and ordered the training to use them. The police began to use modern forensic methods like fingerprinting.

After Twenty Years

by O. Henry

1   The policeman on the beat moved up the avenue impressively. The impressiveness was habitual and not for show, for spectators were few. The time was barely 10 o'clock at night, but chilly gusts of wind with a taste of rain in them had well nigh de-peopled the streets.

2   Trying doors as he went, twirling his club with many intricate and artful movements, turning now and then to cast his watchful eye adown the pacific thoroughfare, the officer, with his stalwart form and slight swagger, made a fine picture of a guardian of the peace.

3   The vicinity was one that kept early hours. Now and then you might see the lights of a cigar store or of an all-night lunch counter; but the majority of the doors belonged to business places that had long since been closed.

4   When about midway of a certain block the policeman suddenly slowed his walk. In the doorway of a darkened hardware store a man leaned, with an unlighted cigar in his mouth. As the policeman walked up to him the man spoke up quickly.

Copyright © American Book Company. DO NOT DUPLICATE. 1-888-264-5877.

5   "It's all right, officer," he said, reassuringly. "I'm just waiting for a friend. It's an appointment made twenty years ago. Sounds a little funny to you, doesn't it? Well, I'll explain if you'd like to make certain it's all straight. About that long ago there used to be a restaurant where this store stands—'Big Joe' Brady's restaurant."

6   "Until five years ago," said the policeman. "It was torn down then."

7   The man in the doorway struck a match and lit his cigar. The light showed a pale, square-jawed face with keen eyes, and a little white scar near his right eyebrow. His scarfpin was a large diamond, oddly set.

8   "Twenty years ago to-night," said the man, "I dined here at 'Big Joe' Brady's with Jimmy Wells, my best chum, and the finest chap in the world. He and I were raised here in New York, just like two brothers, together. I was eighteen and Jimmy was twenty. The next morning I was to start for the West to make my fortune. You couldn't have dragged Jimmy out of New York; he thought it was the only place on earth. Well, we agreed that night that we would meet here again exactly twenty years from that date and time, no matter what our conditions might be or from what distance we might have to come. We figured that in twenty years each of us ought to have our destiny worked out and our fortunes made, whatever they were going to be."

9   "It sounds pretty interesting," said the policeman. "Rather a long time between meets, though, it seems to me. Haven't you heard from your friend since you left?"

10   "Well, yes, for a time we corresponded," said the other. "But after a year or two we lost track of each other. You see, the West is a pretty big proposition, and I kept hustling around over it pretty lively. But I know Jimmy will meet me here if he's alive, for he always was the truest, stanchest old chap in the world. He'll never forget. I came a thousand miles to stand in this door to-night, and it's worth it if my old partner turns up."

11   The waiting man pulled out a handsome watch, the lids of it set with small diamonds.

12   "Three minutes to ten," he announced. "It was exactly ten o'clock when we parted here at the restaurant door."

13   "Did pretty well out West, didn't you?" asked the policeman.

14   "You bet! I hope Jimmy has done half as well. He was a kind of plodder, though, good fellow as he was. I've had to compete with some of the sharpest wits going to get my pile. A man gets in a groove in New York. It takes the West to put a razor-edge on him."

Copyright © American Book Company. DO NOT DUPLICATE. 1-888-264-5877.

15   The policeman twirled his club and took a step or two.

"I'll be on my way. Hope your friend comes around all right. Going to call time on him sharp?"

16   "I should say not!" said the other. "I'll give him half an hour at least. If Jimmy is alive on earth he'll be here by that time. So long, officer."

17   "Good-night, sir," said the policeman, passing on along his beat, trying doors as he went.

18   There was now a fine, cold drizzle falling, and the wind had risen from its uncertain puffs into a steady blow. The few foot passengers astir in that quarter hurried dismally and silently along with coat collars turned high and pocketed hands. And in the door of the hardware store the man who had come a thousand miles to fill an appointment, uncertain almost to absurdity, with the friend of his youth, smoked his cigar and waited.

19   About twenty minutes he waited, and then a tall man in a long overcoat, with collar turned up to his ears, hurried across from the opposite side of the street. He went directly to the waiting man.

20   "Is that you, Bob?" he asked, doubtfully.

21   "Is that you, Jimmy Wells?" cried the man in the door.

22   "Bless my heart!" exclaimed the new arrival, grasping both the other's hands with his own. "It's Bob, sure as fate. I was certain I'd find you here if you were still in existence. Well, well, well!—twenty years is a long time. The old gone, Bob; I wish it had lasted, so we could have had another dinner there. How has the West treated you, old man?"

23   "Bully; it has given me everything I asked it for. You've changed lots, Jimmy. I never thought you were so tall by two or three inches."

24   "Oh, I grew a bit after I was twenty."

25   "Doing well in New York, Jimmy?"

26   "Moderately. I have a position in one of the city departments. Come on, Bob; we'll go around to a place I know of, and have a good long talk about old times."

27   The two men started up the street, arm in arm. The man from the West, his egotism enlarged by success, was beginning to outline the history of his career. The other, submerged in his overcoat, listened with interest.

28   At the corner stood a drug store, brilliant with electric lights. When they came into this glare each of them turned simultaneously to gaze upon the other's face.

Copyright © American Book Company. DO NOT DUPLICATE. 1-888-264-5877.

29   The man from the West stopped suddenly and released his arm.

30   "You're not Jimmy Wells," he snapped. "Twenty years is a long time, but not long enough to change a man's nose from a Roman to a pug."

31   "It sometimes changes a good man into a bad one," said the tall man. "You've been under arrest for ten minutes, 'Silky' Bob. Chicago thinks you may have dropped over our way and wires us she wants to have a chat with you. Going quietly, are you? That's sensible. Now, before we go on to the station here's a note I was asked to hand you. You may read it here at the window. It's from Patrolman Wells."

32   The man from the West unfolded the little piece of paper handed him. His hand was steady when he began to read, but it trembled a little by the time he had finished. The note was rather short.

33   "Bob: I was at the appointed place on time. When you struck the match to light your cigar I saw it was the face of the man wanted in Chicago. Somehow I couldn't do it myself, so I went around and got a plain clothes man to do the job. JIMMY."

1

Based on what you learned from the article "Early Years of the New York City Police," in which decade do you think the story "After Twenty Years" takes place? Why do you think that? Use evidence from the passages to support your answer.

_____

_____

_____

2

Why is it important that the story in "After Twenty Years" happens at night?

_____

_____

_____

Copyright © American Book Company. DO NOT DUPLICATE. 1-888-264-5877.

3

In the story you just read, which of the following best describes the character traits revealed by Patrolman Wells?

A Worldly, fun-loving, risk-taking

B Dutiful, hardworking, focused

C Nostalgic, friendly, restless

D Daring, ambitious, angry

4

In paragraph 10, Bob says "You see, the West is a pretty big proposition, and I kept hustling around over it pretty lively." How does his use of expressions foreshadow what you find out about him later in the story?

A *Proposition* means "something serious to deal with," but it can also mean a *plan*.

B The West is code for having been in a gang, like the outlaws of the Old West.

C *Hustling* means *hurrying*, but it can also mean "making an illegal living."

D He uses the word *pretty*, and his nickname ends up being "Silky Bob."

Writing Task

The waiting man, Bob, tells how he and Jimmy Wells were raised together. They had similar dreams. Over twenty years, they have gone in very different directions. Trace how the author illustrates the different points of view of these two characters—how are they most different, and how are they most alike? What theme does their relationship suggest? Write a brief essay to explain your ideas. Be sure to use evidence from the text.

Copyright © American Book Company. DO NOT DUPLICATE. 1-888-264-5877.

Practice 2: Analyzing Poems

RL 1, 2, 4, 5, 10

DIRECTIONS   **Read these poems, and answer the questions that follow.**

The Fly

by William Blake

Little Fly,

Thy summer's play

My thoughtless hand

Has brushed away.

Am not I

A fly like thee?

Or art not thou

A man like me?

For I dance,

And drink, and sing,

Till some blind hand

Shall brush my wing.

If thought is life

And strength and breath,

And the want

Of thought is death;

Then am I

A happy fly.

If I live,

Or if I die.

Copyright © American Book Company. DO NOT DUPLICATE. 1-888-264-5877.

1

What most likely is the theme of this poem? How does the narrator arrive at his conclusion?

_____

_____

_____

2

How does the structure of this poem contribute to its meaning?

_____

_____

_____

3

What is the fly most likely a symbol for?

A Dancing and singing

B Eternal happiness

C The importance of courage

D The fragility of life

Copyright © American Book Company. DO NOT DUPLICATE. 1-888-264-5877.

Let Love Go On

by Carl Sandburg

Let it go on; let the love of this hour be poured out till the answers are made, the last dollar spent and the last blood gone.

Time runs with an ax and a hammer, time slides down the hallways with a pass-key and a master-key, and time gets by, time wins.

Let the love of this hour go on; let all the oaths and children and people of this love be clean as a washed stone under a waterfall in the sun.

Time is a young man with ballplayer legs, time runs a winning race against life and the clocks, time tickles with rust and spots.

Let love go on; the heartbeats are measured out with a measuring glass, so many apiece to gamble with, to use and spend and reckon; let love go on.

4

What type of poem is this? How can you tell this?

_____

_____

_____

5

What is the effect of repetition in this poem?

A It gives the poem a rhythm.

B It separates the stanzas.

C It explains why love is important.

D It shows that love is tiring.

Copyright © American Book Company. DO NOT DUPLICATE. 1-888-264-5877.

Practice 3: Write a Story

W 3, 4, 5, 10, L 1–3, 5

DIRECTIONS

Use your own paper to write a story based on this prompt.

Think about two people who like each other but have different viewpoints about something they must collaborate on. Write a story (based on real events or made up) that shows how they interact. Do they find a solution? Is it a solution that works for both of them?

Use your own paper to write your story. Make sure your writing is clear and well organized. Be creative, and incorporate literary elements and devices into your writing. Be sure to check for and fix any mistakes.

Activity

SL 1.a–d, 2, 4, 5

Illustrate the story you wrote for Practice 3. Make a series of drawings, storyboards, or cartoons to accompany your story. Or create a collage that embodies the story. You might even pretend that you're creating the cover for your story, just like the ones you see in bookstores. Show your illustration to your working group or to the class, and ask what they think the story will be about. Then read your story, and discuss whether there were any surprises for the listeners.

Participate in discussions of others' work. Provide your feedback on their illustrations and stories too. Be sure to take turns talking, listen to others, and build on their ideas as well as telling your own.

Copyright © American Book Company. DO NOT DUPLICATE. 1-888-264-5877.

Practice 4: Research Project

RL 1, 2, 3, 7, 10, **W** 2, 4–9, 10, **L** 1–3

Complete a project with the following steps.

1. Read one of the books, stories, or plays listed in the pairings below.

2. Then watch the film adaptation of that book. (Be sure to check with your parents if the movie is rated PG or PG-13.) As you watch, make some notes about the film techniques you notice in the adaptation. These include lighting, special effects, camera angles, sound and sound effects, and color choices.

3. Do some research—in books, on the Internet, or by talking with an expert—about how the techniques were used and effects created. If you rent a DVD of the film that has special features, see if there is a "making of" feature. This might provide some insights.

4. Finally, write a report about your experience. Tell how your viewing of the film adaptation was different from reading the book. Provide details about exactly what techniques helped to make it a different experience.

Book	Film adaptation(s)
Twenty Thousand Leagues Under the Sea by Jules Verne	*20,000 Leagues Under the Sea* (1996) starring Richard Crenna, Ben Cross
the Adventures of Huckleberry Finn by Mark Twain	*Adventures of Huckleberry Finn* (1985) starring Lillian Gish, Richard Kiley
The Lion, the Witch and the Wardrobe by C. S. Lewis	*The Chronicles of Narnia: The Lion, the Witch & the Wardrobe* (2005) starring Georgie Henley, Skandar Keynes
"The Gift of the Magi" (story) by O. Henry	*Gift of the Magi* (2010) staring Marla Sokoloff, Mark Webber
Peter Pan by J. M. Barrie	*Peter Pan* (2003) starring Jeremy Sumpter, Jason Isaacs
The Jungle Book by Rudyard Kipling	*Rudyard Kipling's The Jungle Book* (1994) starring Jason Scott Lee, Cary Elwes

Copyright © American Book Company. DO NOT DUPLICATE. 1-888-264-5877.

Copyright © American Book Company. DO NOT DUPLICATE. 1-888-264-5877.

Chapter 5
Understanding Informational Texts

This chapter covers the following seventh grade strand and standards:

Reading: Informational Text

Key Ideas and Details

1. Cite several pieces of textual evidence to support analysis of what the text says explicitly as well as inferences drawn from the text.

2. Determine two or more central ideas in a text and analyze their development over the course of the text; provide an objective summary of the text.

Craft and Structure

4. Determine the meaning of words and phrases as they are used in a text, including figurative, connotative, and technical meanings; analyze the impact of a specific word choice on meaning and tone.

5. Analyze the structure an author uses to organize a text, including how the major sections contribute to the whole and to the development of the ideas.

Range of Reading and Level of Text Complexity

10. By the end of the year, read and comprehend literary nonfiction in the grades 6–8 text complexity band proficiently, with scaffolding as needed at the high end of the range.

Informational texts tell facts and relate true stories. Some can be articles or essays that provide information about a topic. Others can be like stories, telling about actual events or the life of a real person. To get the most out of what you read, you need to be able to pick out central ideas and understand all of the words and phrases that the author uses.

CENTRAL IDEAS

The **central idea** is what a passage is all about. It is the focus of the passage. To identify a central idea, you must first read carefully. A good reader will also look for clues and use thinking questions like these:

- What is the passage mostly about?
- Is there one sentence that states the central idea?
- How can I summarize the passage in my own words?

When you read, you need to be aware of your purpose and vary your speed and strategies to suit the situation. For example, think about reading the newspaper. You might scan the headlines and first sentences of articles to find ones that interest you. You may quickly read for the main ideas in some articles. However, if you find a story that is important to you, you will slow down and read it more carefully so you can get all the facts. You might even read it more than once

Copyright © American Book Company. DO NOT DUPLICATE. 1-888-264-5877.

Many texts have more than one central idea. You should be able to analyze the **development of central ideas** in the text. This means looking at how the author builds the ideas and uses details to support them. It includes exploring how the author uses specific sentence and paragraph structure to make a point. Picking out exactly which part of the text supports an idea can help you answer questions too. When you respond to questions in class and on tests, you will need to cite evidence that supports your analysis of the text.

Read the following text. Then read the questions and explanations that follow.

The Mystery of Easter Island

There are few places on the earth more mysterious and intriguing than Easter Island. It is one of the most isolated islands in the world, with the nearest country over 2,300 miles away. About 1200 years ago, seafarers from a distant culture managed to land upon its remote shores. Over the centuries that followed, a remarkable society developed in isolation on the island.

For reasons still unknown, they began carving giant statues out of volcanic rock. These monuments, known as "moai," are some of the most incredible ancient relics ever discovered. Hundreds of these statues cover the island. Each statue, some over 40 feet tall, has the same appearance: Their stony expressions have no eyes. The statues weigh many tons each, and some wonder how the islanders moved the statues. One legend even claims that the statues "walked" by themselves to their site.

Why an ancient people carved these amazing statues is still a mystery. Some scientists claim that they carved them for protection. Others claim they were made to honor ancestors. Whatever the reason, the statues of Easter Island continue to fascinate scientists and tourists.

What is the central idea of this text?

The author's main point is summed up in the first sentence, "There are few places on the earth more mysterious and intriguing than Easter Island." The rest of the passage explains why the writer makes this claim. To find the central ideas that support this idea are the remoteness of the island, the legendary statues, and why the statues were built. These ideas are developed in a sequential order. The author first tells how the island was settled, then talks about the statues, and finishes up with the fact that they are still a mystery to scientists today.

Copyright © American Book Company. DO NOT DUPLICATE. 1-888-264-5877.

Practice 1: Central Ideas

RL 1, 2, 5, 10

> **DIRECTIONS** Read the following passages, and answer the questions that follow each one.

FDA Issues Warning on Decorative Contact Lenses

Responsible and appropriate use is very important when it comes to contact lenses. That means getting an eye exam and a valid prescription, and buying contact lenses from an eye-care professional licensed to sell them. It's also important to follow directions for cleaning and wearing contact lenses and to have follow-up eye exams.

These precautions apply to all contact lenses, including contact lenses that only change the appearance of the eye in a decorative fashion, such as to turn brown eyes blue.

Fortunately, most decorative contact lenses have been approved for sale by the Food and Drug Administration (FDA). FDA-approved brands of decorative contact lenses are safe when used responsibly. But the FDA has learned that some firms are not seeking FDA approval before marketing decorative lenses. Places such as malls, video stores, and arcades are selling decorative contact lenses that have not been approved by the FDA.

The FDA has received reports of eye problems, such as damage to the cornea and eye infections, connected with decorative contact lenses. Most of the reports involve teenagers. One doctor reported a case of a 16-year-old girl who bought contact lenses at a flea market. "She wore them for a couple of days and ended up in the emergency room with burning, itching, redness, and sensitivity to sunlight," the doctor says. The main problem was poor lens fit. The doctor treated her with antibiotic drops for five to six days, and she recovered.

Others haven't been as lucky. In September 2001, a 14-year-old girl needed treatment after wearing decorative contact lenses she bought for $20 at a video store. "She wanted to turn her brown eyes green to match an outfit," her doctor said. "The result was a lot of pain and suffering."

She had an aggressive infection caused by *pseudomonas* bacterium in one eye. "You can not only lose vision from this infection, but you can lose the eye," the doctor stated. The teenager had to be hospitalized and treated every half hour with drops for four days. The girl was blind in the infected eye for two months. In June 2002, the doctor performed a corneal transplant, which involved removing her diseased cornea and replacing it with a donor cornea. Recovery from this operation takes about a year, and the teenager has still not fully recovered her vision.

Copyright © American Book Company. DO NOT DUPLICATE. 1-888-264-5877.

Along with informing consumers about the potential dangers of decorative contact lenses, the FDA is seizing decorative contact lenses on the market that violate federal law.

The FDA encourages people to discontinue use of decorative contact lenses that were bought without a prescription and a proper fitting. They also recommend contacting your ophthalmologist if you experience any eye problems.

1   After reading this article, where do you think it's safe to buy decorative contact lenses?

   A   A beauty salon

   B   A trusted friend

   C   An eye-care professional

   D   A major shopping mall

2   What is the author's main point in this passage?

   A   People should keep buying and wearing decorative contact lenses.

   B   People should be careful about the dangers of buying decorative contacts.

   C   Decorative contact lenses are safer than corrective contact lenses.

   D   People should avoid wearing contact lenses and should wear glasses instead.

3   What central ideas does the author include? How does the author develop these ideas over the course of the text?

   _____

   _____

   _____

   _____

   _____

Copyright © American Book Company. DO NOT DUPLICATE. 1-888-264-5877.

A Classic Car Story

Sterling McCall began collecting cars in 1979 in a small Texas town. That year, a customer drove a 1927 Ford Model T Doctor's Coupe into McCall's dealership. The customer wanted to trade it for a new car. The Ford Model T was so distinctive and fun to drive, McCall gladly made a deal. He liked the antique car so much that he decided not to sell it and kept it in a barn on his farm outside of Houston.

McCall's hobby of collecting older-model cars became the talk of the town. People began to bring their old cars to the dealership to trade for new cars. In fifteen years, McCall collected so many classic and antique cars he had to build garages all over his farm. A 1941 Buick convertible, a 1948 Lincoln Continental convertible, and a 1946 Plymouth convertible were a few of the valuable and rare classics McCall bought, restored, and drove just for fun.

The definition of a classic varies. However, the Classic Car Club of America states that a car must be at least twenty years old to be considered a classic. Cars that are over forty-five years old qualify as antique cars. Values of these old cars vary widely. Determining factors include the year a car was made, the history of the model, and the demand for a specific car.

McCall's collection of cars totaled eighty-eight when he finally decided to stop building garages on his farm. He decided to open a car museum in Warrenton, a town three miles from his farm. The Sterling McCall Old Car Museum opened in 1998. The museum provides a glimpse into the history of the automobile.

4 What are two central ideas of this passage? How is each one developed throughout the text?

_____

_____

_____

_____

_____

5 Which sentence best supports the idea of Sterling McCall's interest in classic cars?

  A Sterling McCall began collecting cars in 1979 in a small Texas town.

  B That year, a customer drove a 1927 Ford Model T Doctor's Coupe into McCall's dealership.

  C The customer wanted to trade it for a new car.

  D In fifteen years, McCall collected so many classic and antique cars he had to build garages all over his farm.

Copyright © American Book Company. DO NOT DUPLICATE. 1-888-264-5877.

6   Which question is not answered in the passage?

    A   When did McCall begin collecting cars?

    B   Why did McCall begin collecting cars?

    C   What is McCall's favorite car in his collection?

    D   When did the Sterling McCall Old Car Museum open?

MEANING OF WORDS AND PHRASES

Understanding the full meaning of a text depends on knowing what all the words and phrases in it mean. This includes deciphering all of the **figurative, connotative, and technical meanings**. It also includes analyzing how the author's **word choice affects meaning and tone**.

A word or phrase can be used in different ways. An author may choose words to tell plain facts, or an author may choose words to give the text shades of meaning and to add imagery (draw pictures with words).

FIGURATIVE MEANING

In chapter 4, you read about figurative language. This is a technique of using words and phrases that describe one thing in terms of something else. It includes devices like allusion, imagery, metaphor, simile, and symbolism. Authors of informational texts sometimes use figurative language just like authors of literary works.

As you know, the literal meaning of a word or phrase is a factual way to use it. It provides a statement that is understood in just one way. For example, consider "This math problem is difficult to figure out." This sentence is factual: the speaker is having trouble with a math problem.

On the other hand, the **figurative meaning** of a word or phrase has an element of fantasy or exaggeration. It paints word pictures and allows us to "see" a point.

Here is an additional example of figurative language. An **idiom** is a phrase or expression in which the real meaning is different from the literal or stated meaning.

Examples:

        as easy as pie: very easy

        I thought you said this was a difficult math problem. It isn't. In fact, it's as easy as pie.

        drag one's feet: delay; take longer than necessary to do something

        Joe should have finished his project a week ago. Why is he dragging his feet?

Copyright © American Book Company. DO NOT DUPLICATE. 1-888-264-5877.

CONNOTATIVE MEANING

You also read about **connotations** in chapter 4, but let's review this subject. The denotation of a word is its exact meaning as found in the dictionary. A connotation of a word, on the other hand, is meaning that is implied (suggested). To fully understand text that you read, you need to pay attention to both denotations and connotations.

For example, both the words *svelte* and *scrawny* denote "thin." However, without understanding their connotations, these words can be misused. Consider the slight variation in these two sentences:

"Emily, you look positively svelte in your new outfit."

"Emily, you look positively scrawny in your new outfit."

Emily would react very differently to these two statements, wouldn't she? The word *svelte* has a positive connotation of "slender and graceful," particularly when referring to a woman's appearance in a new outfit, while *scrawny* has a negative connotation of "bony and gaunt." So most likely Emily would be flattered by the first statement and offended by the second one.

TECHNICAL MEANING

Technical meaning might be found in texts that are specialized for a specific subject. When you read texts in various subjects, you might find words and phrases used in different ways. Their meanings will depend on the purpose of the texts. You can use the context (what is around the word or phrase), as well as your knowledge of the subject area, to discover meaning. Here is an example of different meanings for different technical areas. Look at this dictionary entry for the word *formula*.

---

formula

noun, plural **-las**, **-lae**

1. An established form or set of words for indicating procedure to be followed or to follow in a ceremony or proceeding

2. Any fixed or conventional way of doing something: *He writes mystery novels based on a successful formula.*

3. *Mathematics.* a. A rule or relationship expressed in symbols.

   b. A symbolic expression.

4. *Chemistry.* An expression of a chemical compound using symbols and figures: *Write the molecular formula for iron.*

5. a. A prescription of ingredients in proportion; a recipe: *The pharmacist used an improved formula to mix the medication.*

   b. A milk mixture for feeding infants

Copyright © American Book Company. DO NOT DUPLICATE. 1-888-264-5877.

Chapter 5

As you can see, the same word would have different meanings. Look at these examples.

What is your formula for saving money?

Which definition fits this use? If you said definition number 2, you are correct.

They make their "special sauce" using a secret formula.

Did you say definition number 5 a? That's right. In this case, formula refers to a recipe for mixing ingredients.

WORD AND PHRASE CHOICE

As you know, an author's **choice of words and phrases affects meaning and tone** in writing. Say an author writes "The oppressive silence held them both in place." The language choices suggest an uncomfortable lack of sound (oppressive silence) that has trapped two people in a moment. The scene seems foreboding and eerie. Now read this similar description: "A sweet stillness lulled them both to rest." The same two people might be in the same place, but the choice of words provides a much different picture. The lack of sound is pleasant (sweet stillness). Instead of being trapped, the people are soothed and relaxed.

Practice 2:   Meaning of Words and Phrases

RL 1, 4, 10

DIRECTIONS Read the passage. Then answer the questions that follow.

Face Value

1   Do you ever have dreams where you don't know who the people around you are? You might "go with the flow" and try to figure things out along the way. Imagine being that confused all the time, even in your waking life. Some people live this way all the time. They suffer from an inability to recognize faces. The problem is, literally, all in their heads—in their brains, to be exact.

2   The brain is a complex organ. For doctors and scientists who seek to understand the processes of learning and memory, it is largely still-uncharted territory. Sometimes a person's brain works differently, resulting in conditions such as dyslexia, in which letters and numbers appear to be reversed and muddled. If you have the unusual condition called synaesthesia, your senses are scrambled. For instance, you might experience a particular taste or color when you hear a certain musical note, or the color red might make a buzzing sound that only you can hear. Small wonder these people feel as if they are "crazy," when their perceptions of the world around them are so confused and mixed up.

Copyright © American Book Company. DO NOT DUPLICATE. 1-888-264-5877.

Page 80

3   Faceblindness is a related brain condition. It's not that the sufferer sees faces as indistinct blurs, but individual details don't seem to stick. The faceblind brain is unable to catalog each face for retrieval later. This makes it difficult to interact with others. Constant cases of mistaken identity abound, creating socially awkward situations.

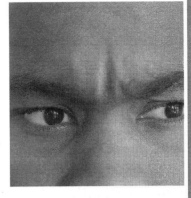

4   Faceblind people often have to play detective. It takes a while before a person becomes recognizable to them. When they finally begin to recognize a person, sometimes it has been a long time since their first meeting, so they have to figure out who exactly this "new person" could be. Sometimes, faceblind people will introduce themselves to those they have known for years.

5   Susie has had faceblindness all her life. It has caused some unusual problems. For example, she was unable to recognize a bully in school. The fact that she seemed to be fearless in the bully's presence made the bully respect her. But Susie had no idea this was happening until much later—it was just accidental luck. Then it frightened her. Uncertain situations such as these have caused her to withdraw from life. She sees her affliction as a weakness that she has to consciously fight. "I just have to accept living in a world full of strangers," she said, shaking her head.

6   Sarah is also faceblind. She teaches children to swim, and this causes her a special problem. When her students get their hair wet, it makes it even more difficult to tell one child from another. Sarah uses different visual and oral cues to tell her students apart. Their distinct voices and mannerisms help her out. Sarah has a much more positive attitude about her faceblindness than Susie does. But both women realize that this is an issue they will deal with all their lives.

7   Faceblindness has only recently been studied by doctors and scientists. Because the condition is little known, faceblind people often feel dumb or out of place. They may become fearful and depressed. But many of them adapt to different lifestyles, where the number of people they interact with is limited. Some of them even have enhanced pattern-recognition abilities in other areas. Their brains seem to compensate by being more attuned to numbers, shapes, or colors in return for the limitations in telling faces apart.

8   Thanks to the complexity of the brain, there will always be areas for brain scientists to study. People like Sarah and Susie may one day have a way out of their world of strangers. In fact, it's not much of a stretch of the imagination to state that one of you reading this right now may be the one who unlocks the secrets of the human brain.

Copyright © American Book Company. DO NOT DUPLICATE. 1-888-264-5877.

Chapter 5

1   In paragraph 2, the author writes that much of the brain is "still-uncharted territory." What kind of language is this, and how does it help the reader to understand the author's point?

_____

_____

_____

_____

2   In paragraph 3, what does <u>catalog</u> mean?

   A   To keep details of   **C**   To compile

   B   To make a list of   **D**   To arrange

3   What mood is conveyed in paragraph 5? What words and phrases most help to create this mood?

_____

_____

_____

_____

4   According to the passage, what is <u>synaesthesia</u>?

   A   Seeing colors that are different from those actually presented before the eyes

   B   Experiencing a sensation in a part of the body other than the part stimulated

   C   Believing that a person you have met before is a complete stranger

   D   Being able to use more senses than the average human being does

Read this sentence from paragraph 6.

Sarah has a much more positive attitude about her faceblindness than Susie does.

5   Due to its connotations, which word could not replace <u>positive</u> in this sentence?

   A   Encouraging

   B   Optimistic

   C   Convinced

   D   Upbeat

Copyright © American Book Company. DO NOT DUPLICATE. 1-888-264-5877.

CHAPTER 5 SUMMARY

Informational texts tell facts and relate true stories.

The **central idea** is what a passage is all about.

Many texts have more than one central idea. You should be able to analyze the **development of central ideas** in the text.

To fully understand a text, you must decipher all of the **figurative, connotative, and technical meanings** of words and phrases in it. This includes analyzing how the author's **word choice affects meaning and tone**.

The **figurative meaning** of a word or phrase has an element of fantasy or exaggeration. For example, an **idiom** is a phrase or expression in which the real meaning is different from the literal or stated meaning.

A **connotation** is an implied (suggested) meaning of a word.

Technical meaning might be found in texts that are specialized for a specific subject.

An author's **choice of words and phrases affects meaning and tone** in writing.

For more practice with this chapter's material, see the Informational Texts Review on page 103.

Copyright © American Book Company. DO NOT DUPLICATE. 1-888-264-5877.

Copyright © American Book Company. DO NOT DUPLICATE. 1-888-264-5877.

Chapter 6
Analyzing Informational Texts

This chapter covers the following seventh grade strand and standards:

Reading: Informational Text

Key Ideas and Details

1. Cite several pieces of textual evidence to support analysis of what the text says explicitly as well as inferences drawn from the text.

3. Analyze the interactions between individuals, events, and ideas in a text (e.g., how ideas influence individuals or events, or how individuals influence ideas or events).

Craft and Structure

5. Analyze the structure an author uses to organize a text, including how the major sections contribute to the whole and to the development of the ideas.

6. Determine an author's point of view or purpose in a text and analyze how the author distinguishes his or her position from that of others.

Integration of Knowledge and Ideas

7. Compare and contrast a text to an audio, video, or multimedia version of the text, analyzing each medium's portrayal of the subject (e.g., how the delivery of a speech affects the impact of the words).

8. Trace and evaluate the argument and specific claims in a text, assessing whether the reasoning is sound and the evidence is relevant and sufficient to support the claims.

9. Analyze how two or more authors writing about the same topic shape their presentations of key information by emphasizing different evidence or advancing different interpretations of facts.

Range of Reading and Level of Text Complexity

10. By the end of the year, read and comprehend literary nonfiction in the grades 6–8 text complexity band proficiently, with scaffolding as needed at the high end of the range.

Writing

2, 4, 9, 10 (in writing tasks)

As you read in the last chapter, understanding informational texts is the first step. The next step is to analyze them. Why? One reason is so that you can decide what you think about them. For example, you might not agree with what an author says in a text. Analysis also helps you to see interactions among people, events, and ideas. In this chapter, you will read about different ways to **analyze informational texts** and to support your analysis with evidence.

Copyright © American Book Company. DO NOT DUPLICATE. 1-888-264-5877.

ANALYZING INTERACTIONS

One way to analyze informational texts is to look for the **interactions among individuals, events, and ideas**. For example, think of reading about the American Civil War. A text might show how conflicting ideas about slavery and business influenced people in the early nineteenth century. Opposing sides then influenced people and events, and this led to the war. The decisions made as a result of the war and its outcome had many influences, of course. This major turning point influenced other events, all Americans, and many new ideas.

Here is a text that you can practice analyzing. Read it, and then explore the questions and explanations after it.

Market Economies

Market economies allow for private ownership of businesses and property. Such economic systems are often called "capitalist" because they encourage capitalism (private ownership of property and the pursuit of profits in business). They have very little government regulation. Market demand determines what will be produced, rather than the government.

A market involves buyers and sellers exchanging money and goods. When you buy a new shirt or a DVD, you are exchanging money in an economic market. In market economies, businesses are free to produce what they choose, and buyers are free to buy what they want. The good thing about market economies is that they tend to operate more efficiently than command economies where production and investment are controlled by a central authority. Since businesses want to make money, they produce only what the market demands. Therefore, if people want shirts, then producers will make shirts until demand is satisfied. Shortages and surpluses usually don't last very long in market economies.

Market economies also produce innovation (new and better ways of doing things). Since businesses are competing with each other, they are always finding ways to make products better or invent new things. To do this, they try to hire the most qualified employees. Therefore, they tend to pay more money to workers who are skilled and do a good job. Workers have an incentive to work hard and obtain more training because it means more personal wealth for them. All this means that economic development tends to occur much faster in market economies than in command or traditional economies.

The downside of market economies is that they often produce "haves" and "have nots." Since financial success depends on one's ability to respond to market demands, market societies tend to consist of a few rich people, a large middle class, and a poor lower class. There is no guarantee of equality in a market economy.

Copyright © American Book Company. DO NOT DUPLICATE. 1-888-264-5877.

How does a market economy affect workers?

The passage tells you that, in a market economy, companies compete for customers. They need to make good products that people will buy. So they hire workers with the most skill and experience. What do you think the workers are likely to do? Well, if they want to work and earn the most money, they will do all they can to become experts at their jobs. This might include education, training, and gaining experiences in several businesses. As the passage says, "Workers have an incentive to work hard and obtain more training because it means more personal wealth for them."

What influence do shoppers have in a market economy?

They have the most influence of all, don't they? As the passage says, "Market demand determines what will be produced," so shoppers basically get what they want. Companies try to persuade people to buy their products. They do this through advertising, word of mouth, and so on. But products that shoppers do not buy are not produced for very long.

ORGANIZATION

How a text is **organized** can also give you clues about the interactions between individuals, events, and ideas in a text. Writers choose the best pattern to present the information and to make a point. Here are some of the common organizational patterns.

Comparison and contrast focuses on how things are similar and different. It is a way to organize and talk about information by looking for similarities and differences. Sometimes you may be asked what is similar and/or different about two or more articles or stories. What you need to find are some points to compare and contrast. Consider the central ideas and details of each text. What people and events are involved? Once you see the facts about each text, consider how the texts relate to each other.

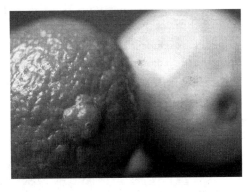

Chronological order (also called time order) means that events happen in sequence. For example, the sequence of events in a biography is typically time order. It begins from the subject's early life and ends with later life. There may be flashbacks (looking back) and foreshadowing (clues to what's ahead). But the events must play out logically in the text. A related pattern is **sequential order**. This is often used for directions or the steps of a process, like making something from a recipe.

Cause and effect explores the relationships between ideas and events. This pattern makes connections about why things happen (the cause) and what happens as a result (the effect). For example, if you eat too much food and do not exercise, you will most likely gain weight.

Copyright © American Book Company. DO NOT DUPLICATE. 1-888-264-5877.

Problem and solution is closely related to cause and effect. It involves looking at the cause of a problem, identifying its effects, and then suggesting a solution. Editorials frequently identify a problem and suggest a solution. Business leaders might use this format when writing proposals. The aim would be to convince companies that a problem exists and a solution can be found for the right price.

The organizational patterns that authors choose affect how ideas are conveyed. Authors strive to use the structures of these patterns to their best effects. When they succeed, each section of a text contributes to the development of the ideas. Your job, as a reader, is to analyze how ideas develop throughout the text. Read this article, and then look at the questions and explanations that follow.

The Importance of Collaboration

Collaboration, or teamwork, is a huge part of our everyday world. Think about it. Adults in the workplace collaborate on projects to produce business plans and marketing ideas. Sports such as soccer, football, lacrosse, and basketball rely on teamwork to win the game. Consider historical feats such as building the pyramids or founding colonies in the New World. How could any of these tasks have been successful without teamwork? It is clear that collaboration is one of the most useful resources for the advancement of mankind.

Understanding that collaboration is important is one thing. However, what does it mean to collaborate effectively? Can a team perform well together if its members are focused on selfish gains? What if there are no established rules? Without a solid foundation, collaboration cannot work. Let's take a look at some of the qualities that make teamwork possible.

One aspect of successful teamwork is sharing a common goal. Consider the game of soccer. What if every player was seeking to kick the ball to a different point? How confusing that would be! Instead, each team has an assigned goal. The object of the game is to kick the ball into that assigned goal. The lesson here is that having a common goal is a part of successful teamwork.

Many coaches of team sports say, "There is no 'I' in team." This cliché is used to remind the team that in order to function as a unit, members of the team must think and behave unselfishly. For example, consider the game of basketball. If there is no one in place to pass the ball to the point guard, how will he or she score? In this case, failure to work as a team will result in failure for the whole team. A good team must banish selfish thinking and behavior.

Copyright © American Book Company. DO NOT DUPLICATE. 1-888-264-5877.

Finally, in order for collaboration or teamwork to be successful, there must be an element of respect. Without respect for one another, members of a team or group will not be able to resolve conflicts or offer one another the trust to do assigned tasks. Think about the last time you worked with a group. If members weren't respectful, what were some of the problems that could have occurred? Without respect, groups will have a hard time establishing a strong bond and working together toward a common goal.

Success in any major endeavor relies on collaboration. This is true in any aspect of life. It is crucial for sports teams. Look at any successful team, and you will find that it has perfected the art of collaboration.

What is the author's central idea, and what organizational pattern is used to convey it?

Which pattern did you choose? This text explains the major aspects of collaboration (working together). The author uses examples of sport teams to illustrate the ideas. There is some comparison and contrast in that it looks at different kinds of teams as well as historical accomplishments to provide examples. But that is not the main pattern used throughout. The passage does not progress in chronological order either. The best answer is that the text follows a cause-and-effect pattern. The author describes the qualities of collaboration. When they are followed, the result is successful teamwork. When team members play well together, the team can win!

How does the body of the article build on the idea that collaboration is important?

The body, or middle paragraphs, gives support to the central idea. In the body, the author must offer reasons and examples to prove that idea. Each major section of this passage contributes an important point. First, the author explains that a team must understand what it means to collaborate. Second, the team must have a shared goal. Third, team members must abandon selfishness. And finally, they need to respect one another. These points logically build on each other to support the central idea.

SUPPORTING YOUR ANALYSIS

No matter what you analyze about a text, you need to use **evidence** to support your ideas. In the last section, you read the article about collaboration. Then you saw questions about it, and explanations to answer them. Did you notice how each answer provided evidence (examples from the text)? It explained why the answer was the best choice based on the article. Anytime you respond to a question, giving evidence will make your answer stronger.

Copyright © American Book Company. DO NOT DUPLICATE. 1-888-264-5877.

Chapter 6

Sometimes you will need to make **inferences** about what the author is saying. You read in chapter 4 about using inference skills when it comes to analyzing literature. These skills are important in any kind of reading. When you make an inference, you are making an educated guess based on facts and details in a passage. By reviewing the ideas and details in a text, you can infer information that is not directly stated.

What is one inference that you can make from "The Importance of Collaboration"? For one example, look at the fourth paragraph. The author mentions team coaches. Not much is said about coaches, but you might know that coaches are important leaders in team sports. They train, motivate, and provide strategies for the team. The author illustrates this with the saying that coaches use to inspire collaboration: "There is no 'I' in team." You could infer that an effective coach or leader is another important factor in successful teamwork.

Practice 1: Analyzing Interactions

RI 1, 3, 5, 10, **W** 4, 9, 10

> **DIRECTIONS** ▶ Read the passage, and answer the questions that follow.

Life in a Sod House Was No Fun at All

1   The Homestead Act of 1862 offered free farm land to any settler over the age of 21 who built a dwelling at least 12 x 14 feet. After the act was passed, pioneers and farmers rushed onto the Great Plains.

2   When these ambitious settlers reached states like Nebraska and the Dakotas, they were startled to find mostly wide open seas of grassy prairie land. Without wood or brick or stone, settlers were forced to build their homes from sod. They plowed up the earth and cut it into rectangular pieces measuring six inches thick and two feet long by one foot wide. These blocks of sod were then stacked one on top of the other, grass-side down, to form a makeshift house.

3   Some settlers sang the praises of their sod homes, claiming that they were not only dirt cheap, but the thickness of their walls kept them cool in the summer and warm in the winter. Others claimed their sod houses were good at holding in the heat from their stoves. But most inhabitants of these sod homes, or "soddies" as they were called, quickly found how hard daily life could be in one of these shelters.

Copyright © American Book Company. DO NOT DUPLICATE. 1-888-264-5877.

4   The shallow roofs were never really waterproof and sometimes even caved in. In a heavy downpour, they would leak from one end to the other and continue to leak for days after a rain. Lids had to be kept tight on the skillets so mud wouldn't fall into the food. During the winter, snow streamed in through every crevice. The earthen dwellings were so cold inside that people often got frostbite even when wrapped in quilts and huddled around their stoves. The floors were compacted dirt, and if straw was brought in to cover them, so too came an army of fleas. Mice and rats burrowed into the walls and were so numerous that settlers constantly had to fend them off with swift kicks.

5   Sod-house dwellers waged a never-ending battle just to keep the outside out. All things considered, as one prairie woman said, "Life is too short to be spent under a sod roof."

1   What is the main organizational pattern of this passage?

   A   Comparison and contrast

   B   Sequential order

   C   Cause and effect

   D   Problem and solution

2   The third paragraph provides some opposing viewpoints to the claim in the passage title that "living in a sod house was no fun at all." Why did the author include this information? Be sure to support your answer with evidence.

   _____

   _____

   _____

   _____

3   Why were settlers willing to live in sod houses at all?

   A   These houses were easier to build than those made from stone or brick.

   B   The cities were getting crowded and offered no room for families.

   C   Settlers wanted the land that the government was offering.

   D   Early settlers were all pioneers with adventurous spirits.

Copyright © American Book Company. DO NOT DUPLICATE. 1-888-264-5877.

4 The author makes the final point: "Living in a sod house was a never-ending battle just to keep the outside out." Name three pieces of evidence in the passage that support this statement.

_____

_____

_____

_____

ARGUMENTATION

You might think this has to do with people having a dispute. But in literature, **argumentation** means writing to persuade. Authors who write to persuade want to influence or convince readers about something. The following are some common examples of persuasive writing.

Campaign speeches	Political articles	Recycling reminders
Editorials	Requests for donations	Sales advertisements

In persuasive writing, the **author's purpose** is to convince readers. Often, an author will put his own **point of view** into what he writes.

When writers wish to change or influence the thinking of their readers, they must present a clear claim. They clarify their ideas by adding their own perspective or bias. But this is not enough for a strong argument. They also should **distinguish the claim from other positions**.

Most importantly, they must offer proof that their claim is valid. They must provide **evidence** that supports the claims they make. Evidence can include examples, definitions, statistics, and expert opinions. All evidence must be **relevant and sufficient to support the claim**. This means the evidence must be connected directly to the subject and shown to support it. For example, a campaign ad might point out that a candidate served in the armed forces. This statement alone is not evidence that directly shows how well this candidate would serve in office. However, say that the military service included a leadership position and proved effective decision-making skills. Then it could be tied to how well the candidate might do in an elected office. This would make the evidence relevant and sufficient to show the candidate's experience.

REASONING

An important part of analyzing arguments is looking at whether they use **sound reasoning**. When reasoning is sound, the conclusions drawn from it come logically from the supporting evidence.

Copyright © American Book Company. DO NOT DUPLICATE. 1-888-264-5877.

Inductive reasoning is the use of observations combined with what you already know to reach a reasonable conclusion. It moves from the specific (observation and prior knowledge) to the general (broad conclusion).

Examples:

Observation: Jana is not at the bus stop this morning.

What you already know: Jana does not like to miss school.

Conclusion: Jana is probably sick.

Observation: Eric failed his Spanish quiz in third period.

What you already know: Eric is a good student who studies hard.

Conclusion: Eric forgot to study for the quiz.

These conclusions aren't proven, but they use sound reasoning. There are many possible reasons for Jana and Eric's unusual behavior. But these are reasonable ones.

Deductive reasoning moves in the opposite direction. Using deduction, you move from the general to the specific. Deductive reasoning is based on facts called premises. One is the major premise, which states a general fact, and the other is a minor premise, which states a more specific fact. From these two premises, you can draw a conclusion.

Example:

Major Premise: Clothes from Express are expensive.

Minor Premise: My friend bought her shirt at Express.

Conclusion: My friend's shirt is expensive.

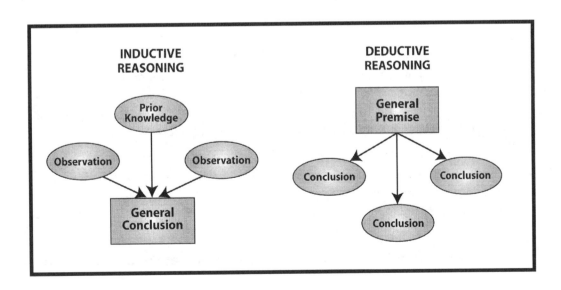

Copyright © American Book Company. DO NOT DUPLICATE. 1-888-264-5877.

Deductive reasoning, like inductive reasoning, can be used incorrectly. Be careful to check that the premises are valid. A conclusion will not be valid if is based on a false premise. A premise is an assumption that must be true in order for the conclusion to be true.

Example:

Major Premise: Boys like to play soccer.

Minor Premise: Ari is a boy.

Conclusion: Ari likes to play soccer.

The false premise here is that all boys like to play soccer. It is a generalization that is invalid. So the conclusion may also be invalid. This is an example of reasoning that is not sound.

COMPARING ARGUMENTS

Sometimes you will read two or more texts about the same topic and find that authors of these texts disagree. You might need to **analyze how two or more arguments differ**. To do this, you first need to understand each text. Then you need to look at how each author uses evidence and emphasizes or interprets certain facts. Now read these two articles, and study the questions and explanations that follow.

The Greenhouse Effect

Over the years, the issue of global warming has become increasingly controversial. Some people think it simply doesn't exist. Others claim that it is a natural cycle that humans have no influence over. But many people believe we are at least partially responsible, and that our coastlines will be underwater in a matter of years! Before getting into the debate, it is important to understand the key concept related to global warming—the greenhouse effect.

The greenhouse effect is not a bad thing in itself. Greenhouse gases, such as water vapor, carbon dioxide, and ozone, naturally exist in the earth's atmosphere. Their job is to trap the sun's heat and keep it in our atmosphere to warm the earth. This is called the greenhouse effect. The heat retained from the greenhouse effect is necessary for our survival. Without it, the planet would be sixty degrees colder!

It stands to reason that if there are more greenhouse gases in the atmosphere, then more heat will be trapped and the earth's average temperature will rise. Many scientists think that our contribution of greenhouse gases is causing the current trend of rising temperatures. And that means we need to change many of our habits that contribute to the buildup of greenhouse gases.

Copyright © American Book Company. DO NOT DUPLICATE. 1-888-264-5877.

Why did the author write this passage?

A To explain the causes of global warming

B To inform people about greenhouse gases

C To clarify the effects of pollution on the atmosphere

D To motivate people to take action on global warming

Which purpose did you choose? At first, the author seems to explain how greenhouse gases work. But read the last paragraph again. Here the author makes a claim that human beings are at least partially responsible for global warming and must take some action.

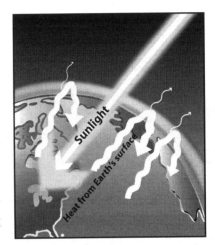

How does the author distinguish the claim from the points of view of others?

The author immediately acknowledges that there are opposing points of view: "Some people think it simply doesn't exist. Others claim that it is a natural cycle that human beings have no influence over."

Does the author offer sufficient evidence to support the claim?

The author provides a bit of background about the global warming debate, explains the greenhouse effects, and then concludes that humans contribute to it. This leads to the call for action to change some of our habits. However, there is no real evidence given for the claim that "our contribution of greenhouse gases is the cause of the current trend of slowly rising temperatures." Which scientists think this? What exactly are they saying? What specifically do humans contribute (emissions, pollution, and so on)? What statistics are available to show cause and effect? All of these are things that readers could look up, but the writer should have done this homework for them.

No Help for Climate Change

A controversy has been raging for years about how much the polluting world population has to do with climate change. The term *climate change* refers to fluctuations in long-range patterns of seasons, temperatures, precipitation, and even wind. Some people are convinced that humans are irreversibly altering the climate.

Many scientists disagree. They recognize there are changes happening. But they maintain that humans are not causing them. For example, there was a period called the Little Ice Age between about 1500 and 1850. These experts say that such trends, which happen every few thousand years, are natural and caused by forces much greater than the human inhabitants of the planet.

Copyright © American Book Company. DO NOT DUPLICATE. 1-888-264-5877.

In 2007, data from a NASA probe showed that Mars was also in a warming trend. Some believe this is evidence that climate changes on both planets are being caused by changes in the sun. It is all part of a natural cycle, as both Earth and Mars experience periodic ice ages. Some people argue that the warming of the two planets is not related, but more evidence certainly needs to be obtained. Then in 2009, scientists met in Denmark for a climate change summit. Based on long-term trends, many presented findings that the earth is actually cooling.

Some people refer to the greenhouse effect. They claim that we have placed so much pollution in the atmosphere, the earth is warming. But many scientists looking at the long-term trends predict the earth is due for another cold period. Meanwhile, activists, governments, and other scientists are still focused on global warming. Instead, we need to prepare for another possible Ice Age.

The earth has a complex set of systems that balance each other. It also has a history of extreme climate fluctuations such as the ice ages. Many people may believe that humans influence the earth's climate, but in the end, it is more likely that we are just along for the ride.

In what way does this author disagree with the author of "The Greenhouse Effect"?

Many issues have more than just two sides. You have to read texts carefully and analyze exactly how authors' viewpoints differ. They are seldom just "opposite" of each other. In this case, both authors agree that there's been a change in global climate. They disagree, however, in how it is happening and whether humans affect it.

Is the author's evidence relevant in "No Help for Climate Change"?

This author refers to some specific data from NASA that supports the claim. The author also mentions a conference at which scientists presented additional evidence. Though the detail about the Little Ice Age is interesting, it is irrelevant without more evidence to support the long-term trend.

How do the authors of "The Greenhouse Effect" and "No Help for Climate Change" interpret similar information in different ways?

Both texts talk specifically about the greenhouse effect. The first passage explains it and provides evidence to support the claim that humans contribute to it. The second passage only briefly mentions it while arguing that some other process is at work.

Copyright © American Book Company. DO NOT DUPLICATE. 1-888-264-5877.

As you can see, the authors of both articles could strengthen their arguments. But this comparison provides some good examples for your analysis. It shows how different authors writing about the same subjects might disagree. It also demonstrates how authors use evidence or interpret facts differently to support their claims.

Practice 2: Argumentation

RI 1, 6, 8, 9, 10, **W** 2, 4, 9, 10

> **DIRECTIONS** **Read the passages, and answer the questions that follow.**

In the Eye of the Shark

Why are people always so shocked and horrified to hear about a shark attack? It's not as though the shark went to someone's home and broke in. Here's a new idea: put yourself into a shark's skin, gliding around alone and hungry. Imagine you feel the emptiness of a creature for whom there is no free lunch, no supermarket, and no way to beg for even a single fish scale. You're that animal.

Cast your gaze through the waters: waters that grow dimmer and lose oxygen every day. As the shark, you don't realize that it is pollution from some very profitable corporations that is suffocating and blinding you. You only know hunger. Now you feel the tugs and swishes in the water that signal food. You move with silent purpose toward it. You feel the weight of the water pressing against your skin as the food bobs in front of your eyes. But your eyes see little through the murky water but the food you need to live, and the urge to live is stronger than the pull of tides.

Now the moment is here, and you open your mouth to grasp the food that comes to you in your own ocean home. As a meat-eater you eat the weak and slow. There is satisfaction and exhilaration as you hold the food that will sustain you. The ache of hunger is gone, and you move to deeper, clearer water.

Listen people: fearing and condemning sharks won't change their natures. So we can take our chances—or stay out of the water.

---

1 Why did the author write this passage?

A He says sharks just do what comes naturally, and it's up to people to avoid them.

B He is advocating better safety measures at beaches to prevent shark attacks.

C He thinks more food should be provided for sharks so they will not attack people.

D He wants big corporations to stop polluting the oceans and killing sharks.

Copyright © American Book Company. DO NOT DUPLICATE. 1-888-264-5877.

Chapter 6

2   What does the author suggest that people should do?

   A   Take up scuba diving to see sharks firsthand.

   B   Make a promise to never swim in the ocean.

   C   Consider the interaction of people and ocean life.

   D   Write an editorial about animals to a newspaper.

3   Is there any evidence in this passage that is not relevant to the claim?

4   The author concludes by telling readers that there are two options for dealing with sharks: "take our chances—or stay out of the water." What does the author mean? Is this choice based on sound reasoning?

Dangerous Predators?

Think sharks are dangerous? Although they are the ocean's most feared and fascinating predators, most sharks, such as the whale shark and the megamouth, are gentle giants. These sharks prefer to dine on algae and small fish rather than large prey and pose no threat to people.

There are, however, a few sharks that prefer larger prey and can be very dangerous to people. The most dangerous sharks include the great white, the hammerhead, the tiger shark, and the bull shark. These sharks have been known to attack humans. Although, according to statistics, shark attacks occur only about a hundred times a year and, out of those, only ten are mortalities. But that's not the idea we get from the media. Sharks are portrayed in movies and even cartoons as big, bad, mean, and predatory. This inspires everyone from kids to adults to fear them even before they know the facts.

Copyright © American Book Company. DO NOT DUPLICATE. 1-888-264-5877.

In contrast, people kill thousands more sharks each year for food and sport than sharks kill people. Shark-fin soup and shark steaks are popular delicacies in many countries. In America, mako is one of the most popular items on the menu. Up until the 1950s, shark liver was used to create vitamin A supplements. Today, sharks are hunted for their fins and their cartilage. Certain shark populations have decreased so dramatically over the last decade that their names have been added to the endangered species list.

From a shark's point of view, people pose a serious threat to shark survival. So, who's the dangerous predator?

5   What is the author's claim in this passage?

_____

_____

_____

_____

6   What is the author's main reason for writing "Dangerous Predators"?

    A   To persuade readers that sharks are a dangerous threat to all of us

    B   To entertain readers with interesting stories about sharks

    C   To convince readers that sharks are not as dangerous as we think

    D   To convince readers to swim with sharks

7   What relevant evidence does the author use to support the claim? Is any of the evidence irrelevant?

_____

_____

_____

_____

_____

_____

Copyright © American Book Company. DO NOT DUPLICATE. 1-888-264-5877.

8 What is the best way to describe how this passage is organized?

    A Chronological   **C** Comparison and contrast

    B Cause and effect   **D** Problem and solution

Writing Task

Both "In the Eye of the Shark" and "Dangerous Predators?" are about sharks. How does the author of each text approach the topic differently? Do their main claims agree or disagree? Write a brief essay in which you compare and contrast how the authors emphasize or interpret facts. Be sure to support your analysis with evidence from the passages.

ANALYZING NONPRINT MEDIA

At times, you might be asked to analyze media like **audio, video, and multimedia**. Often, you will compare and contrast a nonprint version with an original text. For example, you can read the annual state of the union address of our presidents. You can find these online in databases of public documents. Some of these speeches also are recorded. So, after you read a speech, you can listen to it or even watch it on video.

This is a direct transfer of words from one medium to another. Why would you want to both read a speech and listen to it? When you read, you can take your time, go back and reread parts you need to, and look at it several times for analysis. You can figure out the central idea, see what organization pattern is used, and find how evidence for claims is presented. But when you listen to the speech, you can tell where the speaker used special emphasis. You can hear pauses, volume, and emotion. All of these features offer new information for your understanding.

You also can make comparisons of texts and media presentations about the same topic. This is just like when you compare and contrast two passages. For example, you might read about specific events in history in your social studies class. Then you might find an educational series on television about the same events. You can analyze how the facts were presented differently, and why.

Copyright © American Book Company. DO NOT DUPLICATE. 1-888-264-5877.

Activity

RI 7 (SL 1–6)

Visit the online archives of the Miller Center at the University of Virginia (http://millercenter.org/president/speeches). There, you will find various print and non-print versions of speeches made by presidents of the United States. A small icon that looks like an open book means there is a print text version of the speech. Choose a speech, and read it. Then listen to the recorded version—the small icon that looks like a video camera means that a video recording of the speech is available, and the icon that looks like a loudspeaker indicates an audio recording. Take notes about the differences you hear when you listen to the speech. Then present your findings in a group or in class.

Next, listen to or watch a speech *before* you read it. Take notes about what stood out most to you. What do you think the central ideas were? How were they supported? Go by what you remember from listening to the speech. Then read the text version. Does your reading confirm what you heard? Was there anything you missed when you listened to it the first time around? Again, present your findings in a group or in class.

Copyright © American Book Company. DO NOT DUPLICATE. 1-888-264-5877.

CHAPTER 6 SUMMARY

You can **analyze informational texts** so that you can decide what you think about them.

One way to analyze informational texts is to look for the **interactions among individuals, events, and ideas**.

How a text is **organized** can also give you clues about these interactions. Organizational patterns include **comparison and contrast**, **cause and effect**, **chronological or sequential** order, and **problem and solution**.

No matter what you analyze about a text, you need to use **evidence** to support your ideas.

Sometimes you will need to make **inferences** (educated guesses) about what the author is saying.

In literature, **argumentation** means writing to persuade. Convincing readers about his own **point of view** is the **author's purpose**. He or she also should **distinguish the claim for other positions** and provide **evidence** to support the claim. All evidence must be **relevant and sufficient to support the claim**.

An important part of analyzing arguments is looking at whether they use **sound reasoning**. There are two types of logical reasoning: **Inductive reasoning** uses observations combined with prior knowledge to reach a reasonable conclusion; **deductive reasoning** moves from a general premise to a specific conclusion.

You might need to **analyze how two or more arguments differ**, which involves seeing how each author uses evidence and emphasizes or interprets certain facts.

At times, you might be asked to analyze media like **audio, video, and multimedia** and compare and contrast a nonprint version with an original text.

For more practice with this chapter's material, see the Informational Texts Review on the next page.

Copyright © American Book Company. DO NOT DUPLICATE. 1-888-264-5877.

Copyright © American Book Company. DO NOT DUPLICATE. 1-888-264-5877.

Informational Texts Review

This chapter covers the following seventh grade strand and standards.

> **RI** 1–10, **W** 1–4, 7–10, **SL** 1–6, **L** 1–6

This review will give you more practice with the skills you read about in chapters 5 and 6. First, read the passages. Answer the questions that follow. Then you will write about what you read.

Just Like the Old Days

by Jonathan Phillips, Peace Corps Volunteer, Mongolia (2003–2005)

1   Take an imaginary trip with me for a moment. Think of where you live right now. Now imagine it a thousand years ago. That's long before there were big farms, tall skyscrapers, and modern houses. Go back to a time when there were no cars, no plumbing, and no electricity to make your life easier.

2   Now jump ahead in time to today. Have a look around.

3   Well, when I look around in the countryside of Mongolia, where I am a Peace Corps volunteer, I don't have to imagine the past. I see the past every day. The lifestyle of the people and the land itself have remained mostly the same for well over a thousand years. The Mongolia that Marco Polo described some 800 years ago is pretty much unchanged, aside from the capital, Ulaanbaatar, which has grown into a bustling city of nearly a million people. But most Mongolians still live in white felt tents, called *gers*.

4   That's the same way their ancestors lived in the time of Genghis Khan. I recently visited a nomadic family—a family that moves around with the seasons. It almost seemed like a trip to another world. A Mongolian friend, Byamba, is driving his '69 Russian jeep across the steppe—which is a high plain of small, rolling mountains. We are approaching a big *ger*. I have no idea how he has found it, because to me, all *gers* look alike. And this one is way out, away from everything else. The *ger* we're approaching is the one where he grew up. However, his own family has moved away because the local river, where they fished, has dried up. The Gobi Desert is creeping farther north into Mongolia every year.

5   We get out of the car as the family comes out of the *ger*. Two adorable young girls come to meet us. They are wearing Mongolian *dels*, which are long robes with a sash tied around the waist as a belt. The girls have not seen their Uncle Byamba in nearly a year. Judging from the way they look at me, they have never seen someone from another country before.

6   We approach the rest of the family and exchange greetings. A common greeting in summer is, "Are your animals fattening nicely?" Byamba's brother assures me that the horses are fat, and they are also becoming fast. This means that his horses can race in the Naadam holiday that is coming up. Byamba's family is doing just fine. I know almost exactly what will happen, because meetings and behavior inside a *ger* always follow the same pattern. I know what people will say. I know what they will eat. I know what they will drink.

7   I stoop to enter the *ger,* and I see Emee, or Grandmother. She is sitting on a low bed on the right side of the tent. That's the side that people consider most important. She is probably only 55 years old, but her deep wrinkles and hunched posture make her look much older. Living outside on the steppe has aged her quickly. But her toothy smile and her energy with her granddaughters make the room lively.

8   Byamba's father died a few years ago. Today, Byamba's brother, along with his wife and two kids, live in this *ger* with his mother. In Mongolia, families stick together closely. The arrangement in this *ger* is common. Usually one of the family's children marries and stays with the aging parents. That person then takes over the family herd. Grandparents remain important in the family, and receive much respect. When they become sick or too old to perform their usual activities, the rest of the family takes care of them.

9   I once explained the idea of nursing homes and retirement homes that we have in the United States for old people. My Mongolian friends could not understand such an idea.

10   I walk into the left side of the *ger*. That is the custom for guests. They give me a small wooden stool and tell me to sit. Within a minute they hand me a bowl of steaming hot milk-tea. Shortly after, we begin eating *borzag*, which is like a doughnut, but less sweet. We also eat bread with *uuram*, which is the cream skimmed off the top of fresh milk. When I first came to Mongolia, I didn't like these foods. But now, I find them quite tasty.

11   Now the family looks at me. They ask Byamba questions: Who am I? Where am I from? Why did I come to Mongolia? Byamba remains silent as I answer the family's questions. At first they don't talk directly to me. They say their words to Byamba, because they don't think I will understand. It often takes Mongolians a moment to see that I can understand them, even though I am not Mongolian.

Copyright © American Book Company. DO NOT DUPLICATE. 1-888-264-5877.

12   We finish up the snacks and conversation. Soon the family is commencing their work for the afternoon. Byamba's sister-in-law begins chopping meat and rolling out dough for dinner. Emee straps on a huge backpack and grabs a three-foot-long wooden fork. She is going out to collect dried animal droppings. She will burn this in the stove for cooking and for heating the *ger*. Byamba and the young girls take care of the goats. Byamba will comb their fur to get the soft hairs to make cashmere, which is a really soft kind of fabric that fetches quite a price. The girls milk a different group of goats. And I go with Byamba's brother on horseback to round up the livestock that have wandered a few miles away to graze.

13   A newcomer to Mongolia quickly discovers that the hospitality in the countryside is the best in the world. I know that even if I were not with Byamba, this family would take care of me. They would treat me like family. The herder life in the countryside is difficult. People take care of strangers because they know a stranger would always take care of them.

14   The evening becomes chilly as the sun dips below the mountains after 10 o'clock. But inside, the *ger* is alive and warm in dim candlelight. We take turns singing Mongolian songs. After hours of telling stories, playing cards, and singing, the seven of us drift off to sleep. We are resting in our white felt tent, just as people here have been doing on this steppe for a thousand years.

Practice 1: Just Like the Old Days

RI 1–10, **W** 1–2, **L** 4.a, 5.a, 6

DIRECTIONS ➤   **Answer these questions about the passage you just read.**

1

What is the author's attitude toward what he is doing? What words tell you how he feels about his Peace Corps service?

Copyright © American Book Company. DO NOT DUPLICATE. 1-888-264-5877.

2

At the beginning and end of his story, the author says that things are the same now in Mongolia as they have been for a thousand years. Name two central ideas in the passage which support the claim that tradition and routine are important to the Mongolians.

_____

_____

_____

3

In paragraph 7, the author writes, "Living outside on the steppe has aged her quickly." What does this mean?

A Strong family relationships have helped her to mature and become wiser.

B A difficult and work-filled life makes her look older than she really is.

C Without sunscreen, the desert sun has made her skin dry and cracked.

D Isolation in the countryside has made her lonely and depressed.

4

What organizational structure does the author use to relate his experience?

A Comparison and contrast

B Cause and effect

C Problem and solution

D Chronological order

Writing Task

How does the description of one family's daily routine contribute to the overall idea about what Mongolia is like?

On your own paper, write a brief essay that answers this question. Make your writing clear and descriptive. Remember to use evidence from the text and check your writing for errors.

Copyright © American Book Company. DO NOT DUPLICATE. 1-888-264-5877.

Enough to Make Your Head Spin

by Elizabeth (Vernon) Kelley, Peace Corps Volunteer, Bulgaria (2003–2005)

1   "I'll have coffee," I tell the waitress at a cafe during my first week in Bulgaria. She shakes her head from side to side.

2   "OK, tea," I say, thinking that maybe there's something wrong with the coffee machine. Again, she shakes her head.

3   "Um ... cola?" Once more, she shakes her head. By now, she's looking at me like I'm crazy, and I'm totally confused.

4   Then I remember: A shake of the head by a Bulgarian means "yes," and a nod—what the rest of the world does for "yes"—means "no."

5   I knew about this before I arrived in Bulgaria, but it's amazing how something that seems simple and easy enough to remember can lead to so much confusion, and so many funny moments. Early on, when I communicated with Bulgarians, it seemed like my head was moving in ways my brain hadn't told it to. Sometimes I wanted to grab my ears and use them as controls. Learning a language with a completely different alphabet was challenging enough, without trying to figure out whether to nod or shake.

6   When I began teaching, all this head bobbing made communication in the classroom interesting. Although I had made sure my students knew about this cultural difference on the first day of school, we all frequently forgot what we were doing. My students would answer a question correctly or say something really great, and I'd nod. A second later, they were trying to change their answer, since they thought the nod meant they had been wrong. But the confusion went both ways. Sometimes I'd ask a student a yes-or-no question and he or she would answer with a nod or a shake, without saying anything. Not remembering the difference, we'd have to go through the motions several times before I understood. Frequently I found myself saying: "*Da* or *ne*—just tell me one or the other!"

7   I also had to deal with confused colleagues who couldn't figure out why I kept nodding my head while they talked, as if I were arguing with them. In truth, I was just trying to show that I understood and was following along with the story. And then there was the even greater problem of how to act with Bulgarians who spoke English and were aware of the nodding–shaking problem. Was I supposed to nod or shake for "yes" when I was speaking English with them? And what was I supposed to do when we were speaking Bulgarian? What if we were in a situation where both languages were being spoken? To make matters even more complicated, after going a couple of weeks without any contact with other Americans, we'd finally get together and I'd find myself shaking when I should have been nodding. My head was spinning!

Copyright © American Book Company. DO NOT DUPLICATE. 1-888-264-5877.

8   After a year of living here, the gestures have become second nature, and I rarely have to think about what my body language should be. Once in a while, if I'm really tired or not thinking clearly, I find my head moving in a semi-circular nod–shake–wobble, which the Bulgarians find quite amusing.

9   Along with all the funny moments this cultural difference has provided me and my Bulgarian friends, I've come to understand the importance of using all my senses in a new culture, and of not making assumptions that a gesture or other form of communication—even one that seems very simple and universal—means the same thing everywhere. Beyond being conscious of the yes–no difference, I must make sure I am really listening and watching for other clues when someone is communicating with me. Here, a sound along the lines of a cluck of the tongue often accompanies a "no," and being aware of that helps me steer clear of confusion.

10   Tuning in to how the people around me communicate has brought me closer to the people and the culture here. And whenever we slip up and forget to control our heads, the laughter that follows brings us together. Luckily, a smile is a smile the world over.

Practice 2: Enough to Make Your Head Spin

RI 1, 4–6, 10, **L** 4.a, 5.a, 6

> **DIRECTIONS**   **Answer these questions about the passage you just read.**

1

In paragraph 4, the author talks about being confused because Bulgarians shake their heads to agree unlike the "rest of the world," which nods. Why does she claim it is normal for her to be confused? Is her evidence relevant and sufficient to support her claim?

_____

_____

_____

Copyright © American Book Company. DO NOT DUPLICATE. 1-888-264-5877.

2

What is the main way in which the author organizes this text?

A Comparison and contrast

B Chronological order

C Cause and effect

D Problem and solution

3

What is one rule that the author could make in her classroom to avoid miscommunication?

A No one is allowed to ask yes-or-no questions.

B Everyone must respond verbally without gesturing.

C Students must write their answers to questions on paper.

D All students must learn what nods and shakes mean elsewhere.

4

In paragraph 7, what is the literal meaning of the idiom "My head was spinning!"

A I was energized by the conversation.

B My head was circling between a nod and a shake.

C I was confused by all the information.

D My neck was sore from changing between nods and shakes.

Copyright © American Book Company. DO NOT DUPLICATE. 1-888-264-5877.

Practice 3: Compare and Contrast the Passages

RI 1, 3, 6, 9, 10

DIRECTIONS	Now answer these questions about both passages.

1

How do the two authors both use their experience to learn something new? How are their points of view different about what they learn?

_____

_____

_____

2

The authors of "Just Like the Old Days" and "Enough to Make Your Head Spin" are both Peace Corps volunteers. What kinds of challenges do all Peace Corps volunteers face?

A They sometimes have to eat foreign food they don't like just to seem polite.

B They have to learn the languages and customs of the places where they serve.

C They must not describe too much about the way things are done back home.

D They have to make new friends where they serve and can't see other Americans.

Copyright © American Book Company. DO NOT DUPLICATE. 1-888-264-5877.

Practice 4: Write about the Passages

RI 1, 3, 6, 9, W 1–4, 9, 10, L 4.a, 5.a, 6

DIRECTIONS

A. Compare and Contrast Ideas in the Passages

The two passages you read both tell about experiences in the Peace Corps. Jonathan Phillips writes about being in Mongolia. Elizabeth Kelley writes about being in Bulgaria. In what important ways do the settings differ? How do these differences influence the way the authors write about their experiences?

Use your own paper to write an essay that compares and contrasts the two Peace Corps experiences. Make sure your writing is clear and has a beginning, middle, and end. Be sure to use support from the passages in your writing.

DIRECTIONS

B. Write a Story

Think about a time when you experienced a new place or an unfamiliar group of people. It might have been on a trip somewhere. It could have been when you started at a new school or attended summer camp. Write a story that tells about your experience. Use as many details as you can to describe the place, events, and people so that readers will be able to live through that time with you.

Use your own paper to write your narrative. Be creative and descriptive, and remember to check your writing for errors.

Copyright © American Book Company. DO NOT DUPLICATE. 1-888-264-5877.

Practice 5: Research Project

RI 1, 3, 7, 10, **W** 7–10, **L** 4.a, 5.a, 6

DIRECTIONS	Find and read a text, and then listen to a recorded version of the text. Some pairs of texts and their available recordings are listed below, or find another pairing on your own. After you have read the text and listened to its recorded version, analyze the main differences. Does the spoken version provide a different understanding of the text? How so? Is there special emphasis on certain parts? Are there other sounds on the recording that help you understand the meaning or tone of the text? Be sure your writing is well organized and clear. Remember to check for and fix any mistakes.

Note: The URLs below must be typed in exactly as they appear (with capital letters) in order for the links to work.

Possible Pairs of Texts and Audio Versions
"The Birthmark" by Nathaniel Hawthorne (text and audio found at http://www.manythings.org/voa/stories/The_Birthmark_-_By_Nathaniel_Hawthorne.html)
"The Tell-Tale Heart" by Edgar Allan Poe (text and audio found at http://www.manythings.org/voa/stories/The_Tell-Tale_Heart_-_By_Edgar_Allan_Poe.html)
"The 'Great Compromise' on State Representation" (text and audio found at http://www.manythings.org/voa/history/22.html)
Declaration of War (WWII) address by Franklin D. Roosevelt (text and audio found at http://www.historyplace.com/speeches/fdr-infamy.htm)
"The Perils of Indifference" speech by Elie Wiesel (text and audio found at http://www.historyplace.com/speeches/wiesel.htm)

Copyright © American Book Company. DO NOT DUPLICATE. 1-888-264-5877.

Activity

SL 1.a–d, 5, 6

Work in groups. Each group should choose one article or story about an experience (or your teacher can assign texts). Examples of such texts are the two Peace Corps stories you read at the beginning of this review chapter.

Everyone in the group should read the text carefully. Then, collaborate to come up with a skit or one-act play that depicts the experience. Assign parts, and act it out. For example, if you were using the story "Just Like the Old Days," you would act out the day at the *ger*. One student would play Jonathan Phillips, another would play Byamba, and so on.

Be sure to include any multimedia or visual displays that would help viewers to understand your play.

When each play is finished, allow time for questions and answers. Also, discuss the following with the class:

1. What were the central ideas in the presentations?

2. How did the events affect the characters in the play?

3. What ideas did each character have about the situation, and how did their ideas influence the story?

4. What other interactions did you notice among individuals, events, and ideas?

Copyright © American Book Company. DO NOT DUPLICATE. 1-888-264-5877.

Copyright © American Book Company. DO NOT DUPLICATE. 1-888-264-5877.

Chapter 7
Vocabulary

This chapter covers the following seventh grade strand and standards:

Reading: Literature

4. Determine the meaning of words and phrases as they are used in a text, including figurative and connotative meanings; analyze the impact of rhymes and other repetitions of sounds (e.g., alliteration) on a specific verse or stanza of a poem or section of a story or drama.

Reading: Informational Text

4. Determine the meaning of words and phrases as they are used in a text, including figurative, connotative, and technical meanings; analyze the impact of a specific word choice on meaning and tone.

Language

Vocabulary Acquisition and Use

4. Determine or clarify the meaning of unknown and multiple-meaning words and phrases based on *grade 7 reading and content*, choosing flexibly from a range of strategies.

   a. Use context (e.g., the overall meaning of a sentence or paragraph; a word's position or function in a sentence) as a clue to the meaning of a word or phrase.

   b. Use common, grade-appropriate Greek or Latin affixes and roots as clues to the meaning of a word (e.g., *belligerent, bellicose, rebel*).

   c. Consult general and specialized reference materials (e.g., dictionaries, glossaries, thesauruses), both print and digital, to find the pronunciation of a word or determine or clarify its precise meaning or its part of speech.

   d. Verify the preliminary determination of the meaning of a word or phrase (e.g., by checking the inferred meaning in context or in a dictionary).

5. Demonstrate understanding of figurative language, word relationships, and nuances in word meanings.

   a. Interpret figures of speech (e.g., literary, biblical, and mythological allusions) in context.

   b. Use the relationship between particular words (e.g., synonym/antonym, analogy) to better understand each of the words.

   c. Distinguish among the connotations (associations) of words with similar denotations (definitions) (e.g., *refined, respectful, polite, diplomatic, condescending*).

6. Acquire and use accurately grade-appropriate general academic and domain-specific words and phrases; gather vocabulary knowledge when considering a word or phrase important to comprehension or expression.

Learning new **vocabulary** is necessary to develop your reading, writing, and speech. When you come across unfamiliar words, it can create a variety of challenges. There are many ways for you to determine the meaning of an unfamiliar word. These tools will help you correctly use new vocabulary words in reading and writing. You can use these strategies to read with ease and confidence.

Copyright © American Book Company. DO NOT DUPLICATE. 1-888-264-5877.

Context Clues

Context clues are useful for determining the meaning of a word. Context is the words and ideas that surround the unfamiliar word. These words and ideas can give clues to the meaning of the unfamiliar word. Context clues provide a strategy for decoding the meaning of the new vocabulary in the text.

   Example: The neighborhood was <u>opulent</u>, showing the couple it was far beyond their budget.

The second part of the sentence defines the meaning of *opulent* in simpler terms: it was too expensive for the couple. One definition of *opulent* is "affluent or wealthy."

Below you will find a list of the main types of context clues and their signal words.

Context Clues	Signal Words	Example
Comparison	*also, like, resembling, too, both, than*	Look for clues that indicate an unfamiliar word is similar to a familiar word or phrase. Rodney is like a field mouse gathering seeds when it comes to <u>accumulating</u> compact disks.
Contrast	*but, however, while, instead of, yet, unlike*	Look for clues that indicate an unfamiliar word is opposite in meaning to a familiar word or phrase. Lynn has an <u>aesthetic</u> sense in room décor, while her sister Amelie has no artistic tendencies at all.
Definition or Restatement	*is, or, that is, in other words, which*	Look for words that define the term or restate it in other words. The oversized tuxedo made Jesse look <u>preposterous</u>; in other words, he was an amusing sight.
Example	*for example, for instance, such as*	Look for examples used in context that reveal the meaning of an unfamiliar word. Several facts pointed to the man's <u>culpability</u>; for example, he was caught with the weapon in his hand.

Copyright © American Book Company. DO NOT DUPLICATE. 1-888-264-5877.

WORDS WITH MULTIPLE MEANINGS IN CONTEXT

Sometimes you'll encounter **words with multiple meanings**. These words have a clear definition in one context. However, they can mean something entirely different at other times. It all depends on the context. When you spot a word like this, decide which meaning best fits the sentence. Look at the following example:

Example: In the remote forests of Hith, there lived strange and terrible creatures.

Example: Eager to change the channel, Dotty reached for the remote.

In the first sentence, *remote* is an adjective that means "far away." In the second, *remote* is a noun that means "a device used to change TV channels." Can you think of other examples of words with multiple meanings?

Now read this sentence, and answer the question that follows.

It was a sad and haunting strain that met our ears as we entered the old theater. There was a beauty in the voice that we would never forget. This would be a special concert.

Based on context, what does <u>strain</u> mean?

A Effort

B Injury

C Melody

D Filter

Did you choose C? You are right! One way to see which word fits best is to substitute each one for the target word.

GREEK AND LATIN ROOTS AND AFFIXES

Examining **roots** and **affixes** will help you figure out the meaning of a new vocabulary word. A **root word** is a word that has nothing added at the beginning or the end. A new word can be made from a root word by adding an affix to the beginning or ending. A **prefix** is an affix added to the beginning of a root word, while a **suffix** is an affix added to the end of a word. Knowing the meanings of roots, prefixes, and suffixes can help you figure out the meanings of words.

For example, *agree* is a root word. By adding a prefix or suffix, you can make new words that have different meanings.

agree: to have the same view or opinion

*dis*agree: to have different views or opinions

agree*able*: willing or ready to share the same view

Study the following three tables. They contain common roots, prefixes, and suffixes that you will often encounter.

Copyright © American Book Company. DO NOT DUPLICATE. 1-888-264-5877.

SOME COMMON PREFIXES

Prefix	Meaning	Example
pre-	before	precede
de-	away, from	deter
hypo-	under, too little	hypoglycemic
hyper-	over, too much	hyperactive
mal-	bad	malfunction
retro-	backward	retroactive
poly-	many	polyclinic
bi-	two	bicycle
un-	not	unneeded
semi-	half, partly	semicircle
equi-	equal, equally	equivalent
omni-	all, everywhere	omniscient
anti-	against	antibacterial
pro-	forward	propel
inter-	between	interstate
ob-	against	objection
mono-	one, alone	monopoly
epi-	upon	epitaph
mis-	wrong	mistake
sub-	under	submarine
trans-	across, beyond	transcend
over-	above	overbearing
ad-	to, toward	advance
non-	not	nondairy
com-	together, with	composite
re-	back, again	regress
ex-	out of	expel
in-	not	insufficient

Copyright © American Book Company. DO NOT DUPLICATE. 1-888-264-5877.

SOME COMMON ROOTS

Root	Meaning	Example
arch	to rule	monarch
belli	war, warlike	belligerent
bene	good	benevolent
chron	time	chronology
dic	to say	dictation
fac	to make, to do	artifact
graph	writing	telegraph
mort	to die	mortician
port	to carry	deport
vid, vis	to see	invisible

SOME COMMON SUFFIXES

Suffix	Meaning	Example
-able, -ible	able to	usable
-er, or	one who does	competitor
-ism	the practice of	rationalism
-ist	one who is occupied with	racist
-less	without, lacking	worthless
-ship	the art of skill of	leadership
-fy	to make	dignify
-ness	the quality of	kindness
-tude	the state of	rectitude
-logue	a particular kind of speaking or writing	monologue

DICTIONARY SKILLS

The most complete tool for finding a word's meaning is a **dictionary**. In this alphabetically arranged reference source, you can find out what a word means. That way, you can find out if your initial idea about the word's meaning was correct.

Copyright © American Book Company. DO NOT DUPLICATE. 1-888-264-5877.

Chapter 7

Even if you don't own a printed one, you can still use a dictionary. Many free dictionaries can be found by doing a web search for *dictionary*. Below is a typical dictionary entry. You can see the word *efficiency* broken into syllables. The second part shows how to pronounce the word. You then see the word's part of speech and plural form. Finally, *efficiency*'s definitions are covered. Each dictionary is a little different, but most have similar features.

Dictionary Entry

ef·fi·cien·cy (ee-**fish**-uhn-see) *n.* Plural **-cies**

1. The quality of being efficient **2.** Efficient operation **3.** Ratio of energy delivered by a machine to the energy supplied to it

---

Activity

RL 4, **RI** 4, **L** 4.a–d

Read the following passage. On your paper, write each underlined word and what you think it means. Then use a dictionary to look up the words. How precise were you in your ideas about their meanings? Did you need to look up more than one entry for any word? Did you have to choose among several definitions?

The circus is a place full of <u>enchantment</u>. Cheery and <u>whimsical</u> costumes are all around. Clowns try to fill fans with <u>merriment</u>. The crowd is in awe of fearless <u>antics</u>. Some trapeze artists seem to <u>defy</u> the laws of gravity. Not to be outdone, <u>exotic</u> animals come <u>tromping</u> into the ring. Tamers seek to master the <u>ferocity</u> of their lions. Giant elephants show stunning <u>dexterity</u>. For the last act, a motorcycle <u>daredevil</u> lands a huge jump with <u>astounding</u> accuracy. I can't wait to go back to the circus!

A **thesaurus** is also arranged alphabetically. Its purpose is to provide lists of words that have the same, or nearly the same, meanings as the word that you look up. These are called **synonyms**. A thesaurus also gives words with opposite meanings, called **antonyms**. (You will read more about synonyms and antonyms later in this chapter.) A thesaurus comes in handy when you are writing and need to find different ways to express ideas.

A **glossary** is an alphabetical list of specialized words with their definitions. The glossary is usually placed at the end of a book. Glossaries are found in science, social studies, literature, math books, and many others as well.

Page 120

Practice 1: Building Vocabulary

RL 4, RI 4, L 4.a–d, 6

Copyright © American Book Company. DO NOT DUPLICATE. 1-888-264-5877.

> **DIRECTIONS** Read the passages, and answer the questions that follow.

When Is a Star Not a Star?

Have you ever wished on a shooting star? You might be surprised to learn that a falling star is not a star at all. Streaks of light that cut across the night sky are actually meteoroids. Made of tiny bits of dust and grit, meteoroids burn up as they enter the earth's atmosphere. The result is a brief, bright trail of light in the sky.

If you have never seen a shooting star, you may also be surprised to learn that millions of them happen every day. Although the short-lived streaks occur at all times of the day, there are prime times for viewing them. Stargazers are about twice as likely to find a shooting star in the few hours before dawn. At that time, the moon is low in the night sky. From that position, the moon shines much less light across the sky. The result is a dark canvas on which burning meteoroids appear even brighter.

Meteor showers occur at certain times of year when the earth passes through the trail of debris left behind by comets that orbit the sun. On a typical night, you can spot a shooting star every fifteen minutes or so. During a meteor shower, you may see shooting stars streaking across the sky every few seconds. Once in a while, a piece of meteoroid survives the fiery trip and lands on earth. Astronomers call this remnant a meteorite. They study meteorites to learn more about our solar system.

Glossary

Atmosphere – layer of gases surrounding the surface of a planet, moon, or star

Comet – a ball of rock and ice that orbits the sun

Meteorite – the remains of a meteoroid that falls to the earth's surface

Meteoroid – a small solid object moving through space

Meteor shower – a large number of meteoroids that appear together in the same area of the sky

Orbit – to move in a circular path around an object

Solar system – the sun and its surrounding matter, including comets, planets, and moons

1   What makes a meteorite different from a meteoroid?

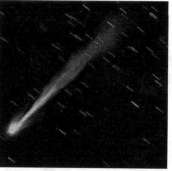

A   A meteorite is much larger than a meteoroid.

B   A meteorite is a remaining piece of a meteoroid found on earth.

C   A meteorite stays in orbit while a meteoroid falls to earth.

D   A meteorite is not at all different from a meteoroid.

2   What does it mean for a comet to orbit the sun?

_____

_____

_____

3   Based on the glossary, which statement could be true?

A   A chunk of the atmosphere has landed in the yard.

B   The science museum has a collection of old meteoroids.

C   People watch comets as they streak across the sky.

D   The meteorite didn't survive its flaming journey in the sky.

4   In the last paragraph, what does the word <u>remnant</u> mean?

_____

5   What is an astronomer?

_____

Walks All Over the Sky: A Traditional Native American Folktale

Long ago, there was a chief that ruled the sky. He had two sons to help him. During this time, life was very serene for the people and animals of the earth. However, there was no light in the sky, so everyone was forced to live out their days in darkness.

One day, the younger son, who was named Walks-All-Over-the-Sky, looked down at the dark world and thought about how beautiful the world would be if it had light. The people of the earth would be so happy! He decided to do something about the darkness that covered the world.

Copyright © American Book Company. DO NOT DUPLICATE. 1-888-264-5877.

As he was gathering wood in the forest of the sky with his older brother one day, the younger son made a mask out of cedar wood and placed it over his face. Then he ignited the mask and began to walk, leaving his bewildered brother standing alone. As the younger son walked, flames shot from his mask and illuminated the Earth. He started running faster towards the west, and the flames grew brighter. He looked down and saw that the people of the earth were joyously celebrating the light. Because he saw how happy the people were, the younger son knew that he had given them a great gift. So, every day, the son ran east to west so that he could continue to light up the Earth. Later, Walks-All-Over-the-Sky decided to sleep. While he slept, sparks flew out of his mouth and turned into stars.

The older brother, Walking-About-Early, wanted to offer something to the people of the world as well. One night, as his younger brother was sleeping, Walking-About-Early rubbed fat and charcoal on his face. With his face shining, he began walking. Walking-About-Early shed light over the world, much like his brother, except this time the light was soft and not quite as bright as the sun. Nevertheless, the people were happy to have this little bit of light with them while the younger brother was sleeping. In this way, the world was never completely dark. All the people of the earth praised the chief and his children for bringing the gifts of the sun, moon, and stars to the world.

6 In the first paragraph, what does <u>serene</u> mean?

_____

7 How is <u>serene</u> pronounced?

   A (**see**-reen)

   B (suh-**rayn**)

   C (**sai**-ruhn)

   D (suh-**reen**)

8 In the third paragraph, what does <u>ignited</u> mean? And how does knowing this word help you to understand a car's ignition?

_____

_____

_____

Copyright © American Book Company. DO NOT DUPLICATE. 1-888-264-5877.

9 What does <u>bewildered</u> mean in the third paragraph?

   A Distracted   **B** Panicky   **C** Unsettled   **D** Puzzled

The third paragraph says "Walking-About-Early <u>shed</u> light over the world." Look at the dictionary entry for the underlined word.

> **shed** (shed) *v.* shed·ding, shed
>
> 1. to emit and let fall, as tears.
>
> 2. to impart or release; give or send forth (sound, fragrance, influence, etc.).
>
> 3. to resist being penetrated or affected by: cloth that sheds water.
>
> 4. to cast off or let fall (leaves, hair, feathers, skin, shell, etc.) by natural process.

10 Which definition is correct for the use of this word in the passage?

   A 1   **B** 2   **C** 3   **D** 4

ANALYZING WORD MEANING

There are several other skills you can use to incorporate your new vocabulary into all that you do. They include getting to know word relationships and shades of meaning that can affect your understanding of what you read.

WORD RELATIONSHIPS

A **synonym** is a word that has the same or a similar meaning as another word. Synonyms often appear in a text to give further meaning. It is helpful to have another word that means the same as the challenging word. The following example shows the use of a synonym as a context clue.

Example: The rider rode at a *brisk* pace so the horse could enjoy a nice *quick* run before returning to the barn.

The word *quick* has the same meaning as *brisk*. They both mean "fast." Having a synonym in the context gives you a clear picture as to the meaning of the unfamiliar word.

An **antonym** is a word that means the opposite of another word. When the antonym is familiar, it makes it easier to understand the meaning of its opposite.

Example: The child was taught to *suppress* her laughter rather than *release* her amusement.

The word *release* is the opposite of *suppress*. *Release* means "to let go," whereas *suppress* means "to control."

Copyright © American Book Company. DO NOT DUPLICATE. 1-888-264-5877.

CONNOTATIVE AND DENOTATIVE MEANINGS

The **denotation** of a word is its meaning as found in the dictionary. On the other hand, a **connotation** of a word is meaning that is implied (suggested). People assign these connotative shades of meaning to words over time. To fully understand a text that you read, you need to pay attention to both denotations and connotations.

For example, both the words *notorious* and *celebrated* denote being well known. However, you also need to know their connotations. If you don't, you might misuse these words. Read the following sentences.

Suzette was notorious for her delicious gourmet cooking.

Tex felt celebrated when he made the "Ten Most Wanted" list.

In sentence 1, the word *notorious* seems awkward. That is because of its connotation as "scandalous" rather than "famous." In sentence 2, the word *celebrated* seems awkward. Its connotation is "acclaimed" rather than "infamous."

Consider the words *vagrant* and *homeless*. Both of these words refer to the same individuals: people with no fixed or permanent address. But they evoke very different images in the minds of readers. *Vagrant* generally brings to mind someone who is a public nuisance. But someone described as *homeless* is usually looked upon with compassion or even pity. Given the different connotations of the words, a volunteer working for a food bank would probably choose the word *homeless*. On the other hand, someone writing an editorial letter about cleaning up an inner-city park might use the word *vagrant*.

Activity

RL 4, RI 4, L 1.a–d, 5.c

Fill in the blanks in each sentence pair with the appropriate word choice. You can use a dictionary or a thesaurus to help you.

variable

inconsistency

1. The missing _____ needed to solve the mystery was the time of the crime.

2. The _____ of the musician kept the orchestra from playing in tune.

forceful

assertive

3. The hockey player was penalized for his _____ check of the opposing left winger.

4. Kyle is very _____ of his right to be at the meeting.

elderly

veteran

5. The _____ player taught the rookie a few lessons.

6. The _____ couple lived on a hill near Tyler.

Copyright © American Book Company. DO NOT DUPLICATE. 1-888-264-5877.

Many words and phrases have **nuances** of meaning, which are small differences. But these slight variations can change the meaning of a text. Some words mean almost the same thing. But there are always small differences in meaning—otherwise there would not be different words for similar objects or ideas! Or they might have taken on different connotations over time. You need to be aware of subtle variations and how they affect overall meaning.

FIGURATIVE LANGUAGE

In chapter 4, you read about **figurative language**. It encompasses devices that authors use to make their writing livelier and more interesting. It also helps to convey meaning and tone. When you recognize literary devices, you can appreciate the full meaning of a text.

Review figurative language in chapter 4, if you need to. For now, let's look at two specific devices: **allusions** and **analogies**. Allusions are references to well-known people, historical events, myths, works of art, places, or even other literary texts. Analogies are relationships between two sets of ideas. Look at these examples.

Allusion example: "It's pouring!" Giles shouted. "If this rain doesn't let up soon, we'll need to build an ark!" This statement is an allusion to the biblical story of Noah and the ark. Allusions sometimes refer to literary, religious, or mythological texts.

Analogy example: "A child's life is like a piece of paper on which every person leaves a mark." The author is comparing the way in which people make impressions on the mind of a young child to the way that a pencil or pen writes on paper.

Practice 2: Analyzing Word Meaning

RL 4, L 5, 6

DIRECTIONS	Read the passage, and answer the questions that follow.

The Deserted House
by Alfred Tennyson

Life and Thought have gone away
Side by side,
Leaving door and windows wide:
Careless tenants they!

5   All within is dark as night:
In the windows is no light;
And no murmur at the door,
So frequent on its hinge before.

Copyright © American Book Company. DO NOT DUPLICATE. 1-888-264-5877.

> Close the door, the shutters close,
> Or thro' the windows we shall see
> The nakedness and vacancy
> Of the dark deserted house.
>
> 10 Come away: no more of mirth
> Is here or merry-making sound.
> The house was built of the earth,
> And shall fall again to ground.
>
> Come away: for Life and Thought
> 15 Here no longer dwell;
> But in a city glorious—
> A great and distant city—have bought
> A mansion incorruptible.
> Would they could have stayed with us!

1   What most likely does the deserted house represent?

   A   Someone who is traveling   **C**   Someone who has died

   B   A house that needs repair   **D**   An abandoned dream

2   Which word is an antonym for <u>vacancy</u> as it is used in line 11?

   A   Job   **C**   Opportunity

   B   Emptiness   **D**   Post

3   What most likely are the speaker's feelings about what has happened? Support your answer with examples from the passage.

   _____
   _____
   _____
   _____

Copyright © American Book Company. DO NOT DUPLICATE. 1-888-264-5877.

4 Based on this poem, which analogy is true?

    A Ears are like shutters.

    B Silence is like an empty house

    C Death is like a closed door.

    D Eyes are like windows.

5 What does the word <u>incorruptible</u> mean in line 21?

    A To corrupt easily

    B Not well corrupted

    C To be morally right

    D Morally questionable

6 At the end, the speaker says that Life and Thought are no longer here but "in a city glorious—/A great and distant city—have bought/A mansion incorruptible." What allusion is he making here? Why do you think so?

_____

_____

_____

_____

Copyright © American Book Company. DO NOT DUPLICATE. 1-888-264-5877.

CHAPTER 7 SUMMARY

Learning new **vocabulary** is necessary to develop your reading, writing, and speech.

Context clues are used to determine the meaning of a word based on the words and ideas that surround it.

Sometimes you'll encounter **words with multiple meanings**—meanings that are determined by the context.

Examining **roots** and **affixes** will help you figure out the meaning of a new vocabulary word. A **root word** is a word that has nothing added, and a new word can be made from it by adding affixes. A **prefix** is an affix added to the beginning of a root word, while a **suffix** is an affix added to the end of a word.

Reference sources for finding word meaning include a **dictionary** (which provides meaning, pronunciation, part of speech, and more), a **thesaurus** (which provides synonyms and sometimes antonyms), and a **glossary** (like a mini-dictionary at the end of a chapter or book).

Word relationships can help you figure out unfamiliar words.

A **synonym** is a word that has the same or a similar meaning as another word.

An **antonym** is a word that means the opposite of another word.

The **denotation** of a word is its meaning as found in the dictionary. On the other hand, a **connotation** of a word is meaning that is implied (suggested).

Many words and phrases have **nuances** of meaning, which are small differences.

Figurative language encompasses devices that authors use to make their writing more interesting and helps to convey meaning and tone. Two specific devices include **allusions** and **analogies**.

Copyright © American Book Company. DO NOT DUPLICATE. 1-888-264-5877.

CHAPTER 7 REVIEW

RL 4, RI 4, L 4–6

> **DIRECTIONS** Read the following passages, and answer the questions after each one.

Excerpt from "Ali Hafed's Quest"

by Orison Swett Marden

1   Happy and contented was the good Ali Hafed, when one evening a learned priest of Buddha, journeying along the banks of the Indus, stopped for rest and refreshment at his home, where all wayfarers were hospitably welcomed and treated as honored guests.

2   After the evening meal, the farmer and his family with the priest in their midst gathered around the fireside, the chilly mountain air of the late autumn making a fire desirable. The disciple of Buddha entertained his kind hosts with various legends and myths, and last of all with the story of the creation.

3   He told his wondering listeners how in the beginning the solid earth on which they lived was not solid at all, but a mere bank of fog. "The Great Spirit," said he, "thrust his finger into the bank of fog and began slowly describing a circle in its midst, increasing the speed gradually until the fog went whirling round his finger so rapidly that it was transformed into a glowing ball of fire. Then the Creative Spirit hurled the fiery ball from his hand, and it shot through the universe, burning its way through other banks of fog and condensing them into rain, which fell in great floods, cooling the surface of the immense ball.

4   "Flames then bursting from the interior through the cooled outer crust, threw up the hills and mountain ranges and made the beautiful fertile valleys. In the flood of rain that followed this fiery upheaval, the substance that cooled very quickly formed granite, that which cooled less rapidly became copper, the next in degree cooled down into silver, and the last became gold. But the most beautiful substance of all, the diamond, was formed by the first beams of sunlight condensed on the earth's surface."

Copyright © American Book Company. DO NOT DUPLICATE. 1-888-264-5877.

1 In paragraph 1, what does <u>learned</u> mean? Look at this dictionary entry.

> learned (**lur**-nid for 1–3; lurnd for 4) *adj.*
>
> 1. demonstrating much knowledge; scholarly; erudite
>
> 2. associated with the pursuit of knowledge or aimed at scholars: *He consulted a learned text.*
>
> 3. displaying learning or knowledge; well-informed: *She is learned about how people behave.*
>
> 4. acquired by experience, study, or conditioning

Choose the definition that is the best fit for how the underlined word is used in the text.

A 1   **B** 2   **C** 3   **D** 4

2 Paragraph 1 says "wayfarers were hospitably welcomed." Which word is a synonym for <u>hospitably</u> as it is used here?

A Strongly   **B** Carefully   **C** Dutifully   **D** Sociably

3 In paragraph 4, look at the parts of the word <u>upheaval</u>, and analyze what it means based on those parts.

_____

_____

_____

_____

4 Which word is an antonym for the word <u>condensed</u>, which appears in the fourth paragraph?

A Reduced   **B** Diluted   **C** Concentrated   **D** Thickened

5 What allusion in the story makes it seem more realistic?

_____

_____

_____

_____

Copyright © American Book Company. DO NOT DUPLICATE. 1-888-264-5877.

Scorpions

1   Scorpions are odd-looking creatures. They have short front limbs with large pincers. Their long tails can curl up over their entire bodies. Their hard exoskeletons protect them. In order to grow, they must molt, or shed, these exoskeletons frequently. The layer under the one they shed hardens into a new exoskeleton. Due to fluorescent chemicals in their bodies, scorpions glow green under ultraviolet light.

2   Like many things about them, scorpion reproduction is sort of unusual. Although they're like spiders, scorpions do not lay eggs. Mothers birth scorplings one at a time in litters of up to one hundred. Newborns look just like tiny adults. They all cling to their mother's back as she walks. Then again, considering how human parents ferry their kids around in vehicles, maybe scorpions aren't so unusual.

3   Scorpions live in many areas of the world. There are over two thousand species, and most of them prefer warm areas where weather stays above sixty-eight degrees Fahrenheit. If they must, they can survive the cool weather of a desert night. All species reside within forty-nine degrees of the equator, which is roughly the middle third of the earth.

4   Scorpions make most people think of deadly stings. So people fear all scorpions. Since its venom is meant to subdue very small prey, the average scorpion's sting can't harm humans who aren't allergic. However, some kinds have potent venom that can seriously harm most people.

5   People often pass along misinformation about scorpions. According to one popular myth, if a scorpion is too close to fire, it will sting itself to death. This is not true; a scorpion is immune to its own venom. This assumption probably came from observations of scorpions coming too close to heat sources. Because they are cold-blooded, their nervous systems short circuit when exposed to extreme heat. A jolting scorpion would indeed look like it was stinging itself.

6   Any Americans worried about lethal scorpion stings can rest easy. Most dangerous scorpions live outside of the United States. The Arizona bark scorpion is a major exception. Its sting can cause intense pain, breathing problems, and muscle spasms. Luckily for those in the other forty-nine states, the scorpion is true to its name and stays in Arizona.

Copyright © American Book Company. DO NOT DUPLICATE. 1-888-264-5877.

6   In the first paragraph, the prefix in the word <u>exoskeleton</u> means what about the scorpion's skeleton?

    A   The scorpion's bones are multilayered.

    B   The scorpion has a shell it can crawl into.

    C   The scorpion does not have a skeleton.

    D   The scorpion's skeleton is on the outside.

7   In paragraph 5, people passing along <u>misinformation</u> means that they —

    A   make up things about what scorpions can do.

    B   tell lies because they hate scorpions.

    C   spread rumors without verifying the truth.

    D   create fun stories about scorpions.

Read this sentence from paragraph 4.

Since its venom is meant to subdue very small prey, the average scorpion's sting can't harm humans who aren't allergic.

8   Give two synonyms for <u>subdue</u>.

_____

_____

Read this sentence from paragraph 6.

Any Americans worried about lethal scorpion stings can rest easy.

9   What does <u>rest easy</u> mean?

_____

_____

Copyright © American Book Company. DO NOT DUPLICATE. 1-888-264-5877.

Read this sentence from paragraph 6.

Its sting can cause forceful pain, breathing problems, and muscle spasms.

10 What would be the best replacement for <u>forceful</u>?

   A Intense

   B Weighty

   C Impressive

   D Robust

Copyright © American Book Company. DO NOT DUPLICATE. 1-888-264-5877.

Chapter 8
Research

This chapter covers the following seventh grade strand and standards:

Writing

2. Write informative/explanatory texts to examine a topic and convey ideas, concepts, and information through the selection, organization, and analysis of relevant content. (in writing task)

Research to Build and Present Knowledge

7. Conduct short research projects to answer a question, drawing on several sources and generating additional related, focused questions for further research and investigation.

8. Gather relevant information from multiple print and digital sources, using search terms effectively; assess the credibility and accuracy of each source; and quote or paraphrase the data and conclusions of others while avoiding plagiarism and following a standard format for citation.

9. Draw evidence from literary or informational texts to support analysis, reflection, and research.

    a. Apply *grade 7 Reading standards* to literature (e.g., "Compare and contrast a fictional portrayal of a time, place, or character and a historical account of the same period as a means of understanding how authors of fiction use or alter history").

    b. Apply *grade 7 Reading standards* to literary nonfiction (e.g. "Trace and evaluate the argument and specific claims in a text, assessing whether the reasoning is sound and the evidence is relevant and sufficient to support the claims").

Range of Writing

10. Write routinely over extended time frames (time for research, reflection, and revision) and shorter time frames (a single sitting or a day or two) for a range of discipline-specific tasks, purposes, and audiences.

Speaking and Listening

Comprehension and Collaboration

1. Engage effectively in a range of collaborative discussions (one-on-one, in groups, and teacher-led) with diverse partners on grade 7 topics, texts, and issues, building on others' ideas and expressing their own clearly.

    a. Come to discussions prepared, having read or researched material under study; explicitly draw on that preparation by referring to evidence on the topic, text, or issue to probe and reflect on ideas under discussion.

Some people believe research is difficult. They might hear the teacher assign a research paper and groan. But we all do research every day. Think about when you want to go see a movie. You need to see what's playing, when, and in which theater. You also might want to check if there is a time of day when you might get a discounted ticket. To find out all of this information, you must know where to look and what questions to ask. That's research!

Copyright © American Book Company. DO NOT DUPLICATE. 1-888-264-5877.

RESEARCH QUESTIONS

After you choose a topic, you need to decide how you will approach it. Asking **research questions** will help you focus on what exactly you will talk about. For example, say your topic is the poet Emily Dickinson. Well, that is a very broad topic! An effective research question helps to narrow it.

 Example: How did Emily Dickinson's life influence her poetry?

As you can see, this question provides a direction for your research. A strong research question passes the "So what?" test. In other words, it asks an interesting question that invites discussion. It is not so broad that it cannot be answered in an essay.

Focused research questions also help you find topics for further research. For example, say that you want to write a paper about US politics. The topic "US politics" is very broad. It would be difficult to write a research paper that is not extremely long. A more focused research question could deal with one specific aspect of US politics. For example, you could write a paper about negative campaigning in a recent race for office. The topic is much more focused, making it easier to research and write an effective and well-developed essay.

RESEARCH SOURCES

The next step is to find **research sources**. You need to know how to make sense of various sources. These include the following:

Print Sources

- **Literary and informational texts** you read will often be sources for papers that you write. You will use these sources to draw evidence for your ideas. When you analyze them, you must use examples from these texts to support your analysis.

- An **encyclopedia** is a reference work that contains articles about a variety of topics. It is a good place to begin your research as it provides a broad overview of a topic.

- An **almanac** is a book of data and facts about a variety of topics, organized in a format similar to an encyclopedia. An almanac is a good source to use if you want to find basic historical and statistical information about a city, state, or country.

- A **journal** is a publication that focuses on topics relevant to a specific industry or area of study. Journals contain articles written by experts in that particular field; therefore, the information in them tends to be specific and focused. Examples of journals for American literature include *Comparative Literature* and *Poets & Writers*.

- **Newspapers** present current events and include daily newspapers such as the *Times-Picayune* and the *New York Times*, as well as weekly newsmagazines like *Time* and *U.S. News & World Report*.

Copyright © American Book Company. DO NOT DUPLICATE. 1-888-264-5877.

Research

Digital Sources

Using the **library catalog** at your local library, you can find the research materials you seek. Although they may not be as popular now due to the Internet, **CD-ROMs** and **microfilm** archives are still excellent resources.

A **search engine** is the easiest way to find things on the **Internet**. Google (google.com) is the most popular search engine. Yahoo! (yahoo.com) and Ask (ask.com) are also widely used.

To use a search engine, type a **key word** into the search bar. Key words are just what they sound like—key, or important, words. The best way to explain keywords is to use an example. Search for the key word *whales*. The engine delivers a list of hyperlinks related to whales.

When you find good pages, you should save them for later. If you're at home, you can **bookmark** pages to your own computer. Use the Help menu on your web browser to find out how. If you are on someone else's computer, either e-mail links to yourself or use a free bookmarking site like www.del.icio.us.

EVALUATING SOURCES

Some sources are more reliable than others. You want to find sources that are **credible** (trustworthy) and **accurate** (factual and in agreement with several other sources). Sources that are most balanced also are most reliable. If a source shows bias (one-sided opinion), chances are that some information about other viewpoints has been left out. You can use these sources, of course. But you need to balance the equation yourself by finding sources that offer other viewpoints.

Here are some examples of sources and how credible and accurate they can be.

Books and journals can be reliable sources if they are written by experts. Look for texts written by authorities in their field. You can also check who published the texts. For example, university presses publish texts that are reliable. There are many respected publishers that produce volumes about certain subjects. Just as with authors, look for experts in the publishing of particular materials.

Eyewitness accounts come from people who actually saw what happened or were present at an event. These accounts are often reliable. Keep in mind, though, that eyewitnesses might view and/or remember the same event differently. Therefore, it is best to rely on more than just one eyewitness.

Newspaper articles are often viewed as reliable sources. Newspapers must follow strict rules about verifying their own sources before printing a story. However, keep in mind that news reporters do sometimes allow their own opinions to influence the way they report. It is best to read several articles that report on an issue or event. That way, you can compare the various articles to determine what information is most reliable.

Copyright © American Book Company. DO NOT DUPLICATE. 1-888-264-5877.

Supermarket tabloid articles are usually considered fairly unreliable. This is because these newspaper and magazines focus on sensational stories. Often, tabloid stories are not true or only partially true. A good researcher will hardly ever rely on tabloids as reliable sources of information.

Internet sources make research easier than ever before. But you must be careful. Some online resources are reliable, but others are not. Keep in mind that anyone can post anything on the World Wide Web. Personal websites and chat rooms, for example, are not reliable sources of facts. It is important to learn which sites are good resources, such as educational (.edu), government (.gov), and certain organizational (.org) sites.

Practice 1: Research Sources

w 7–10

| DIRECTIONS | Choose the best answer for each question. |

1   To find facts about the world's fastest airplane, which key words would provide the best results?

   A   Airplane speeds throughout world

   B   Highest speeds of vehicles worldwide

   C   World's fastest airplane

   D   Which airplane is the fastest in the world?

2   What is one question you might ask yourself to judge the credibility of information you find in a resource?

   A   Does the author have strong beliefs that might have influenced his views?

   B   Do I agree with this source?

   C   Does the title of this work seem appropriate considering the content?

   D   Was this material written while I was alive?

3   What would be the best source to use to find when writer Ernest Hemingway lived?

   _____
   _____
   _____
   _____

Copyright © American Book Company. DO NOT DUPLICATE. 1-888-264-5877.

4   You are interested in researching the history of American automobiles. You want to find out which American car has proved to be the most reliable. Which source would probably show the most bias?

A   A journal article from a noted automobile historian

B   An encyclopedia entry about the invention of the automobile

C   An interview with a curator from the National Automobile Museum

D   An article written by a representative of Ford Motor Company

5   Kerry is writing about the reasons that Langston Hughes wrote his poetry. A search engine gave Kerry these results. Which would be most likely to help her with her paper?

A   Collected Poems of Langston Hughes – Buy for $8.99

B   Complete Online Archive of Langston Hughes Poems

C   "Why I Love Langston Hughes Poems" by David Jones

D   How the Inspired Life of Langston Hughes Inspired His Poems

6   You're doing online research about the history of the African American Civil Rights Movement. Which of these would be the best link to click on?

A   The History of the Women's Rights Movement

B   People with Disabilities Seek Their Own Civil Rights Movement

C   The Road to Civil Rights for the Black Community

D   Civil Rights in Ancient Europe

7   You need to find an article comparing modern and classical painters. What would be the best key words to search?

_____

_____

USING SOURCES IN YOUR WRITING

Now that you have reviewed how to find and evaluate sources, it's time to use them. There are many ways for you to incorporate what you've learned into a research paper.

Direct quotations are the exact words of the original author or speaker. Use quotation marks around the quoted words and attribute the words to the person who said or wrote them.

Example: Hester Prynne of *The Scarlet Letter* is described by Hawthorne as "ladylike, too, after the manner of the feminine gentility of those days."

Copyright © American Book Company. DO NOT DUPLICATE. 1-888-264-5877.

Paraphrasing (also called an indirect quotation) is restating the words of another person in your own words. Paraphrasing does not use quotation marks, but it does give credit to the person who originally said it.

Original material:

> President John F. Kennedy said, "Let every nation know…whether it wishes us well or ill…that we shall pay any price, bear any burden, meet any hardship, support any friend, oppose any foe, to assure the survival and the success of liberty. This much we pledge … and more."

Paraphrase:

> In his inaugural address, President John F. Kennedy told all nations that America would do what it must to survive and stay free.

Summarizing is used for longer passages or entire works. It puts the original author's main idea into your own words. When you summarize, you only include the main point and major details. Summaries provide a much shorter overview of the original material.

> **Example:** *Beowulf* tells the story of a hero (Beowulf) who successfully battles three creatures during his life, although the third creature fatally wounds him.

CITING SOURCES

To include research in your paper, you need to paraphrase it in your own words or quote it. To **cite sources** is to show readers where you found your information. This is also a way of giving credit to the original source. Taking credit for someone else's work is a form of cheating called **plagiarism**.

When it comes to citing sources and writing bibliographies, your school will probably have its own style and rules. These may vary from the examples we've listed. Ask your teacher for the preferred way to document sources.

Let's say you want to use an idea you found in an encyclopedia. You found it in an entry about mountains. The entry shows a table of the longest mountain ranges on Earth; the Andes range is listed as the longest. Most writers would cite that source this way:

The Andes is the world's longest mountain range, according to the *Encyclopaedia Britannica*.

Or it could be written this way:

The Andes is the world's longest mountain range (*Encyclopaedia Britannica*).

Copyright © American Book Company. DO NOT DUPLICATE. 1-888-264-5877.

The Modern Language Association (MLA) style uses parenthetical **in-text citations**, which means a reference to a work is placed in parentheses after a quote, paraphrase, or summary. A citation is a brief reference in a text to another source that acknowledges where a quote or idea came from.

MLA requires citations to be listed as follows:

For a work <u>by one author</u>, list the author's last name and the page number where the material is taken, with no comma between.

> **Example:** Two examples of the theory are explained (Dankin 185).

Notice the end punctuation goes after the parenthetical citation.

When material is summarized from <u>more than one page</u>, give the page range.

> **Example:** (Dankin 185–187)

When the author is already mentioned in the text, put only the page number in parentheses.

> **Example:** Dankin gives us two examples of the theory (185).

At the end of your paper, you'll have a list of all the sources that you cited. This list is called your **bibliography**. All information on this page must be written in a specific format, according to the style guide you use. Ask your teacher about the guide you should be using.

To demonstrate citations in this book, you will read about MLA style. The guidelines for citing sources and writing a bibliography are explained in the MLA style guide, titled *MLA Handbook for Writers of Research Papers*. In this style, the page is called "Works Cited" and contains sources that you used in your research report. Entries are listed in alphabetical order by the author's last name. Here are examples of several bibliographical entries, using MLA style.

Documenting a Book:

Twain, Mark. <u>Life on the Mississippi</u>. New York: Penguin Classics, 1984.

Newspaper Article:

Anderson, Ed. "Jindal does about-face on raise veto." <u>New Orleans Times-Picayune</u> 30 June 2008 A1.

Offline Encyclopedia:

Wallace, Daniel. "Iron Man." <u>The Marvel Encyclopedia</u>. Ed. Alastair Dougall. New York: DK Publishing, 2006. 146–147.

Web Article:

Kanamori, Hiroo. "The Energy Release in Great Earthquakes." <u>Journal of Geophysical Research</u> Volume 82, (1977): p. 2981. 1 May 2008. <http://adsabs.harvard.edu/>.

[Note: Instead of the Web address, uou might be asked to list the source medium at the end. Ask your teacher the preferred way to list Internet sites.]

As you know, the titles of long works, like books and newspapers, should be in italics. But when you write a bibliographic entry by hand, it is hard to make it look italicized. So use an underline instead.

Copyright © American Book Company. DO NOT DUPLICATE. 1-888-264-5877.

There are many other kinds of texts that you may find yourself citing. These are just a few samples to give you an idea. Ask your teacher for handouts or websites you can use to check your citations and bibliography.

Practice 2: Evaluating and Using Sources

W 7–10

> **DIRECTIONS**   Read the research sources, and answer the questions that follow.

Talking with Hands: The Next Big Thing?

by Margaret O'Sullivan

Back in the '90s, the cool phrase was "talk to the hand." Well, that phrase might not be popular anymore, but there may be a better use for it anyway. Since its early development in the 1800s, American Sign Language (ASL) has continued to develop as a language among a special group of individuals—deaf people and those with hearing loss. It was not an easy road, though.

In 1817, Thomas Hopkins Gallaudet founded the American Asylum for the Deaf and Dumb. The school is now known as the American School for the Deaf. He and other professors tutored hearing impaired students from around America and taught them sign language. Since the variety of students was so large, many different skills blended. This created the basis for ASL. However, critics argued that signing was not a language. William Stokoe, a professor of English at Gallaudet University, changed this thinking. In 1955, he became very interested in ASL and began serious study of it. He wrote many articles in scholarly journals about ASL linguistics. Eventually, Stokoe was able to convince skeptics that ASL was a natural language just like English.

Sign language has become especially popular with parents of infants. Many parents teach basic signs to their children at an early age. Some of these signs are *Mama*, *Daddy*, *milk*, *more*, *eat*, and *no*. Studies have shown contact with sign language can have positive effects on children's social well-being, whether they are hearing-impaired or not. When babies are taught early in life to communicate, they tend to have faster language development later on.

Today, American Sign Language is a distinct language. It has its own grammar rules and syntax. ASL classes are offered as language courses in many secondary and postsecondary schools. It looks like people have started talking with their hands, instead of to them.

– from *Hearing Now* magazine, June 2011

Copyright © American Book Company. DO NOT DUPLICATE. 1-888-264-5877.

Web search for "American Sign Language"

Results **1 - 6** of about 7,440,000 for English american sign language [definition]. (0.15 seconds)

ASLHistory.net
Includes many links to ASL information: timelines, famous hearing impaired people, charts, and pictures. The history of ASL can be explored at ASLHistory.net.

HelenKeller.net
Almost everyone has heard of Helen Keller and her instructor, Anne Sullivan. But what do you really know about them? What were their dreams and ambitions? Learn about these two amazing women, along with photos and journal entries, here at HelenKeller.net.

Deafspeak.org
The Deaf and Hearing Loss Society's home page. We have chapters in all fifty states, and our members are comprised of students from across the United States. To learn more about the DHLS, visit deafspeak.org.

SigningMadeEasy.com
Want to learn American Sign Language? Don't have the time to take a multi-week seminar? Visit our Web site for fast tips and illustrated learning guides. Be able to talk with any hearing impaired person in less than three weeks! Visit signingmadeeasy.com.

TalkASL.com
Need help learning American Sign Language? Join this forum! Membership includes daily ASL tips and videos, access to message boards to ask questions to other ASL beginners, and weekly quizzes and puzzles to sharpen your ASL skills. All this and more at TalkASL.com.

ASLcamp.com
Want your kids to have a fun-filled, yet educational, summer? This six-week program will introduce your child to the joy of sign language. Every day the children will learn new signs and ways to incorporate them into everyday conversation. Sign up now at ASLcamp.com.

1 2 3 4 5 6 7 8 9 NEXT ▶

Copyright © American Book Company. DO NOT DUPLICATE. 1-888-264-5877.

Copyright Page from *The Basics of American Sign Language*

Artwork by Richton Design Studio

Cover Photo: Desiree Johannson

Published by: Botkins Press

47 W. Reese Ave.

Chicago, IL

Copyright © 2007 by Werner C. Moreland

All rights reserved. Printed in the United States of America. Except as permitted under the United States Copyright Act, no part of this publication may be reproduced, stored, or retransmitted in any form without prior written permission of the publisher.

Copyright © American Book Company. DO NOT DUPLICATE. 1-888-264-5877.

ASL Alphabet Chart from *The Basics of American Sign Language*

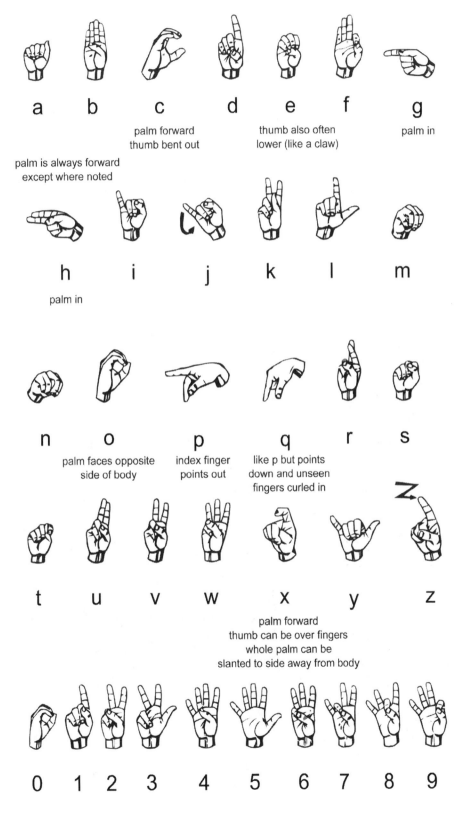

Copyright © American Book Company. DO NOT DUPLICATE. 1-888-264-5877.

Chapter 8

"Fingerspelling" passage from *You Can Sign Too*

There are plenty of signs in the ASL vocabulary. There are also plenty of reasons to fingerspell. Fingerspelling is exactly what it sounds like—spelling out words with signs that match each letter of the word. There are quite a few different manual alphabets throughout the world. A typical ASL user would learn the American Fingerspelled Alphabet.

The American Fingerspelled Alphabet consists of twenty-two handshapes that stand for the twenty-six letters of the American alphabet. Why are there only twenty-two handshapes? Well, the handshapes of some letters are very similar. They can be used in various positions or movements. Depending on which you use, the different letters are produced. For example, the letters *K* and *P* use the same handshape—except one is made facing up to the ceiling, and the other is made facing down toward the floor.

Why fingerspell? Simply put, some words just don't have signs. Many names of people, places, titles, and brands are fingerspelled. Sometimes fingerspelling is easier in the conversation. For example, the sign for *cat* is very simple, but in the context of the conversation, it may be just as easy or even faster to fingerspell *C-A-T*. When you are learning ASL as a hobby or to talk with a deaf friend or relative, chances are you may forget a sign every now and then. If you forget a word's sign, you don't have to stop talking, you can simply fingerspell it.

Learning your American Fingerspelled Alphabet can give you a good basis for learning sign language. Many signs use basic alphabet handshapes to form the word. It is also good to know your alphabet for everyday conversation.

1   To find information about the history of American Sign Language, which link from the web search would be most useful?

   A   ASLCamp.com

   B   Deafspeak.org

   C   ASLHistory.net

   D   TalkASL.com

2   What cannot be determined using the ASL Alphabet Chart from the book *The Basics of American Sign Language*?

   A   Basic vocabulary signs in ASL

   B   The handshapes of the letters

   C   The letters of the ASL alphabet

   D   Movements that accompany different letters

Copyright © American Book Company. DO NOT DUPLICATE. 1-888-264-5877.

3 What is the main idea of the article "Talking with Hands: The Next Big Thing?" from *Hearing Now* magazine?

    A American Sign Language is fun for everyone to learn and speak.

    B American Sign Language has a distinct history and continues to grow in popularity.

    C American Sign Language is just for deaf people and babies.

    D American Sign Language should not be considered a language because it does not use the voice.

4 What is the acceptable bibliographic entry for the book *The Basics of American Sign Language*?

_____

_____

5 After reading from the chapter on "Fingerspelling" in *You Can Sign Too*, you decide you want to learn more about it. Which website contains tips, quizzes, and practices for learning ASL?

_____

PREPARING FOR DISCUSSIONS

In addition to finding sources for your writing, there is another reason to read about topics. You need to **prepare for discussions** in class or in groups of which you are a member. When you know you will talk about a topic, you need to read assigned texts. You can also do additional research so you are ready to add to the discussion.

Copyright © American Book Company. DO NOT DUPLICATE. 1-888-264-5877.

CHAPTER 8 SUMMARY

Asking **research questions** will help you focus on exactly what you will talk about.

Focused research questions also help you find topics for further research.

The next step is to find **research sources**. **Print sources** include **literary and informational texts**, **encyclopedia articles**, **almanac** and **journal** entries, and **newspapers**. **Digital sources** include the **library catalog**, **CD-ROMs** and **microfilm**, and the **Internet**.

Next, you need to evaluate sources to make sure they are **credible** and **accurate**. Examples of reliable sources are **books and journals** by experts, **eyewitness accounts**, and authoritative **Internet sources**. Other sources like **supermarket tabloid articles**, personal websites, or chat rooms are not reliable sources for facts.

Now you need to incorporate your research into your own work. **Direct quotations** are the exact words of the original author or speaker. **Paraphrasing** is restating the words of another person in your own words. **Summarizing** is used for longer passages or entire works and includes the main point and major details summed up in your own words.

No matter how you include your research, you must **cite sources** to show readers where you found your information and avoid **plagiarism**. Use **in-text citations** in your writing, and list the works you used in a **bibliography**.

In addition to finding sources for your writing, you need to **prepare for discussions** in class or in groups.

Copyright © American Book Company. DO NOT DUPLICATE. 1-888-264-5877.

CHAPTER 8 REVIEW

W 2, 7–10, SL 1.a

> **DIRECTIONS** | Say you are doing a research project about Hawaii. You find the following sources. Read them, and answer the questions that follow.

Almanac Fast Facts

Flag:

Capital: Honolulu (on Oahu)

State Abbreviation/Postal Code: HI

Organized as Territory: 1900

Entered Union (rank): Aug. 21, 1959 (50)

State Flag of Hawaii

Motto: *Ua mau ke ea o ka 'aina i ka pono* (The life of the land is perpetuated in righteousness.)

State Symbols

    Flower: Hawaiian hibiscus (1988)

    Song: "Hawaii Pono'i" (1967)

    Bird: nene (goose) (1957)

    Tree: kukui nut (1959)

Nickname: Aloha State (1959)

Origin of Name: May have been named after Hawaiki, the mythical homeland of the Polynesians, or Hawai'iloa, the hero of a Hawaiian legend.

Highest Peak: Mauna Kea (13,796 ft)

Largest Volcano (by volume): Mauna Loa (13,679 ft)

Major Points of Interest:

Haleakala National Park (Maui)

Hawaii Volcanoes National Park (Hawaii)

'Iolani Palace, the only royal palace in the United States (Honolulu)

National Memorial Cemetery of the Pacific (Oahu)

Pearl Harbor (Oahu)

Polynesian Cultural Center (Oahu)

Waikiki Beach (Honolulu)

Copyright © American Book Company. DO NOT DUPLICATE. 1-888-264-5877.

Exotic Travel

August 1, 2008

Mauna Loa
by Malachi Cornell

Mauna Loa is the largest volcano on Earth. It is located in the Hawaiian Islands. Mauna Loa means "Long Mountain" in Hawaiian, which is quite an accurate name. In fact, the volcano is so large that it covers half of the island of Hawaii. By itself, it amounts to about 85 percent of all the other Hawaiian Islands combined. Its altitude reaches more than 13,680 feet and has a volume of about 9,600 cubic miles. Mauna Loa's sides do not have a steep slope, but its lava is very fluid. For these reasons, Mauna Loa is considered a shield volcano. This volcano has been around for centuries. It is among the world's most active volcanoes. Mauna Loa has erupted around thirty-three times since the first known event in 1843. The last recorded eruption was in 1984.

Most of Mauna Loa's eruptions caused only property damage. It ruined villages in 1926 and 1950. No recent eruptions have caused deaths. The two main dangers of this volcano are lava flows and flank collapses. Many volcanoes have lava that advances at a walking speed. However, lava flow from Mauna Loa comes from a much more intense eruption. In 1984, Mauna Loa released so much lava in three weeks' time that it was like three years' worth of an average volcano's lava flow. With faster flow, lava can cover more land and harm more ground. In fact, the town of Hilo is almost entirely built on lava flow. It is in danger of further lava flows in the future.

Another perilous but rare hazard at Mauna Loa is the possibility of flank collapse. Hawaiian mountainsides are sloped downwards because of the deep faults; the most well-known being the Hilina Slump. The danger looms that an earthquake could heave the volcano's flanks into a landslide. In turn, the substantial landslide could trigger a tsunami, putting surrounding land and people in further danger.

Because of these risks, Mauna Loa is a closely monitored volcano. Its large size, even considering its dangers, makes it a fascinating sight to visit.

23

Copyright © American Book Company. DO NOT DUPLICATE. 1-888-264-5877.

Major Eruptions of Mauna Loa in the Twentieth Century		
Year	Area (square miles)	Eruption Source
1907	10.8	Southwest Rift
1919	10.8	Southwest Rift
1926	13.5	Southwest Rift
1933	2.3	Summit
1940	5.0	Summit
1942	13.1	Northwest Rift
1949	8.5	Summit
1950	43.2	Southwest Rift
1975	5.0	Summit
1984	18.5	Northwest Rift

1   Which of the following questions was not answered by the magazine article "Mauna Loa"?

   A   How big is Mauna Loa?

   B   What caused Mauna Loa to erupt?

   C   What are two dangers of Mauna Loa?

   D   What does Mauna Loa's name mean?

2   According to the chart, in which year did an eruption cover the most area?

   _____

3   According to the "Almanac's Fast Facts," which of these is not a major point of interest in Hawaii?

   A   Polynesian Cultural Center

   B   Pearl Harbor

   C   Dole Plantation

   D   Waikiki Beach

4   What does the magazine article describe as the two main dangers of Mauna Loa?

   _____

Copyright © American Book Company. DO NOT DUPLICATE. 1-888-264-5877.

5 Kieran wants to include the information "Mauna Loa is considered a shield volcano" in a paper he is writing. How should he write his in-text citation?

A "Mauna Loa is considered a shield volcano," Malachi Cornell, "Mauna Loa," *Exotic Travel*, p. 23.

B "Mauna Loa is considered a shield volcano" (Cornell 23).

C Cornell says "Mauna Loa is considered a shield volcano."

D "Mauna Loa is considered a shield volcano" (Cornell, "Mauna Loa," *Exotic Travel*).

6 In a class discussion about volcanoes, a fellow student comments about the fact that many eruptions happened in the 1940s. Where else can you point to in the research sources that discusses periods of most destruction?

_____

_____

Writing Task

There are many legends and myths about volcanoes. Throughout history, people who did not know how volcanoes worked created stories to explain them. Find a story that focuses on volcanic activity. Compare and contrast how it portrays what happens with the facts you have learned about volcanoes. On your paper, write an essay that discusses the fictional and factual ideas. Make sure your writing is clear and well organized. Be sure to check for and fix any mistakes.

Copyright © American Book Company. DO NOT DUPLICATE. 1-888-264-5877.

Chapter 9
The Writing Process

This chapter covers the following seventh grade strand and standards:

Writing

4. Produce clear and coherent writing in which the development, organization, and style are appropriate to task, purpose, and audience.

5. With some guidance and support from peers and adults, develop and strengthen writing as needed by planning, revising, editing, rewriting, or trying a new approach, focusing on how well purpose and audience have been addressed.

6. Use technology, including the Internet, to produce and publish writing and link to and cite sources as well as to interact and collaborate with others, including linking to and citing sources.

Range of Writing

10. Write routinely over extended time frames (time for research, reflection, and revision) and shorter time frames (a single sitting or a day or two) for a range of discipline-specific tasks, purposes, and audiences.

Language

1–3 (in proofreading reference)

At some point, you will need to write an essay in response to a writing prompt. You might write essays that are narrative, expository, or persuasive. We'll talk more about these modes (types) of essays in this chapter. You will also review ways to write an effective essay and practice writing on your own.

Every process has steps, and the **writing process** is no different. The steps are planning, drafting, revising, proofreading/editing, and finally publishing. Let's look at each step and the activities it includes. When you practice these steps, you will be able to get through them quickly as you write an essay for a test.

STEP 1: PLANNING

Planning is important when writing an essay. Before you can write about a specific topic, you must plan your course of action. This includes making sure you fully understand the writing prompt, developing your ideas, and other steps. You will review all of these skills in this chapter. Then you will use the skills to prepare your essay. However, we need to go over some basic elements of an essay first.

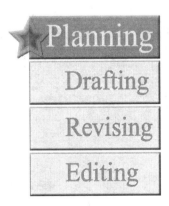

Copyright © American Book Company. DO NOT DUPLICATE. 1-888-264-5877.

Essays have a basic structure. Some are shorter and some longer, but they all need to have a clear beginning, middle, and end. Here are the parts of an essay:

- The **introduction** is the first paragraph of your essay. It gets the reader's attention and contains the central idea (what the essay is all about).

- The **body** usually consists of two to four paragraphs. Each of these paragraphs supports and elaborates on the controlling idea. Each paragraph focuses on a different supporting point from the thesis.

- The **conclusion** is the last paragraph of your essay. It reinforces the main idea of your essay with a strong summary. It ties everything together and convinces the reader of your position. The conclusion should summarize the points you made but not repeat them word for word.

The first step in writing a good response is to read the writing prompt carefully. Make sure you understand what topic you should write about. This is usually clearly stated in the prompt. You also need to understand what mode (narrative, expository, or persuasive) you should write in. There are clues about this in the prompt. Now, we will look at two other important things to know before you begin writing—your purpose and your audience.

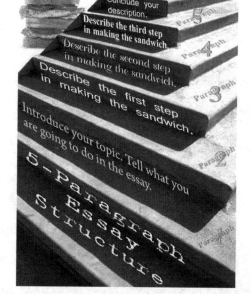

PURPOSE FOR WRITING

Just as people read for different reasons, authors write with various purposes in mind. A **purpose for writing** is your reason for whatever you write. Consider the following types of writing: a novel, a textbook chapter, a friendly letter, and an editorial. Each has a certain purpose. As an author, you may have more than one reason to write a particular piece of writing, but one purpose is usually the most important. When you are writing for the writing assessment, your purpose will be mentioned in the prompt you're given.

There are quite a few reasons to write. However, in general, people write for the purposes of **entertaining**, **informing**, or **persuading**. These also correspond to the three modes in which you are expected to write effectively in seventh grade: narrative, expository, and persuasive.

AUDIENCE

Once you are clear about your purpose for writing, you must consider your **audience**, the person(s) who will read what you write. Unless you are writing in your journal or taking notes in class, you are always writing for a particular audience. It may be your teacher, a friend, your parents, or fellow students. Knowing your audience gives you important information, including the following:

Copyright © American Book Company. DO NOT DUPLICATE. 1-888-264-5877.

the audience's interest	what topics or information is of interest to the audience (so you can capture the interest of your readers)
the audience's prior knowledge	what the audience already knows (so you don't tell the readers something they already know, and you can draw on that prior knowledge)
the audience's vocabulary	words that the readers understand (so you don't use words that are too easy or too difficult)
what the audience needs to know	information or explanations that you want the audience to know (so you can make sure everything is properly covered)

Of course, when you write as part of a test, your real audience will be the professional scorers who will grade your response. However, a prompt might give you a specific audience to address. You need to know how to write for all kinds of possible readers.

DEVELOPING IDEAS

Once you clearly understand the writing prompt, you can begin generating ideas to use in your response. You may have many good ideas, but they aren't useful until you get them out of your head and onto the paper. Then you can work with them, organize them, and add examples and evidence that will **develop your ideas** into useful material for your essay.

Graphic organizers can be very helpful. They include diagrams like the **Venn diagram**, **spider map**, **plot diagram**, and others into which you can visually place your ideas.

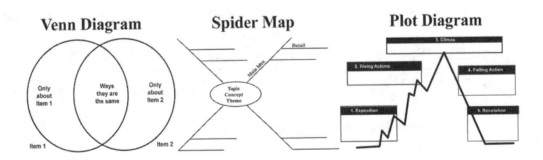

For example, a **Venn diagram** is useful when comparing and contrasting ideas. It is a quick visual way to see points that are alike and those that are different. Draw two circles that intersect, labeling both for the items or ideas that you are comparing. Write the points that are unique to each item in its own circle. The overlapping part of the circles contains the similarities between the two. To compare and contrast three items, you can add a third circle.

Copyright © American Book Company. DO NOT DUPLICATE. 1-888-264-5877.

Chapter 9

A **spider map** is helpful for almost any topic to decide the main points to cover. You write the central idea in the center, and then you write each main point about it on the lines radiating outward like legs. Supporting details go on the smaller lines off of each leg. This graphic organizer also works well to develop ideas for cause and effect. For example, you can write a cause in the center and the effects that happen as result on the lines. Conversely, the effect can go in the middle, with the causes that led to it on the lines.

A **plot diagram** is excellent for mapping out the stages of a narrative. You can jot a summary of the story's beginning, middle, and ending. This gives you a good reference as you start to fill in the story details.

Whichever method you use to generate ideas, keep your goal in mind. You want to be able to use whatever notes you made as a road map to follow as you begin to write. Once you have your ideas in a usable list or organizer, it's time to begin drafting. As you write, and later revise, you will develop your ideas further by adding details and linking everything together in a logical way.

Practice 1: Purpose, Audience, and Ideas

> **DIRECTIONS**
>
> **A. For each of the following topics, determine the purpose for writing an essay about it. Then describe the interest, knowledge, and vocabulary of the given audience, as well as what you think the audience should know. The first one is completed for you.**

1. **Topic:** babysitting

Purpose: persuade potential employers to hire you to babysit

Audience: parents of the children

Audience Interest: wants a hardworking, responsible person who has skills in dealing with children

Audience Knowledge: knows the discipline and compassion needed for children

Audience Vocabulary: probably knows popular, informal language, including childcare terms

Audience Should Know: your willingness to work hard and care for their children

Copyright © American Book Company. DO NOT DUPLICATE. 1-888-264-5877.

2. Topic: the arts (music, fine arts, performing arts) in school

Purpose: _____

Audience: school board members

Audience Interest: _____

Audience Knowledge: _____

Audience Vocabulary: _____

Audience Should Know: _____

3. Topic: the arts in school

Purpose: _____

Audience: students

Audience Interest: _____

Audience Knowledge: _____

Audience Vocabulary: _____

Audience Should Know: _____

Copyright © American Book Company. DO NOT DUPLICATE. 1-888-264-5877.

4. Topic: <u>having a safety plan in case of fire</u>

Purpose: _____

Audience: <u>readers of the local newspaper</u>

Audience Interest: _____

_____

Audience Knowledge: _____

_____

Audience Vocabulary: _____

_____

Audience Should Know: _____

_____

---

5. Topic: <u>doing homework</u>

Purpose: _____

Audience: <u>students</u>

Audience Interest: _____

_____

Audience Knowledge: _____

_____

Audience Vocabulary: _____

_____

Audience Should Know: _____

_____

B. Choose one of the topics in part A of this practice. Use the planning methods of your choice to develop ideas for your essay about the topic.

Note: Keep your notes and papers from this chapter review in a folder for later use. You will use the work you do here in other practices and chapter reviews.

Copyright © American Book Company. DO NOT DUPLICATE. 1-888-264-5877.

STEP 2: DRAFTING

Now you are ready to start **drafting**. Remember, when you write a draft, it does not have to be perfect on the first try. You have time to revise and proofread later. As you write, leave wide margins and plenty of space between each line. That way, you will have room to make changes later.

As you practice writing, you will develop your own personal writing process. Some writers follow their outlines exactly. Other writers begin with the body paragraphs, write a strong conclusion, and then go back and write an introduction. There are no rules for this part of writing. Find the best way for you to get your ideas on paper.

CLARITY AND COHERENCE

Clarity refers to how easily readers can understand what you write. Your writing is clear when it uses precise language and logical organization. This goes hand in hand with **coherence**, which means "to stick together." When your essay has coherence, it means the ideas stick together. They are connected and lead from one to the other. Tying your ideas together is important to help the reader understand your writing. Three ways you can link the ideas and make them clearer include **organization**, **using transitions**, and **repeating key words and phrases**.

ORGANIZATION

Organizing your ideas is the first step to developing a coherent essay. As you know, there are several ways to organize your ideas. These are called **organizational patterns**. In chapter 6, you read about how authors use some of these patterns. You will also use these ways to organize your own essays.

A common pattern is **chronological order**, which starts with a first event, followed by a second event, then a third event, and so forth. This pattern works well for writing a narrative. A similar pattern is **sequential order**. This pattern is perfect for describing how to do something or get somewhere.

You can also compare and/or contrast ideas to make a point. This is the **comparison and contrast** pattern. You can make a strong case by comparing your position with similar ideas that are proved. Or you can contrast your position with its opposite, pointing out differences to show why your position is better. This pattern works for persuasive and expository essays.

Copyright © American Book Company. DO NOT DUPLICATE. 1-888-264-5877.

Explaining **cause and effect** is another way to organize. For example, say that you are writing an essay about your favorite class in school. You would probably explain the causes for liking this subject. You can use transitions to make the causes and effects clear. Cause and effect can be used to organize an expository essay.

Another way to organize a paragraph is in **order of importance**. All of the points should be relevant to the topic, but some points can be emphasized more than others. You can place the most important idea in the first body paragraph, and then follow it with less-important ideas mentioned in other paragraphs. Or you can build up to the most important point, placing it in the last body paragraph. This pattern works well for any type of essay.

USING TRANSITIONS

Transitional words and phrases link ideas from one sentence to another. They also link ideas between paragraphs. They help an essay "stick together." Without these transitional words and phrases, the writing becomes less interesting or even less understandable.

Each organizational pattern has transitional words and phrases that help make it clear. For example, consider these transitions: *like, similarly, just as, however, on the other hand, yet, but*. They all signal that comparison/contrast order is being used. When you choose a pattern to organize your writing, don't forget the transitions! (We'll talk more about transitions when we discuss each type of essay in the next chapter.)

REPEATING KEY WORDS AND PHRASES

You don't want to say the same thing over and over. But **repeating key words and phrases** can improve the reader's understanding of the topic. Key words or ideas from your main idea can be included in the topic sentences of your paragraphs. This will make it easier for the reader to follow your train of thought. These repeated words are like landmarks along the road of your essay. They remind the reader where you have been and where you are going. For example, look at the following plan for an essay in which the topic sentences repeat key words from the central idea:

Central Idea: Citizens of the United States could greatly improve the country by obeying the law, protecting the environment, and being kind to each other.

Topic Sentence: The most basic step to improve the country is to obey the law.

Topic Sentence: In addition, citizens can make this country even more beautiful by protecting the environment.

Topic Sentence: A third way to make the United States a better place to live is for citizens to reach beyond their own self-interest and be kind to one another.

Do you see how repeating the steps and various terms for "improve" tied together all the main points? This also helps focus on the main idea through the whole essay. Yet the phrasing is varied enough so that it does not become boring.

Copyright © American Book Company. DO NOT DUPLICATE. 1-888-264-5877.

Read this excerpt from a newspaper editorial. Then answer the questions that appear after it, and read the explanations for each one.

People should always be aware of their surroundings. This is particularly true in parking lots at night. First, they need to look around the lot carefully. It is important to see any potential danger spots. This includes especially dark areas. Next, drivers should find their keys ahead of time and have them in hand. The police encourage people to have their car keys already in hand, so they are not fumbling around for them, unable to get into their car. In addition, keys can serve as a weapon in case someone does jump out and try to assault a driver. The alarm button for a car found on many key chains also can be helpful in case of emergency. Finally, before actually getting in the car, drivers also should look through the car windows to make sure no one is hiding inside.

What organizational pattern does the writer use?

If you said chronological or sequential order, you are correct. The author walks readers through a series of safety tips for going to their cars in a parking lot at night.

What transitions provide clues to this pattern?

The transition words *first*, *next*, and *finally* help readers to understand the order in which the sequence takes place.

What else does the author do to bring coherence to the passage?

The author introduces the idea of safety in the opening sentence. The second sentence narrows down surroundings to parking lots. Each point is reinforced with an example or a related idea. For instance, the passage mentions "drivers should find their keys ahead of time and have them in hand." The next sentence reinforces this idea by saying what police have to say about it. These related details throughout the passage build coherence.

Practice 2: Drafting

W 4, 5, 10

> **DIRECTIONS** **A. Go back to your notes from Practice 1. Choose one of the topics for which you filled in the purpose and audience details. Now develop ideas for this topic, and write a draft of your essay.**

Copyright © American Book Company. DO NOT DUPLICATE. 1-888-264-5877.

DIRECTIONS **B. Here is another writing prompt for more practice. Read the prompt carefully. Then complete the planning and drafting steps of the writing process.**

When learning new skills and becoming a more mature person, it is helpful to have a good role model. A role model can be a friend whom you admire, an adult you know, or someone you only know about through the news.

Before you write, think about someone you look up to and want to be like. What are the reasons for your admiration? How does this person's life influence what you do?

Write a multi-paragraph essay about someone you look up to as a role model. Tell why you see that person as someone to emulate (be like) and how this person has influenced you.

Using this prompt, begin your planning. Decide how you should address the topic for the audience and what mode of writing to use. Then develop some ideas about the topic, and write a first draft. Review the "Drafting" section of this chapter for important concepts to keep in mind while drafting.

Save your work. You will further develop this essay later in the chapter.

STEP 3: REVISING

Even if you plan your writing well and draft carefully, you will still have room to improve. The next step of the writing process is **revising**. This is the time to make your essay the best it can be. Sometimes that means making small changes like changing words to be more precise. Other times it might mean **rewriting** sections for better organization or to add details.

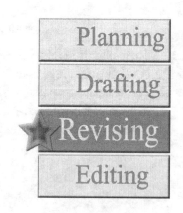

There is one other possibility that you should be prepared for. Once in a while, you may need to **try a new approach**. As you revise, you might see that changes you have made just don't work. Maybe you discover that using your first plan won't properly answer the question in the prompt. When this happens, consider starting over. If you have the time to do so, go back to the planning stage and try a different way to approach the task.

Copyright © American Book Company. DO NOT DUPLICATE. 1-888-264-5877.

GUIDANCE AND SUPPORT

During revising is a good time to get **guidance and support**. For example, you can conference with your teacher or a tutor about how to improve your writing. You can also work with other students to review each other's writing.

When you ask others to look at your draft and offer suggestions on how to improve it, be sure to tell them what advice you need. For example, as they read your draft, have them consider the following questions:

- Are the ideas easy to understand?
- Is each paragraph clearly about one idea?
- Does your essay flow logically from beginning to end?

MAKING IMPROVEMENTS

Read your essay as if you were the audience. Put yourself in the place of the people who will be reading it, and read it as if you were seeing the essay for the first time. Here are some questions you can ask yourself to help pinpoint what revisions you need to make.

❏ Did I write on the assigned topic?
❏ Did I present a clear central idea?
❏ Did I give enough details to elaborate my main idea?
❏ Did I present my supporting points in a logical order?
❏ Did I write with my audience in mind?
❏ Did I use vocabulary that expresses my meaning well?
❏ Did I use sentences that make my main idea interesting to my audience?
❏ Did I write in complete sentences and use a variety of sentence patterns?

When you write your draft, you know what you mean, but you want to be sure it will be clear to your audience. As you revise your essay, imagine that you are the reader. Do you have enough information? Do you still have questions? Are there details missing? Would adding an example improve the writing? When you revise, you can **add support and details** to make your ideas clearer.

Using sentence variety means writing sentences of different kinds and lengths. It includes using different types of phrases. Varying sentences make your writing more interesting. This includes combining simple sentences into longer ones or starting a sentence differently, like with a phrase or dependent clause. Simple, direct sentences can be the best way to say what you mean. But if you use only simple sentences, your writing becomes repetitive and boring.

Copyright © American Book Company. DO NOT DUPLICATE. 1-888-264-5877.

Deleting unrelated sentences helps focus the reader's attention on your topic. As you saw, you might need to add details to parts of your essay. In other cases, you will want to delete unrelated sentences. This means eliminating ideas, statements, or examples that do not relate directly to the topic of your essay.

DEVELOPING STYLE

Writers use language to convey **style**. A writer's style is a unique way of conveying a point. It becomes almost like a signature. All writers have a style and voice, from the giants of literature to the most inexperienced writing student. You have a voice yourself, and though you are just beginning to develop it, it is your own. Word choice is a key component of creating your own style. Your style is the way that you use language and tone in your writing.

Part of style depends on the words and phrases you use. Vivid writing helps readers understand your ideas. Try to use clear, precise language and details that appeal to the senses. Choosing the right words helps readers know what you mean, creates images, and sets a tone.

When you write a school assignment or an essay on a test, you should use **formal style**. You can write more informally when you send e-mail to friends or make notes in your journal. Here are some qualities of formal and informal language.

Formal Language	Informal Language
includes broader vocabulary	uses simple vocabulary words
uses complex sentence structure	contains simple sentences
maintains proper grammar	loosely follows grammar rules

For example, look at this sentence:

> As its super-hot outside layer got cooler and hardened into different kinds of rock, the moon was totally messed up by enormous asteroids and teeny flying bits.

The language is informal; it sounds like something you would tell your best friend about a new space movie. Now look at this sentence:

> As its molten outer layer gradually cooled and solidified into different kinds of rock, the moon was bombarded by huge asteroids and smaller objects.

This sentence is much more formal; it is probably used in a science book.

Copyright © American Book Company. DO NOT DUPLICATE. 1-888-264-5877.

SAMPLE ESSAY

Read this essay written by a student named Garrett. His assignment was to explain something or someone of importance in his life. He needs to describe this item or person and say why it is important to him. He chose to write about his dog, Max. After reading his essay, study the questions and explanations that follow.

> Dogs come in many sizes, shapes, and colors. Some dogs are large while others are small. I have a Labrador retriever, an interesting breed of dog. Learning about this dog can help anyone who wants a Lab for a pet.
>
> My veterinarian, Dorothy Howe, says Labrador retrievers originally came from Canada. These dogs stand about 2 feet tall and weigh between 60 and 75 pounds. They come in black, yellow, or chocolate, and they are sometimes used for bird hunting. Howe says the personality of a Lab should match that of the dog's owner, so before choosing a Lab, a person should observe its personality and behavior. Labrador retrievers can live 8–12 years or longer depending on the owners' attention to their health.
>
> Care of the Labrador retriever involves regular feeding, usually two cups of food each day with plenty of fresh water. Dog experts recommend a high-quality dog food with a few nutritious snacks now and then. Labs should never be allowed to overeat. Labrador retrievers love to play fetch, so always keep a Frisbee or rubber bone handy. Labs are also very strong dogs who will drag you along on their leash unless they are trained to walk with you. They also must learn not to chase other dogs or cars.
>
> I learned that Labrador retrievers can get diarrhea, worms (especially heartworm), and distemper. They also can become blind, and get hip disease or a skin infection. They need checkups and shots on a regular basis. As puppies, Labs can get sick and die if they become too cold. Both puppies and adult Labs are fun-loving, affectionate, and protective of their owners.
>
> Most people enjoy Labrador retrievers. They're playful, loyal, and good hunting dogs too. When I look into my Lab's eyes, I see a smart and lovable dog. That's what makes him interesting to me.

Take a look back at the checklist for making improvements.

How did Garrett do in all these areas?

He did write on the assigned topic, but only partially. He provides much interesting information about Labs, but he does not say specifically why his dog is important to him. The main points—about how Labs look, how to care for them, and some specific physical needs—are well developed and organized. But the introduction is vague and does not really grab the reader. It needs much more descriptive language. It also needs to better state the purpose of the essay.

Copyright © American Book Company. DO NOT DUPLICATE. 1-888-264-5877.

What did Garrett leave out? Are there details and examples that he should add?

Garrett has some excellent supporting details, especially the ones that come from an expert—the veterinarian. But when you read this essay, you might think of some questions that you would want to ask Garrett. He does not say much about his own dog. He does not even tell readers Max's name or how long Max has been in the family. These are important details to add so that he can answer the part of the writing assignment about why Max is important to him.

Garrett also makes a few statements that need some elaboration to support them. For example, he writes, "Labs should never be allowed to overeat." Readers might wonder why that is. He also says, "They also must learn not to chase other dogs or cars." Again, an explanation is needed to tell the reader why this is important. In addition, he could explain better why Labs tend to get the health conditions he writes about.

What other changes can Garrett make in words, phrases, and sentences to improve his essay?

There are many ways in which Garrett could revise his writing to make it livelier and more interesting. One example is to take out any information that is not relevant, such as the idea that Labrador retrievers are originally from Canada. Another example is combining sentences in a way that makes more sense, so that related ideas are together. Look at this original part of the second paragraph:

> "My veterinarian, Dorothy Howe, says Labrador retrievers originally came from Canada. These dogs stand about 2 feet tall and weigh between 60 and 75 pounds. They come in black, yellow, or chocolate, and they are sometimes used for bird hunting."

Here it is again with the reference to Canada taken out. Garrett arranged and linked the sentences more logically. He added some information that develops his own writing style and offers a peek at his own dog, Max:

> "Adult Labs stand about 2 feet tall and weigh between 60 and 75 pounds. They come in black, yellow, or chocolate. Max is a chocolate Lab with a smooth, shiny coat. My veterinarian, Dorothy Howe, says Labrador retrievers are sometimes used for bird hunting. This makes sense, seeing how fast they run and how well they can be trained. Max doesn't go on hunts, but he sure pays attention to birds in the neighborhood."

There are many other improvements that Garrett could make. These examples show how important revising is after you have drafted your essay.

Copyright © American Book Company. DO NOT DUPLICATE. 1-888-264-5877.

Practice 3:   Revising

W 5

DIRECTIONS	Take out the draft you wrote for Practice 2. You will now revise it.
	If you can, get guidance and support from a teacher or tutor. You can also work with other students using peer review. Read over your own paper, and make improvements to it. Be sure it is clear, coherent, and descriptive.
	Save your work. You will work on this essay again in Practice 4.

STEP 4: PROOFREADING AND EDITING

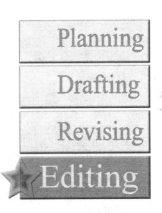

The final steps of going over your essay are some of the most important. In the last few steps, you will look for errors in spelling, punctuation, and grammar that can bring down your grade. Making sure your writing is error-free in these areas is called **proofreading**. Correcting these errors is called **editing**.

Don't try to proofread as you revise. You will not be able to sort out your ideas, refine word choices, and add details at the same time that you look for spelling and punctuation errors. You will miss more mistakes that way. Take it one step at a time. It makes more sense to look for errors when the essay is completed.

Again, read your composition as if you were the audience. Put yourself in the place of the people who will be reading it, and read your words as if you were seeing them for the first time. Make your changes by using the spaces in between the lines and in the margins. Here are some questions to ask yourself at this point. (You can also check chapter 11 in this book for a few of the conventions to focus on.)

- [ ] Did I write using appropriate subject-verb agreement, verb tenses, word meaning, and word endings?
- [ ] Did I write using correct punctuation?
- [ ] Did I write using correct capitalization?
- [ ] Did I write using appropriate formatting (e.g., indentations, margins)?
- [ ] Did I write using correct spelling?
- [ ] Did I remember to print or write neatly?

Copyright © American Book Company. DO NOT DUPLICATE. 1-888-264-5877.

Practice 4: Proofreading and Editing

W 5, L 1–3

> **DIRECTIONS**
>
> Take out the draft you revised for Practice 2. You will now proofread it.
>
> Chapter 11 covers some of the conventions you should know. Review that chapter, and then proofread your essay. If you need more practice with conventions, review the grammar book you use in school, or practice using American Book Company's *Basics Made Easy Grammar and Usage Review.*
>
> Then come back to this chapter to take the final step in the writing process and to complete the chapter review.
>
> Save your work. You will have one final step to take with your essay in Practice 5.

Step 5: Publishing

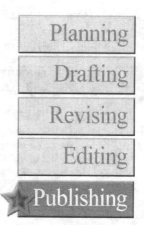

When you write reports for class, the final step might be **publishing** your work. After revising your essay and completing your final draft, you can share it with others. Publishing allows others to view and read what you have written. You might want to print out a clean copy of your essay for your classmates to read. You could post your essay to a blog or website using the Internet. However you choose to publish your work, you are allowing others to read and comment about what you have accomplished.

Before you publish, make sure that you have **cited your sources** and have a **bibliography** ready.

A great thing about today's technology is that it allows multimedia interaction. Therefore, you can even **link to sources** that are available online.

Whether you print your paper in hard copy or post it online, you can add graphics to enhance it. These can help your readers to better understand what you have written. Keep in mind that images, just like texts, have creators and owners. You must give credit (use citations) for the graphics you use, just as you must for quoted text.

Copyright © American Book Company. DO NOT DUPLICATE. 1-888-264-5877.

Practice 5: Publishing

W 6

DIRECTIONS	Take out the essay that you drafted, revised, proofread, and edited. You are now ready to publish it.
	Choose a medium for publishing your work, and print or upload your essay with any accompanying media it needs. Then ask your teachers, tutor, and/or classmates to read it and give you their feedback.
	As a final step, make yourself notes about what you would do differently in the writing process next time.

Copyright © American Book Company. DO NOT DUPLICATE. 1-888-264-5877.

CHAPTER 9 SUMMARY

The **writing process** includes the steps of **planning**, **drafting**, **revising**, **proofreading/editing**, and **publishing**.

Planning includes making sure you fully understand the writing prompt, develop your ideas effectively, and other steps.

Keep in mind that the structure of an essay includes an **introduction**, **body**, and **conclusion**.

A **purpose for writing** is your reason for whatever you write. In general, people write for the purposes of **entertaining**, **informing**, or **persuading**.

Once you are clear about your purpose for writing, you must consider your **audience**, the person(s) who will read what you write.

During planning, you will **develop your ideas**. **Graphic organizers** like the **Venn diagram**, **spider map**, **plot diagram**, and others can help you visually place your ideas.

Drafting involves getting your ideas down on paper.

This is the time to work toward **clarity** (making sure readers can understand what you wrote) and **coherence** (ensuring that ideas stick together), which are affected by **organization**, **using transitions**, and **repeating key words and phrases**.

Revising is the time to make your essay the best it can be. Sometimes that means making small changes, sometimes it involves **rewriting**, and once in a while it means you need to start over and **try a new approach**.

This is an excellent time to get **guidance and support** such as conferencing with a teacher or tutor or working with other students.

As you revise, you can **add support and details** to make your ideas clearer. **Using sentence variety**, **deleting unrelated sentences**, and developing your own writing **style** are also effective ways to improve your essay. Remember to write in a **formal style** for school assignments and tests.

The final step is **publishing** your work by printing it or posting it online. Remember to include source **citations**, a **bibliography**, and **links to sources**.

Copyright © American Book Company. DO NOT DUPLICATE. 1-888-264-5877.

CHAPTER 9 REVIEW

W 4–6, 10, L 1–3

| DIRECTIONS | 1. Practice reviewing an essay by another student. |

Chad's assignment was to write an informational essay about how to perform an activity that he knows well. Read and evaluate Chad's essay. Rate the essay on a scale of one to four, with one being the lowest rating and four being the highest. (See chapter 1 for more about scoring essays.) Use the material in this chapter to develop particular reasons for the rating that you choose. Share your results with the class or with your teacher.

> The sure-fire way to sink a free throw every time is to practice, practice, practice. A basketball free throw is just what it sounds like: an opportunity to toss the ball thru the hoop while you are free from other players trying to distract you. You just stand at the free throw line (fifteen feet from the basket), with no other players defending you, and take a shot. It should be easy but many players miss because they don't practice the essential elements of free throw shooting.
>
> The first thing you want to do is to relax. Free throws are the easiest shots in the game, so just take it easy and let your practice pay off. When you practice your shot, set your feet shoulder width apart with your shooting foot slightly forward of the other foot. In other words, if you shoot with your right hand, put your right foot slightly foward. Then, you should look at the hoop to let your eyes register the distance. This lets your brain know where you want the ball to go.
>
> After you bounce the ball a few times to relax your shooting muscles, hold the ball gently but with confidence. Make sure your shooting hand is directly under the ball and your elbow is pointing down at your knee. Then, look again at the hoop, take a deep relaxing breath, bend your knees, and take your shot. After you release the ball, remember to follow through with your fingers pointing toward the hoop, and watch the ball "swish" through the net.
>
> Finally, repeat these steps, establish a routine that works for you, and practice it regularly. Stand in the same place on the free throw line, bounce the ball the same number of times. Take your breath at the same time. Keep your routine the same. In this way, every time you step up to the free throw line, you don't have to think. Your body goes on automatic pilot, and you sink the free throw every time!

| DIRECTIONS | 2. Work further on your own essays. |

Take out any other essays that you have drafted. Take them through the rest of the writing process by applying the steps of revision, proofreading, and publishing.

Copyright © American Book Company. DO NOT DUPLICATE. 1-888-264-5877.

DIRECTIONS 3. Write essays based the following writing prompts. Ask your teacher or tutor which ones to complete first.

Carefully follow the steps of the writing process to complete an essay based on the prompt. Share your essay with your teacher, tutor, or classmates. For more practice, complete essays based on the other prompts.

Write a persuasive essay telling a classmate or friend why you would or would not recommend a book you read recently. Include examples from the book's text to support your opinion.

Many professional athletes earn millions of dollars each year. At the same time, teachers, nurses, firefighters, and law-enforcement officers earn much less per year. Is it fair that professional athletes earn such high salaries compared to people who perform these important services? Why or why not? Write a persuasive essay focusing on whether professional athletes should earn higher salaries than public servants.

If you could live in any country in the world, which would it be? Explain why you would want to live there. Before you begin writing, think about all the countries you could pick from. Which would you choose? Why? What would be different about living there?

It has been said that opposites attract. Think of someone you are friends with who may be very different from you. Does he or she have different taste in music or wear a different style of clothing? What features do you have in common? Write an essay explaining the differences and similarities that exist between you and this particular person. Be sure to include specific details and examples in your writing.

For a long time, many people have been interested in space and the possibility of life beyond Earth. Imagine your visit to a strange new planet that no human has seen before. Are there other creatures living there? Can you move around in the same way you do on earth? Write an essay in which you describe your day on this planet.

Copyright © American Book Company. DO NOT DUPLICATE. 1-888-264-5877.

GRADE 7
COMMON CORE
ENGLISH LANGUAGE ARTS

Chapter 10
Types of Writing

This chapter covers the following seventh grade strand and standards:

Writing

Text Types and Purposes

1. Write arguments to support claims with clear reasons and relevant evidence.
   a. Introduce claim(s), acknowledge alternate or opposing claims, and organize the reasons and evidence logically.
   b. Support claim(s) with logical reasoning and relevant evidence, using accurate, credible sources and demonstrating an understanding of the topic or text.
   c. Use words, phrases, and clauses to create cohesion and clarify the relationships among claim(s), reasons, and evidence.
   d. Establish and maintain a formal style.
   e. Provide a concluding statement or section that follows from and supports the argument presented.

2. Write informative/explanatory texts to examine a topic and convey ideas, concepts, and information through the selection, organization, and analysis of relevant content.
   a. Introduce a topic clearly, previewing what is to follow; organize ideas, concepts, and information, using strategies such as definition, classification, comparison/contrast, and cause/effect; include formatting (e.g., headings), graphics (e.g., charts, tables), and multimedia when useful to aiding comprehension.
   b. Develop the topic with relevant facts, definitions, concrete details, quotations, or other information and examples.
   c. Use appropriate transitions to create cohesion and clarify the relationships among ideas and concepts.
   d. Use precise language and domain-specific vocabulary to inform about or explain the topic.
   e. Establish and maintain a formal style.
   f. Provide a concluding statement or section that follows from and supports the information or explanation presented.

3. Write narratives to develop real or imagined experiences or events using effective technique, relevant descriptive details, and well-structured event sequences.
   a. Engage and orient the reader by establishing a context and point of view and introducing a narrator and/or characters; organize an event sequence that unfolds naturally and logically.
   b. Use narrative techniques, such as dialogue, pacing, and description, to develop experiences, events, and/or characters.
   c. Use a variety of transition words, phrases, and clauses to convey sequence and signal shifts from one time frame or setting to another.
   d. Use precise words and phrases, relevant descriptive details, and sensory language to capture the action and convey experiences and events.
   e. Provide a conclusion that follows from and reflects on the narrated experiences or events.

7–10 (in persuasive writing task)

Language

Knowledge of Language

3. Use knowledge of language and its conventions when writing, speaking, reading, or listening.
   a. Choose language that expresses ideas precisely and concisely, recognizing and eliminating wordiness and redundancy.

Copyright © American Book Company. DO NOT DUPLICATE. 1-888-264-5877.

There are three basic types of essays that you should be able to write: **persuasive**, **informative**, and **narrative**. In grade 7, you will mostly write essays to analyze topics, but you might also write some stories. This chapter will help you review the key concepts for writing each type of essay.

PERSUASIVE WRITING

You need to be able to **write arguments** (known as **persuasive writing**) that convince readers about your thoughts or viewpoints. To do this, you have to make a **strong claim**. Then you must support your position with **clear and relevant evidence**. Your reasons and evidence must be **logically organized**.

Persuasive writing is used to convince readers about a point of view. It is also used to motivate people to do (or not do) something. Persuasive writing can be seen most often in the following places:

- Advertisements
- Editorials
- Letters to the editor
- Essays
- Speeches
- Research reports

When writing persuasively, you need to build an argument. This includes making a claim and supporting it with solid evidence and logical reasoning.

MAKE A CLAIM

First, you have to pick a side. This is called **making a claim**. Your essay must have a clearly stated opinion. Before you write, make sure you know what you will be arguing. Consider exactly which position you will take!

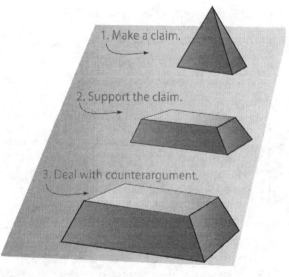

SUPPORT THE CLAIM

Next, you need to **support the claim**. In other words, you must provide reasons for your argument. Use as many details as possible to show why your reasons are valid. Include examples and facts. Organize these facts and details logically so that the audience can see how your evidence supports your argument.

Copyright © American Book Company. DO NOT DUPLICATE. 1-888-264-5877.

Persuasive details should include facts. Facts are statements that can be proved. "Alaska was the forty-ninth state admitted to the Union" is an example of a fact. "Alaska is the best place to spend a summer vacation" is an example of an opinion. An opinion is a personal viewpoint on a topic that everyone might not agree about. Sometimes you will need to use opinions. After all, your argument *is* an opinion! But be aware that your whole essay cannot be based only on opinions.

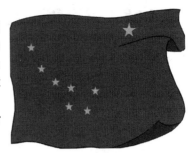

Once you make a statement, you must support it. You can give **evidence** that will make your opinion believable. In other words, the evidence you provide helps support your claim. You must consider the topic and your audience to decide the best kind of evidence to use.

Strong evidence includes relevant examples, quotes from experts, studies, and statistics. Weak evidence includes irrelevant examples, vague details, and generalizations. Read the following claim and the two pieces of evidence that follow. Which piece of evidence best supports the claim?

Claim: Martin Luther King Jr. was an influential leader of the civil rights movement.

Evidence

Example 1: King organized speeches, marches, and nonviolent protests to spread the word about racial tolerance. He also received many awards for his efforts, including a Nobel Peace Prize.

Example 2: King did not like the way African Americans were being treated. So he decided to do something about it. He worked very hard to obtain rights for African Americans.

If you chose Example 1, you are right. It gives specific ways in which Dr. King led African Americans in the civil rights movement. Example 2 offers only general statements and is not strong evidence to support the claim. It is vague and general. Not giving enough solid information will weaken your argument. This is what you want to avoid when you are writing.

Another effective way to support a claim is by using logic. **Logical reasoning** is the rational way of reaching a conclusion. A strong argument supports an opinion using facts in a valid way. A weak argument lacks logic. It does not have the evidence a reader needs to be persuaded. There are different ways to build a logical argument.

For example, you could say, "I am a human. Humans need sleep. Therefore, I need sleep." This is a simple example of reasonable logic.

However, if you said, "Humans need sleep. My dog, Fluffy, needs sleep. Therefore, my dog, Fluffy, is a human." This example would be an example of logical fallacy. Animals, like humans, need sleep. It does not mean, however, that they are human.

Copyright © American Book Company. DO NOT DUPLICATE. 1-888-264-5877.

USE PERSUASIVE LANGUAGE

When you write to persuade, you need to use **persuasive language** that will convince readers to agree with your stance. You need to emphasize important points and express them in a way that that attracts your audience. You also need **create cohesion** (unified ideas) by linking your claims and evidence. Finally, for school essays and writing on tests, remember to use a **formal style** that incorporates a respectful tone and correct grammar and usage.

Imagine that LuAnne wants to work at a music store. She is trying to convince the owner to hire her for an after-school job. Which of LuAnne's approaches would be more persuasive to the store owner?

Example 1: I really like music and listen to it all the time. You should hire me because I will be on time and do what you tell me.

Example 2: I am familiar with all kinds of music, so I could help customers find what they need. I could even recommend new music. My hard work, attention to detail, and ability to follow complex procedures, such as working the cash register, make me an ideal employee.

If you said Example 2 is more persuasive, you're right! In Example 1, LuAnne focuses on herself. It's great that she likes music, but how does that benefit her potential employer? She makes a statement that the store owner should hire her because she will be on time and follow directions. This is weak language, stating the minimum a worker needs to do. She does not include enough details or use strong words to tell why she should be hired. It is not a convincing argument.

In Example 2, LuAnne turns her love of music into a way to make more sales. She points out the reason why her interest in music will benefit customers. She also provides details about what will make her a good employee. She uses convincing and formal language like "hard work, attention to detail, and ability to follow complex procedures." The second example is much more likely to get LuAnne hired!

ACKNOWLEDGE OPPOSING CLAIMS

When building an argument, you need to **acknowledge opposing claims** and tell why they are not as strong as yours. This shows that you understand the argument and the opposition but believe your argument is the strongest. Look at this example.

Make a claim: Students should not be allowed to bring their cell phones to class.

This sentence makes a strong claim. The writer is clearly arguing against cell phones in class.

Copyright © American Book Company. DO NOT DUPLICATE. 1-888-264-5877.

Types of Writing

Support the claim:

Fact: Cell phones distract students from learning and staying focused.

Fact: In addition, cell phones with text capability give students an opportunity to cheat.

Example: I can't tell you how many times a variety of ringtones from all over the room has interrupted a class I've been in!

Example: Even when phones are on silent mode, people are texting instead of studying.

Answer objections: Many students say that they need their phones for safety and emergencies. That's fine. But they should leave them in their lockers when they come to class. They are unlikely to encounter many true emergencies in history or math!

The writer thinks about an opposing claim someone could make. Then the writer answers this objection, showing that it really does not apply to the classroom.

PROVIDE A STRONG CONCLUSION

Many writers focus attention on making a strong claim and supporting it. That's great. But remember that it is just as important to have a **strong conclusion** in your persuasive essay. In your last paragraph, you want to make the most of the final opportunity to refresh your audience about your claim and how you proved it. This is the place to reinforce the main idea of your essay with a strong summary. It should tie everything together and convince readers of your position. The conclusion should summarize the points you made but not repeat them word for word.

Read this sample prompt from a test that Michael took. Then read her written response to the prompt. Afterward, you will see a discussion about how well she addressed the points needed to write an effective persuasive essay.

> **Writing Prompt**
>
> Officials in your school district are considering making uniforms mandatory for students. They believe it would help students feel more equal and help teachers who would no longer need to deal with dress code issues. Do you think this is a good idea? Write an essay that persuades readers to your opinion about this topic.

Copyright © American Book Company. DO NOT DUPLICATE. 1-888-264-5877.

Michael's Persuasive Essay

Some school officials are talking about making school uniforms mandatory. They say that uniforms are a way to make sure all students feel equal. Also, teachers would not have to enforce the dress code. However, there will always be something that students do to show their individuality. Making them wear uniforms is just an easy way to solve an immediate problem, but kids won't learn anything from it and will just be frustrated. Uniforms will not solve any problems. The school board should not make uniforms mandatory.

By wearing the same clothes as everyone else, students are not allowed to have much social identity. One of their few ways to express their individuality is taken away. Wearing the clothes they like is one way teens have of being creative. If something really is not appropriate for school, parents should be advised to talk to their kids about it. If that doesn't work, there are many alternatives, like detention, for enforcing the dress code.

This decision would not affect just the students. School uniforms would be an added expense to the already tight budgets of most families. People would have to spend more money on an extra set of clothes.

In the end, the students themselves need to learn how to dress in public. After all, when they are not in school, they will need to make clothing choices that work. A better answer might be to turn a dress-code problem into a way to teach students what they should wear. Isn't that what school is all about? We need to prepare for the rest of our lives.

School uniforms are not the answer. Making students wear uniforms takes away student individuality, adds expense to family budgets, and does not teach students anything. We should find a more creative solution to help kids realize why they should dress properly for school.

Let's look at how Michael addressed each step of writing a strong persuasive essay.

First, what is his claim? At the end of his introduction, the first paragraph, he clearly states, "The school board should not make uniforms mandatory." There is no question about his position. Remember that it is important to be clear and unwavering when stating which side of an argument you are on.

Copyright © American Book Company. DO NOT DUPLICATE. 1-888-264-5877.

Next, how does he support the claim? His main points are the topic sentences of his body paragraphs:

> "By wearing the same clothes as everyone else, students are not allowed to have much social identity."

> "This decision would not affect just the students."

> "In the end, the students themselves need to learn how to dress in public."

Having written this essay for a test, Michael could not do any research to find evidence to use. But he uses evidence from his own personal experience. He is one of the students, and he knows about how teens express themselves through wearing the clothes they like. In addition, he uses the same fact used in the argument for uniforms to argue against it. He points out that it would be a financial hardship for many families to have to buy uniforms. Finally, he argues that school is all about learning, and students being taught what to wear in public could be part of it. By offering a suggestion for another solution, Michael makes it clear that there is not just one way to solve the dress code issue.

Michael uses persuasive language by making strong statements like these:

> "Uniforms will not solve any problems. The school board should not make uniforms mandatory."

> "We need to prepare for the rest of our lives."

> "School uniforms are not the answer."

He acknowledges opposing claims right in his introduction. Then he creates cohesion by refuting them with "However, there will always be something that students do to show their individuality." This is like saying, "Here's what other people say, but this is why it is not a good argument." By making statements and then following them up with examples and reasons, he gives his argument cohesion. (You can review cohesion in chapter 9.)

Finally, Michael finishes with a strong conclusion. He restates his position clearly. Then he refreshes his main points for his audience: "Making students wear uniforms takes away student individuality, adds expense to family budgets, and does not teach students anything." He leaves readers with a final thought about finding a different solution.

When you write for class, you will be able to research your topic and include evidence that you find in sources. When you write on tests, you will often be responding to a text. In that case, you will use evidence from the text to support your ideas. In any scenario, however, you will need to take the same step to build a strong argument.

Copyright © American Book Company. DO NOT DUPLICATE. 1-888-264-5877.

Chapter 10

Practice 1: Persuasive Writing

W 1.a–e, 7–10, L 3.a

DIRECTIONS	Read the passages, and then answer the questions that follow.

Develop a persuasive essay for one of the prompts below. Conduct some brief research to find out about the topic and to gather evidence for your viewpoint. Remember to make a strong claim, support your claim, maintain a formal style, provide coherence and transitions, respond to counterclaims, and close with a strong conclusion. As always, check your essay for errors, and fix any you find. For more practice, write essays for additional topics from this list or from ideas that you develop on your own.

The editors of a health and fitness magazine are having a contest. Contestants must write a paper convincing the readers to pick one exercise as the healthiest physical activity to improve their lives. What physical activity do you think is the healthiest?

Should the personal life of the president of the United States reflect the high moral standards on which this nation was founded? Or is the personal life of the president of the United States irrelevant to his or her public contribution? Take a position on this issue and argue for your point of view.

Citizens and conservationists alike are concerned about the poor air quality in many big cities. Cars, buses, planes, and industry contribute to this pollution. You have been asked to speak to fellow students about this issue. Convince your audience of the best ways to improve air quality in your community.

One day on your school campus, you see a dog and a police officer who are at the school to check the grounds for the presence of drugs. Some students are thankful that the dogs are there, while other students are complaining that their privacy is being invaded. What do you think?

Copyright © American Book Company. DO NOT DUPLICATE. 1-888-264-5877.

Activity

W 1.a–e, 2.a–f

Look through the editorial sections of newspapers and magazines. Find three letters or articles that interest you. For each one, write a response that agrees or disagrees with the author's point of view. If you agree, be sure to add your own evidence and a specific reason why you are adding your voice to the argument. If you disagree, make sure to acknowledge and refute the opposing claim.

INFORMATIVE WRITING

You will often need to write informative or explanatory texts. As you can probably guess, the purpose of **informative writing** (also called **expository writing**) is to explain a topic. This kind of essay can be about anything. Look at these titles of example expository essays:

"How to Hit a Homer in Baseball"

"The Secret Lives of Ferrets"

"Why Astronauts Visit Space"

"Cooking for One"

From these examples, you can see that expository writing gives information. It helps you learn more about the world. You can find expository writing in many places. Here are some examples:

- Newspapers
- Magazines
- Internet
- Cookbooks
- Instructional manuals
- School textbooks
- Menus
- Food labels
- Product brochures

Just as you do for persuasive writing, you need to provide **relevant evidence** in informative writing. Here, this evidence does not really support a claim. But it helps readers to understand your topic. Include relevant **facts**, concrete **details**, expert **quotations**, and other examples to make your descriptions complete and clear. In addition, be sure to use **precise language** and specific vocabulary to your subject. Be sure to include a **strong conclusion** to sum up your ideas and leave the reader with a final thought.

Copyright © American Book Company. DO NOT DUPLICATE. 1-888-264-5877.

ORGANIZE FOR CLARITY

In informative writing, you can explain how something works. You can also tell why an event happened. Or you may simply give facts about a topic. These are all purposes of informative essays, and each type may require a different kind of **organization**. (You can read more about organizational patterns in chapter 9.)

For example, you might write to explain a concept like courage. You could organize this essay in order of importance, based on which points you think are most important down to the least. Alternatively, you might be asked to write about how to perform a task. The best organization for a process essay is sequential order. At other times, you might write about how someone has affected your life or why something happens. These types of prompts call for a cause and effect essay. And finally, you might need to write about similarities and differences between people, places or idea. This requires a comparison and contrast organization. Be sure to use the right **transitions** to show readers which organization you are using. Transition words and phrases help show the relationships between ideas in your essay.

There are two additional organizational patterns that you might use when writing informative essays.

CLASSIFICATION

Classification is something you are probably familiar with from science class. Scientists use classification to group animals, plants, rocks, and all sorts of things. When classifying items, they are grouped by some sort of characteristic. Animals are grouped first by whether they are vertebrate and invertebrate, and then each of those is broken down by other characteristics. All sorts of topics can be discussed and written about by classification. Imagine if you were going to write about "Types of Music I Like." You could start with some general categories like "popular music" and "classical music." Within each of those you could break it down into further subcategories and groups. This type of sorting is often a good basis for how to arrange the information in your essay.

DEFINITION

You may think of a definition as only a short statement in a dictionary. That is one type of definition, but another type is more like an essay. While a dictionary definition will be brief and to the point, an essay that focuses on definition can discuss the literal meaning of a word or an idea and the special qualities that distinguish it from other things. It can also explore the other ideas and emotions the word is related to. For example, if you were assigned to write an essay about freedom, you might start with the literal definition. After that, you could move to the more abstract concept of the personal freedoms that we have in the United States. You could

Copyright © American Book Company. DO NOT DUPLICATE. 1-888-264-5877.

also go on to discuss examples of freedom that the readers could be taking for granted and might not realize they have. There is an important point to remember when using definition as an organizational pattern. When the readers are finished, they should have a very thorough and complete view of the topic. Ideally, they should also have been exposed to some aspects of the topic that were fresh and new to them. But it is not enough to explain what something means. You must apply the definition to your argument in a meaningful way.

SUPPORT READER UNDERSTANDING

There are several creative ways to help readers understand your informative writing. These include formatting, graphics, and multimedia.

As you know from reading, informative texts include **formatting** to help you understand the text better. Formatting draws your eye and helps you to see where certain information is located. When you write, you can use these same features.

Formatting Features	
Title	can tell a great deal about the topic of the text. Informative materials usually have titles that tell exactly what the articles are about.
Headings	act as the titles of sections in a text. The major heading is usually the document's title. All sections after that may have **headings** and even subheadings to identify smaller portions of those sections.

Information presented as a type of picture is called a graphic. **Graphics**, including graphic organizers, allow a reader to examine information at a glance. Because graphics provide information visually, they are often used in magazines, newspapers, advertisements, and on the Internet. Knowing how to read graphics is an important skill. It can help with research and decision making. Ask your teacher about the many kinds of graphics, such as outlines, schedules, flow charts, and tree diagrams.

Types of Graphics	
Graphic	**Description**
Graphs	show large amount of information in a small space. Graphs often use numbers to present data.
Maps	show the geographic location or setting of a certain event or trend. Maps can be as detailed or as general as needed.
Tables	show data arranged in rows and columns. This helps the reader find and compare the information. The rows of a table go across; the columns of a table go up and down.
Timelines	help organize ideas and events into chronological order so that one event follows another in a time sequence. They are useful graphic aids for showing historical information or biographical information about people.

Copyright © American Book Company. DO NOT DUPLICATE. 1-888-264-5877.

Writing that is published online also can have **multimedia** components. Say that you write a report about how ants work together in a community. You publish it to your classroom webpage. What might you include to help readers understand the text about the ant activities? A picture of ants and their anthill would be helpful. But online, you can include even more visual information. A video of ants actually going about their daily tasks would be a great addition for reader comprehension.

Practice 2: Informative Writing

W 2.a–f, L 3.a

> **DIRECTIONS**   **A. Read the passages, and then answer the questions that follow.**

During the night, if a fire starts in your home, follow these steps for survival. First, roll out of your bed, staying low. Next, crawl to the door, and feel the door. If it is hot, do not open the door. Or if you open the door, but then smoke or hot gases rush into the room, close the door as fast as you can, and find another method of escape. Third, if the door is not hot, brace yourself against it, and then crack the door open very slowly. Toxic gases or fire may be on the other side. If no smoke enters the room, cover your nose and mouth with a moist cloth, and open the door enough for you to exit the room. Then crawl quickly to safety. Most importantly, get out by the quickest, safest route. Finally, if you are on an upper floor, use an escape ladder, knotted rope, or a fire escape to leave your home. Or you may be able to climb out a window onto the roof and drop to the ground. Then find a phone, and call the fire department.

---

1   What is the organizational pattern of this writing?

   A   Definition

   B   Cause and effect

   C   Sequential order

   D   Comparison and contrast

2   In the passage above, underline the transition words and phrases that provide clues about the organization of the passage.

_____

_____

Copyright © American Book Company. DO NOT DUPLICATE. 1-888-264-5877.

A Healthy Choice

Thai food is the healthiest food you can eat. It contains much less fat than typical American food and numerous herbs and spices that help digestion.

Medical Study

Block Medical Center recently conducted a study on patients with high cholesterol. Patients substituted lower-fat foods five times a week for their typical meals. The study found that the majority of the patients lowered their cholesterol twenty percent or more.

Preparation is Key

Part of the reason why Thai food is so healthy is because of the way it is prepared. Thai food is often grilled, boiled, or stewed. These methods lower fat and maintain vitamins and nutrients in the food. American food is often deep-fried or pan-fried in grease or oil.

Healthy Ingredients

Another reason Thai food is so healthy are the ingredients. Lemon grass, ginger, garlic, basil, and lime are all used in Thai cooking and are very good for you. Many believe these ingredients can cure a headache, relieve pain, and even cure the flu or the common cold.

Best Food for Your Health

Thai food really is the healthiest food you can eat. No other food comes close to providing such a balanced, nutritious diet.

3   What is the fastest way for a reader to find facts about how Thai food is prepared?

   A   Find places where the article mentions food.

   B   Look up Thai food preparation online.

   C   Look at the title of the article.

   D   Read the section headings.

4   Which sentence can be added to the second paragraph to strengthen the author's point?

   A   The lower-fat foods fed to the patients in the study came from a Thai restaurant.

   B   Block Medical Center conducts many different studies and publishes them regularly.

   C   My cousin and her family love Thai food and eat it for dinner almost every night.

   D   American restaurants outnumber Thai restaurants more than twenty to one.

Copyright © American Book Company. DO NOT DUPLICATE. 1-888-264-5877.

5   What would be the best graphic or multimedia element to add to this text to help readers understand it? Describe it in detail. Explain your reasons for your choice.

_____

_____

_____

_____

> **DIRECTIONS** **B. Choose three to four texts from newspapers, magazines, textbooks, or online. Articles about science, technology, or history may be best. Examine each selection. Then, on your own paper, answer the following questions.**

1   What primary organizational pattern can you identify?

2   What key words indicate the organizational pattern? Underline the transitions in the passage.

3   Determine why the writer chose the particular organizational pattern. How does the pattern add to the reader's understanding or strengthen the writer's position?

4   Are there formatting features or graphics (or multimedia features, if online) that help you understand the text? How do they help specifically with reading comprehension?

> **DIRECTIONS** **C. Write an informative essay about a topic of your choice, or pick one of the subjects below.**

What makes a good team member? Think about a person you have worked with on a team at school, at home, or in your community. What about this person made him or her a good team player? Write about what you think makes an effective team member and how this person fulfills that role.

You have heard about and studied many discoveries and inventions. Choose one that you see as being extremely important. Describe it, and tell why you think it was a critical discovery or invention.

What is your favorite pastime? It might be a pursuing a hobby or a talent you have. Tell what this activity is, when you make time for it, and steps you take to stay good at it.

Copyright © American Book Company. DO NOT DUPLICATE. 1-888-264-5877.

NARRATIVE WRITING

Narrative writing tells a story. Like the other essays you have read about in this chapter, it needs to be well organized. It needs a logical order with appropriate transitions. It also should have precise language and a suitable conclusion. But as a story, it can include some creative elements that other essays might not.

As you read in chapter 3, stories have several distinctive elements. One is a setting or **context**. Whether you are writing about something true that happened to you or about a made-up character, you should describe where and when your story takes place. Another element is the plot. When you write a narrative, you should focus on the **sequence of events**. You don't necessarily need to tell a story in the same order it happened. But the event sequence needs to make sense. It should also have **pacing** that makes the rising action, climax, and falling action flow naturally. Another element in stories is the **characters**. Is one of these characters the **narrator**? What **point of view** is the story told from?

On top of these elements, you can use the literary devices you read about in chapter 4. Characters can speak to each other in **dialogue**. **Sensory language** and **descriptive details** can capture the events and experiences of the characters.

Now read this writing prompt.

> In school, teachers help you discover new things and learn about them. You too have skills and ideas that you can teach others. Think about a time you taught a person something (maybe a younger sibling), or consider how you might teach what you know. How did you, or would you, give information to show what you mean?

How would you respond to this prompt? You might try writing a response, and then come back to read the sample essay.

Here is the draft of a student essay written as a response to the prompt. Read the essay and the questions that follow.

Delia's Narrative Essay

I sat on the steps in front of my house. I had finished my homework, so I was playing my harmonica. I like the harp (which is a nickname). It sounds nice and is small enough to carry around. It would be nice, though, to have a friend to play harmonica along with me.

After a while, my friend Chelsea came over. "I wish I could play," Chelsea said. It was great to hear her say that, all on her own. I told her that I would teach her. But she needed her own harp because you can't share when it's been in your mouth. A plain harmonica is not expensive, and I told where she could get one. The next day, she came back with her own harp.

First, I showed Chelsea how to hold the harp. She got that pretty quickly. Then, we practiced exhaling and inhaling. Both are used to make sounds. The sounds she was making were pretty bad at first.

Copyright © American Book Company. DO NOT DUPLICATE. 1-888-264-5877.

> What Chelsea could not figure out was how to make a single note. "A bunch of notes play together every time," she said. She looked very frustrated. I told her to put her tongue over some of the note holes, but then she didn't make any sound! I finally said, "Pretend that you're going to whistle." She tried it, and a single, clear note came out!
>
> Chelsea was excited. I gave her some practices to do. We agreed to meet on weekends so I could teach her more. It felt good to teach Chelsea something I was good at, and it made her feel good too.

What do you think of Delia's response? First, look at these questions.

Does Delia's essay address the writing topic well?

Delia does a good job of focusing on what she can teach and telling how she did it.

Why does Delia use dialogue?

It helps to bring the characters to life and to develop the plot.

How can Delia improve the description of the setting?

Delia tells where the story take place, but she does not provide any descriptive details. What is the neighborhood like? What color are her front steps? What kind of day was it when Chelsea came over? Any of these details paint a picture for readers and make it easier to visualize the scene.

Delia made some revisions on her essay. Now read Delia's revised version.

Delia's Revised Narrative Essay

Last Saturday, I sat on the brick steps in front of my house. It was just me and my mom's ailing little petunias. It was a sunny April day, and I had finished my homework, so I was playing my harmonica. I like the harp (which is its nickname). It sounds cheerful and is small enough to carry around. It would be nice, though, to have a friend to play harmonica along with me.

Shortly after lunch, my friend Chelsea came over. "I wish I could play," Chelsea said. I told her that I would teach her. But she needed her own harp because you can't share an instrument that you put in your mouth. A plain harmonica is not expensive, and I told Chelsea she could get one at the discount store on the corner. On Sunday, she came back with her own harp.

First, I showed Chelsea how to hold the harp. The fingers of the left hand have to wrap around the top and bottom, not blocking any of the air holes. She got that pretty quickly. The right hand can be added to help move the harp and also to cup the air in front of it for a sound effect. I told Chelsea we'd get to that later. Next, we practiced exhaling and inhaling. Both methods are used to make sounds. The sounds she was making were ear-splitting at first.

Copyright © American Book Company. DO NOT DUPLICATE. 1-888-264-5877.

What Chelsea could not figure out was how to make a single note. "A bunch of notes play together every time," she whined. She looked very frustrated. I told her to put her tongue over some of the note holes, but then she didn't make any sound! I finally said, "Pretend that you're going to whistle." She tried it, and a single, clear note came out!

Chelsea was as excited as a kid opening a present. I gave her some practices to do. We agreed to meet on weekends so I could teach her more. It felt satisfying to teach Chelsea something I was good at, and it delighted her too.

What do you notice about Delia's changes? First, she added details in the first paragraph to better describe the setting. Now we know it's a sunny Saturday in April, the steps are made of brick, and there's a plant next to Delia. In other paragraphs, Delia added more precise wording, like *ear-splitting*, *satisfying*, and *delighted*. She also added details that help readers picture what she describes, like holding the harmonica. Finally, she used figurative language by adding a simile to tell how excited Chelsea was: "Chelsea was as excited as a kid opening a present." As you can see, all of these improvements make the story more interesting to read. As you work on your narrative essay, try to use what you have learned about how to make a story fun to read.

Practice 3: Narrative Writing

W 3.a–e, L 3.a

> **DIRECTIONS**   **A. Read and answer these questions.**

Practice making precise and descriptive word choices. Fill in the blanks below with more specific and very specific terms for the general words that are provided.

General	More Specific	Very Specific
1. athlete	soccer player	David Beckham
2. to walk		to tiptoe
3. animal		rabbit
4. vehicle	car	
5. cold		twenty-three degrees
6. celebrity		Taylor Swift
7. politician	governor	
8. to like		
9. sad		
10. happy		

Copyright © American Book Company. DO NOT DUPLICATE. 1-888-264-5877.

> | DIRECTIONS | **B. Write a narrative essay. Choose your own subject, or let one of the topics below provide inspiration.** |

Look through a magazine, and find a picture that appeals to you. Cut it out, paste it in your notebook, and write a story about it.

Write a dream that a plant, a fish, a star, or a stone might have.

Write about an event in your life. First, write it from your perspective. Then, write it from the perspective of someone else who was present.

Invent a new myth that explains the beginning of the universe.

Write about the worst mistake you ever made.

If you had wings, where would you fly to, and why? Write about one day in which you have a pair of wings.

Think of a very unusual pet (one that you could never have in real life). Write a story about how the pet comes into your life and what happens next.

Say your school is having a "turnabout day," an event when selected students get to be the principal and teachers. You have been designated as the principal for a day. Write about your day as principal of your school.

Copyright © American Book Company. DO NOT DUPLICATE. 1-888-264-5877.

CHAPTER 10 SUMMARY

There are three basic types of essays that you should be able to write: **persuasive**, **informative**, and **narrative**.

You need to be able to **write arguments** (known as **persuasive writing**) that convince readers about your thoughts or viewpoints.

First, you have to make a **strong claim**.

Then, you must support your position with **clear and relevant evidence**.

Your reasons and evidence must be **logically organized**.

You also need to **acknowledge opposing claims** and tell why they are not as strong as yours.

Finally, you need a **strong conclusion** to remind your audience about your claim and how you proved it.

You will often need to use **informative writing** (also called **expository writing)** to explain a topic.

As always, you need to provide **relevant evidence** including **facts**, concrete **details**, expert **quotations**, and other examples.

Be sure to use **precise language** and vocabulary specific to your subject.

A **strong conclusion** should sum up your ideas and leave the reader with a final thought.

There are many informative essays, and each type may require a different kind of **organization**. You can use order of importance, sequential order, cause and effect, comparison and contrast, **classification**, and **definition** patterns. Be sure to use the right **transitions** to show readers which organization you are using.

You can add **formatting** features like **headings**, **graphics**, and **multimedia** to your writing to help make your meaning clearer to readers.

Narrative writing tells a story. Like all other essays, it needs to be well organized, with a logical order with appropriate transitions, and should have precise language and a suitable conclusion.

Distinctive elements of narrative writing include setting or **context**, a plot with its **sequence of events** and **pacing**, and **characters**. Remember to decide who will be the **narrator** and from what **point of view** you will tell the story.

You also can use **dialogue**, **sensory language**, and **descriptive details** to bring the story to life.

Copyright © American Book Company. DO NOT DUPLICATE. 1-888-264-5877.

Chapter 10

CHAPTER 10 REVIEW

W 1–3, L 3.a

> **DIRECTIONS** 1 Choose one of the prompts below, and write a well-organized persuasive essay. Be sure to clearly state your claim and logically support your ideas with relevant evidence. Use language to create cohesion among claims and counterclaims. Be sure to check your work for errors.

Think about what you have read, seen, and heard recently. Was there something about which you said, "I should say something about that!" Many people express their opinions by writing letters to the editor or personal essays for newspapers and magazines. Write an essay about a topic you feel strongly about in a way that explains your point of view to those who read it. State your opinion clearly, and provide reasons for it.

Write an essay telling a classmate or friend why you would or would not recommend a book you read recently. Include examples from the book to support your opinion.

In addition to school, what activity is most important for young people to participate in? It might be family dinners or discussions, sports, playing an instrument, or taking up a hobby. Describe the activity you feel is vital for young people, and persuade readers about why it is so important.

> **DIRECTIONS** 2 Write an informative essay. Don't forget to include a central idea, relevant supporting details, and a strong conclusion. Decide on your own topic, or choose from the list below.

an animal	a food	a movie	a store
a book	a game	a relative	a trend
a celebrity	an invention	a sport	a vacation spot

Copyright © American Book Company. DO NOT DUPLICATE. 1-888-264-5877.

Page 192

| DIRECTIONS | 3 | Choose one of the prompts below, and write a well-developed narrative essay. Engage the reader, use a variety of narrative techniques, include vivid description and sensory details, and provide an appropriate conclusion. |

Some teens say their parents lecture them too much; parents say they want to pass on their knowledge to give their kids an edge. If you were suddenly a parent, what important knowledge would *you* want to pass on to the next generation? Make sure your essay is well developed and logically organized. Check for errors, and fix any you find.

Have you ever had to make a tough decision? Tell about a time when you had a difficult choice, but you made the right decision in the end. Write a story about the events leading up to this decision. Be sure to include specific details.

There is an old saying about friends: "A true friend walks in when the rest of the world walks out." Do you have a friend who fits this description? Tell about a time when your best friend stood by you even though the rest of your friends abandoned you. Be sure to include specific examples.

Copyright © American Book Company. DO NOT DUPLICATE. 1-888-264-5877.

Copyright © American Book Company. DO NOT DUPLICATE. 1-888-264-5877.

Chapter 11
Conventions

This chapter covers the following seventh grade strand and standards:

Language

Conventions of Standard English

1. Demonstrate command of the conventions of standard English grammar and usage when writing or speaking.

   a. Explain the function of phrases and clauses in general and their function in specific sentences.

   b. Choose among simple, compound, complex, and compound-complex sentences to signal differing relationships among ideas.

   c. Place phrases and clauses within a sentence, recognizing and correcting misplaced and dangling modifiers.

2. Demonstrate command of the conventions of standard English capitalization, punctuation, and spelling when writing.

   a. Use a comma to separate coordinate adjectives (e.g., *It was a fascinating, enjoyable movie* but not *He wore an old[,] green shirt*).

   b. Spell correctly.

Knowledge of Language

3. Use knowledge of language and its conventions when writing, speaking, reading, or listening.

   a. Choose language that expresses ideas precisely and concisely, recognizing and eliminating wordiness and redundancy.

By this time, you have learned many **conventions** of Standard American English. Your teachers expect you to use them in your writing. When you take a test, there may be questions about them. Conventions include using language correctly in the following areas:

- Capitalization
- Punctuation
- Sentence structure
- Subject-verb agreement
- Spelling
- Verb tense

There are many rules for all of these conventions. You can use a style guide or grammar book to review these rules. In this chapter, you will review some specific conventions that you are focusing on this year.

WORKING WITH SENTENCES

In this section, we'll go over types of sentences. We'll also look at parts of sentences and how they work together. Knowing these can help you as a writer and reader.

Copyright © American Book Company. DO NOT DUPLICATE. 1-888-264-5877.

TYPES OF SENTENCES

There are four different types of sentences.

- A **simple sentence** has one independent clause. An **independent clause** is a group of words, containing a subject and a predicate, that can stand alone as a sentence.

  Examples: Juan and Emily eat lunch together every day.
  Did Henry kick a field goal?

- A **compound sentence** contains two independent clauses. The clauses can be joined by a comma and a coordinating conjunction (*and, but, or, nor, for, so,* or *yet*) or with a semicolon.

  Examples:

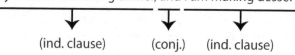

My mother is cooking dinner, and I am making dessert.

(ind. clause)   (conj.)   (ind. clause)

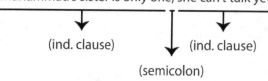

Muhammad's sister is only one; she can't talk yet.

(ind. clause)   (ind. clause)

(semicolon)

- A **complex sentence** contains one independent clause and one or more dependent clauses. A **dependent clause** cannot stand alone as a sentence.

  Examples:

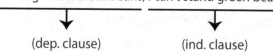

Although I like black beans, I can't stand green beans.

(dep. clause)   (ind. clause)

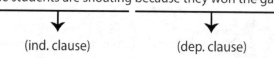

The students are shouting because they won the game.

(ind. clause)   (dep. clause)

- A **compound-complex sentence** contains at least two independent clauses and at least one dependent clause.

Copyright © American Book Company. DO NOT DUPLICATE. 1-888-264-5877.

Examples:

Though Padma prefers mysteries, she tried the historical novel, and she really enjoyed it.

(dep. clause)   (ind. clause)   (conj.)   (ind. clause)

My aunt is coming to visit, but I hope she leaves soon because I have a lot of homework.

(ind. clause)   (conj.)   (ind. clause)   (dep. clause)

Practice 1:   Types of Sentences

ELA-3-M3-GLE 24

DIRECTIONS	Identify the types of sentences.

1 Jennifer went to school, but Eli stayed home because he had the flu.

A   simple   C   complex

B   compound   D   compound-complex

2 I missed the bus this morning.

A   simple   C   complex

B   compound   D   compound-complex

3 Although three hundred volunteers searched, no one found the lost hiker.

A   simple   C   complex

B   compound   D   compound-complex

4 Ethan raked the leaves, and Laura picked up sticks.

A   simple   C   complex

B   compound   D   compound-complex

5 My dog and I like to go for walks in the woods.

A   simple   C   complex

B   compound   D   compound-complex

Copyright © American Book Company. DO NOT DUPLICATE. 1-888-264-5877.

6 If you want, we can ride our bikes to Lake Claiborne and go for a swim.

    A simple   C complex

    B compound   D compound-complex

PHRASES

A **phrase** is a group of related words that does not include a subject and verb. There are several different types of phrases. Let's take a look at each of them.

A **prepositional phrase** always begins with a preposition. A preposition is a word that shows a relationship between nouns or pronouns and other words in a sentence. Commonly used prepositions are *of, to, in, for, with,* and *on*. A preposition links the phrase to the rest of the sentence. The rest of the phrase is the object of the preposition (any nouns or pronouns after the preposition).

Examples: The keys are on the table. (preposition – *on*; object – *table*)

              The shelter is for the homeless. (preposition – *for*; object – *homeless*)

Remember to place prepositional phrases closest to the objects they modify in a sentence.

Example: I ran to chase around the kitchen table my cat, Whiskers. (incorrect)

The prepositional phrase "around the kitchen table" modifies the verb *ran*, so it needs to be next to it in order for the sentence to make the most sense.

Example: I ran around the kitchen table to chase my cat, Whiskers. (correct)

An **appositive phrase** explains or identifies another part of a sentence.

Example: Jamie, born fifteen days ago, is the most beautiful child we've ever seen.

"Jamie is the most beautiful child we've ever seen" can function as a sentence. The information between the commas is an appositive that describes Jamie.

An **infinitive phrase** contains an infinitive (the word *to* plus the base form of a verb) and any words associated with it.

Examples: I want to eat dinner at six.

              Eileen will forget to wash the car.

When using infinitives, be careful not to split the *to* and the verb.

Examples: Keeley wanted to generously sprinkle the cupcake with candy jewels. (incorrect)

              Keeley wanted to sprinkle the cupcake generously with candy jewels. (correct)

Copyright © American Book Company. DO NOT DUPLICATE. 1-888-264-5877.

MODIFIERS

A **modifier** is a word or phrase that describes something. Modifiers should be placed close to the thing that they are describing so that the meaning is clear. A modifier that is put in the wrong place can make the meaning of the sentence unclear, or worse, nonsensical. Such modifiers are called **misplaced** or **dangling** modifiers. Read the following examples in which the modifiers are incorrectly placed.

Example 1: Baking in the oven, Mr. Mobley smelled the cherry pie.

The placement of words in the sentence confuses the meaning. It sounds like Mr. Mobley is baking in the oven! This is because *Mr. Mobley* is the noun closest to the phrase *baking in the oven*. To correct the sentence, move the modifier closer to what it is describing.

Corrected: Mr. Mobley smelled the cherry pie baking in the oven.

Example 2: We almost sang all of the songs in the show.

The placement of words in the sentence confuses the meaning. If we *almost sang*, does that mean we were just talking part of the time? What the writer meant to say is that we sang *almost all* of the songs. To correct the sentence, move the modifier *almost* closer to what it is describing.

Corrected: We sang almost all of the songs in the show.

As you work with sentences, take note of how they change what you read. You will see that different structures can slightly change meaning. For example, separate clauses that follow each other signal that ideas are separate. However, if these ideas are joined in clauses and phrases, you can see more of a relationship in the ideas. When you combine different structures with the correct transition words, the relationships become even clearer. Look at these examples.

Separate clauses:

The knight rode to the dragon's lair. The dragon was not there. It might return at any time. He had to be ready. Everyone was counting on him. He had to triumph.

Obviously, these ideas are related. We can see the progress of the action in this brief scene. However, the ideas are disjointed, just like the structure of these short simple sentences.

Clauses combined with phrases and transitions:

The knight rode to the dragon's lair, but the dragon was not there. It might return at any time, though, so he had to be ready. Because everyone was counting on him, he had to triumph.

It's more interesting now, isn't it? There is a more immediate connection between the knight looking for the dragon and not finding him. There is also a direct relationship between having to be ready and the reason for that readiness—because the dragon might be back any moment. Finally we see that it is precisely because everyone is counting on him that the knight knows he must win.

When you read, watch how sentences and phrases relate to one another. See how the right structures help meaning and tone to come alive. Try to incorporate the same structures into your own writing.

Copyright © American Book Company. DO NOT DUPLICATE. 1-888-264-5877.

Chapter 11

Practice 2: Phrases and Modifiers

L 1.f, 3

DIRECTIONS ▶ Read the passage, and answer the questions that follow.

Bending along the rifts of the white water, you wonder if the bow of the rubber raft will rise enough to clear the raging rapids ahead. Whoosh! It does, and the boatman guides it around the bulging boulders skillfully. This is one of the thrills of floating the Rio Grande. Each of the rapids presents a special navigation problem, so the guide's experience, knowledge, and strong arms serve to keep the boat off the rocks and you out of the water. Most people who ride the river arrange for an outfitter to provide everything. You have the option of sitting back and enjoying the ride, at least until the next wave of white water washes over you. The biggest thrill besides wondering if you'll fall out of the raft comes at Rock Slide Rapid. Once you pass it, you might like to take a turn with the oars, but soon your shoulders will scream for a break. Listen to them. Listen to the soothing sounds of the river. Let yourself float like a leaf. The trip to Santa Elena Canyon is twenty miles of constantly changing landscape. When you finally reach the canyon, you will be greeted by spectacular canyon walls that rise 1,500 feet above you.

Read the first sentence.

Bending along the rifts of the white water, you wonder if the bow of the rubber raft will rise enough to clear the raging rapids ahead.

1   What change should be made to correct the misplaced modifier?

_____

_____

_____

_____

Copyright © American Book Company. DO NOT DUPLICATE. 1-888-264-5877.

Read this sentence.

It does, and the boatman guides it around the bulging boulders skillfully.

2   What is the best position for the modifier <u>skillfully</u>?

    A   It does, and the skillfully boatman guides it around the bulging boulders.

    B   It does, and the boatman skillfully guides it around the bulging boulders.

    C   It does, and the boatman guides it around skillfully the bulging boulders.

    D   Correct as is

Read this sentence.

Each of the rapids presents a special navigation problem, so the guide's experience, knowledge, and strong arms serve to keep the boat off the rocks and you out of the water.

3   Which part of this sentence is an infinitive phrase?

_____

Read this sentence.

The biggest thrill besides wondering if you'll fall out of the raft comes at Rock Slide Rapid.

4   How should this sentence be punctuated?

    A   The biggest thrill besides wondering, if you'll fall out of the raft comes at Rock Slide Rapid.

    B   The biggest thrill besides, wondering if you'll fall out of the raft comes, at Rock Slide Rapid.

    C   The biggest thrill, besides wondering if you'll fall out of the raft, comes at Rock Slide Rapid.

    D   Correct as is

WORKING WITH ADJECTIVES

Adjectives are detail words and can tell us things about a noun's appearance and characteristics. They answer the question, "What kind of (noun) is it?"

    Examples of adjectives:

An <u>excited</u> poodle yapped at my feet. (What kind of poodle is it? An *excited* poodle.)

Caroline cried when she outgrew her <u>furry</u>, <u>yellow</u> slippers. (What kind of slippers are they? *Furry, yellow* slippers)

Copyright © American Book Company. DO NOT DUPLICATE. 1-888-264-5877.

In the second example, you see two **coordinate adjectives**. Coordinate adjectives are adjectives that appear in sequence and modify the same noun. When this happens, they need to be separated by a comma. Here is a little trick: if you can insert "and" between the two adjectives, they probably need a comma between them.

Example: That is one <u>mean</u>, <u>hungry</u> bear. (The bear is mean AND hungry.)

You should not use a comma if the first adjective described the second adjective.

Example: I got a pair of <u>warm flannel</u> pajamas for my birthday. (The flannel pajamas are warm. The word *warm* describes the quality of the flannel.)

SPELLING

Spelling correctly is not only an important tool for writing; it also plays an important role in vocabulary building and reading comprehension. There is no magic way to learn to spell, but you can improve your spelling by using some of the following methods. Memorizing rules and spelling lists also helps you learn to spell accurately.

1   In a notebook, keep a list of words that you find challenging to spell. Circle the part of the word you have difficulty with, and master the correct spelling of the word.

2   Pronounce the word correctly. This can often help you correctly spell the word.

3   Learn to spell by syllables if you have trouble spelling long words or tricky-sounding words.

4   Instead of guessing at the spelling of a word, use a dictionary, a thesaurus, a glossary, or your computer's spellchecker. A dictionary will also give you the correct pronunciation and the division of the word into syllables.

SOME SPELLING RULES

Rule 1 Put *i* before *e*, except after *c*, or when sounded like *a* as in *neighbor* and *weigh*.

Examples: fr*ie*nd, rec*ei*ve, *ei*ght, perc*ei*ve

Exception 1: Most of the time, rule 1 gives you the correct spelling of a word. However, there are some words that do not follow this rule: *foreigner, forfeit, height, leisure, neither, science, scientific, seizes,* and *weird*.

Copyright © American Book Company. DO NOT DUPLICATE. 1-888-264-5877.

Rule 2 When prefixes are added to root words, the spelling of the root word does not change.

> **Examples:** dis + satisfied = *dis*satisfied; un + noticed = *un*noticed;
> over + see = *over*see il + logical = *il*logical; un + selfish = *un*selfish;
> in + exact = *in*exact

Rule 3 When a suffix starting with a vowel is added to a word ending in a silent *e*, such as *receive* and *smile*, the *e* is dropped, making words such as *recei*ving and *smil*ing; imagine + able = *imagin*able, continue + ous = *continu*ous.

Exception 1: The *e* is not dropped when it would change the meaning of the root word.

> **Examples:** dye + ing = *dye*ing (not dying); singe + ing = *singe*ing (not singing)

Exception 2: The *e* is not dropped if the *e* clarifies pronunciation.

> **Examples:** flee + ing = *flee*ing (not fleing); toe + ing = *toe*ing (not toing)

Exception 3: The *e* is not dropped if the sound *c* or *g* must be kept soft.

> **Examples:** notice + able = *notice*able (not noticable); courage + ous = *courage*ous
> (not couragous)

Rule 4 If the suffix starts with a consonant, keep the *e*.

> **Examples:** large + ly = larg*e*ly; excite + ment = excit*e*ment; state + ly = stat*e*ly;
> force + ful = forc*e*ful; brave + ly = brav*e*ly

Exceptions: true + ly = *tru*ly; argue + ment = *argu*ment; whole + ly = *whol*ly;
awe + ful = *aw*ful; judge + ment = *judg*ment

Rule 5 When a suffix is added to root words ending in *y*, change the *y* to an *i*, such as in sill*i*ness and beaut*i*ful.

Exception 1: Keep the *y* if the suffix being added is *-ing*.

> **Examples:** fly + ing = fl*y*ing (not fliing); try + ing = tr*y*ing (not triing)

Exception 2: Keep the *y* if a vowel in the root word comes before the *y*.

> **Examples:** stay + ed = *stay*ed (not staied); play + ful = *play*ful (not plaiful)

Exception 3: Keep the *y* in some one-syllable base words.

> **Examples:** dry + ness = *dry*ness (not driness); shy + er = *shy*er (not shier)

Rule 6 If a word ends in a consonant + vowel + consonant, if the suffix begins with a vowel, and if the word contains only one syllable or an accented ending syllable, double the final consonant. Otherwise, do not double the last consonant in the root.

> **Examples:** stop + er = sto*pp*er; sun + ed = su*nn*ed; occur + ed = occu*rr*ed;
> drop + ed = dro*pp*ed; sit + ing = si*tt*ing; begin + ing = begi*nn*ing

Rule 7 English words that have non-English roots form the plural according to their original language.

Copyright © American Book Company. DO NOT DUPLICATE. 1-888-264-5877.

CONCISE LANGUAGE

In addition to following these rules, there is another way to use your knowledge of conventions to improve your writing. When you know the rules, they can help you to **choose precise and concise language** to express ideas.

Precise words and phrases tell exactly what you mean. This is one place that correctly spelling words helps. How? Well, you don't want to use the wrong word in place of one that is similar but spelled differently. This can lead to misunderstandings.

For example, look at this sentence: "Pete, did you right the report?" It looks like this sentence is asking if Pete made something correct on a report that was wrong. Most likely, what the author meant to ask is "Did you <u>write</u> the report?" The words *right* and *write* sound alike, but they are spelled differently. There are other words that mean similar things but have different connotations. No matter what the differences, you should know them—or look them up—and always use the most effective and correct word or phrase for each context.

Concise language means there are no unnecessary words or phrases. When you write a draft, you might go on and on or repeat ideas as you try to make a point. but when you revise, you can check for wordiness and redundancy.

Here is an example of redundancy: "People who are always late and never get anywhere on time do not show respect for the people who are waiting for them." What is wrong here? The phrases "are always late" and "never get anywhere on time" are saying the same thing. A more concise way to write this sentence is this: "People who are always late do not show respect for the people who are waiting for them."

Copyright © American Book Company. DO NOT DUPLICATE. 1-888-264-5877.

Practice 3: Conventions

L 1–3

Doc Holliday

1 Doc Holliday struggled to fit in from the time he was born. John Henry Holliday was born in 1851 in Griffin, Georgia, with a cleft palate and a cleft lip. His uncle was a surgeon and corrected the birth defects by performing an operation. The child had to be fed carefully, or he could choke to death, so he was given liquids from a shot glass. The childhood experience must have inspired the boy; by the age of 22, John Holliday had his Doctor of Dental Surgery degree. He had also contracted tuberculosis and was told that he had only a few months to live. Heeding the advice of his uncle to move to a drier climate, Doctor John Holliday boarded a train for Dallas. The year was 1873.

2 "Doc" Holliday began to practice in Dallas. But his disease continued to bother his body. He would have problems in the middle of working on patients with coughing spells. His dental practice declined, and Doc turned to gambling for a living. In the old west, a gambler stood alone and had to defend himself. Doc Holliday was well aware of this and faithful practiced with six-guns and knives. He was a hot-tempered southern gentleman who would never step aside for any man. This led to one confrontation after another. After sending many bullies and gunmen to meet their maker Doc moved from one western town to another narrowly avoiding being hanged.

3 By the time he reached Tombstone, Arizona, Doc Holliday had a reputation as one of the fastest guns in the west. His trail was littered with the bodies of dead men who had underestimated his skill. In Tombstone, he was reunitted with his old friends, the lawman Wyatt Earp and his brothers. There, he took part in the well-known gunfight at the OK Corral. Afterwards, the gang continued to ambush the Earps, maiming Virgil and eventually killing Morgan. Wyatt, Holliday, and a few loyal deputies, hunted down the ruthless vicious members of the outlaw cowboy gang for the murder and maiming of numerous dedicated lawmen. Many outlaws died in Wyatt's ride of revenge, some at the end of Holliday's smoking pistol.

Copyright © American Book Company. DO NOT DUPLICATE. 1-888-264-5877.

4   Doc Holliday had come west knowing that he was living on borrowed time. He always thought he would die by a bullet, with a knife in his ribs, at the end of a rope, or by drinking himself to death. He maintained that he would not die in bed of a coughing fit. Yet that is what fate had in store for him. May of 1887 found him in a convalescent hospital in Glenwood Springs, Colorado, dying of tuberculosis. He spent his last fifty-seven days in bed, delirious for the last two weeks. Finally, on November 8, he woke up clear-eyed. He asked for a shot of whiskey. He drank it down with great relish. Pondering his condition and the irony of his life he said "This is funny" and he died.

Read these sentences from paragraph 1.

Heeding the advice of his uncle to move to a drier climate, Doctor John Holliday boarded a train for Dallas. The year was 1873.

1   What is the best way to combine these sentences?

  A   Heeding the advice of his uncle to move to a drier climate, Doctor John Holliday boarded a train for Dallas, and the year was 1873.

  B   Heeding the advice of his uncle to move to a drier climate in 1873, Doctor John Holliday boarded a train for Dallas.

  C   In 1873, heeding the advice of his uncle to move to a drier climate, Doctor John Holliday boarded a train for Dallas.

  D   Doctor John Holliday, in 1873, boarded a train for Dallas, heeding the advice of his uncle to move to a drier climate.

Read this sentence from paragraph 1.

His uncle was a surgeon and corrected the birth defects by performing an operation.

2   Which part of the sentence can be deleted?

_____

_____

Read this sentence from paragraph 2.

But his disease continued to bother his body.

3   What is a more precise word to use in place of <u>bother</u>?
  A Assault   B Smash   C Thrash   D Remove

Copyright © American Book Company. DO NOT DUPLICATE. 1-888-264-5877.

4 In paragraph 2, what is the best way to revise this sentence to eliminate the misplaced modifier?

He would have problems in the middle of working on patients with coughing spells.

_____

_____

Read this sentence from paragraph 2.

Doc Holliday was well aware of this and faithful practiced with six-guns and knives.

5 How should the word <u>faithful</u> be written?

   A Faithly   **B** Faithfully   **C** Faithlessly   **D** Correct as is

Read this sentence from paragraph 2.

After sending many bullies and gunmen to meet their maker Doc moved from one western town to another narrowly avoiding being hanged.

6 What is the correct way to use commas in this sentence?

   A After sending many bullies and gunmen, to meet their maker Doc moved from one western town, to another narrowly avoiding being hanged.

   B After sending many bullies, and gunmen to meet their maker, Doc moved from one western town to another narrowly avoiding, being hanged.

   C After sending many bullies and gunmen to meet their maker, Doc moved from one western town to another narrowly, avoiding being hanged.

   D After sending many bullies and gunmen to meet their maker, Doc moved from one western town to another, narrowly avoiding being hanged.

7 Which word in paragraph 3 is misspelled?

   A Reputation

   B Littered

   C Reunitted

   D Revenge

Copyright © American Book Company. DO NOT DUPLICATE. 1-888-264-5877.

Read this sentence from paragaph3.

Wyatt, Holliday, and a few loyal deputies, hunted down the ruthless vicious members of the outlaw cowboy gang for the murder and maiming of numerous dedicated lawmen.

8   Should any of the adjectives have commas between them because they are coordinate adjectives? Identify the pairs of adjectives, and explain why they do or do not need commas.

_____

_____

_____

_____

Read these sentences from paragraph 4.

He asked for a shot of whiskey. He drank it down with great relish.

9   What is the best way to write this part of the text?

   A   He asked for a shot of whiskey but drank it down with great relish.

   B   He asked for a shot of whiskey; he drank it down with great relish.

   C   Asking for a shot of whiskey, he drank it down with great relish.

   D   Asking for a shot, he drank down the whiskey with great relish.

Read this sentence from paragraph 4.

Pondering his condition and the irony of his life he said "This is funny" and he died.

10   Where should you place commas in this sentence?

_____

_____

Copyright © American Book Company. DO NOT DUPLICATE. 1-888-264-5877.

CHAPTER 11 SUMMARY

You have learned many **conventions** of Standard American English and are expected to use them in your writing. Conventions include correctly using language in areas such as punctuation, sentence structure, and spelling.

Types of sentences include the **simple sentence**, **compound sentence**, **complex sentence**, and **compound-complex sentence**. A complete sentence is also known as an **independent clause**.

A **phrase** is a group of related words that does not include a subject and verb. Types include the **prepositional phrase**, **appositive phrase**, and **infinitive phrase**.

A **modifier** is a word or phrase that describes something and should be placed close to what it describes. When in the wrong place, **misplaced** or **dangling** modifiers can make the meaning of the sentence unclear or even nonsensical.

Adjectives are detail words and can tell us things about a noun's appearance and characteristics. **Coordinate adjectives** are adjectives in sequence that modify the same noun and need to be separated by a comma.

Spelling correctly is an important tool for writing and plays an important role in vocabulary building and reading comprehension. There are many spelling rules to study.

CHAPTER 11 REVIEW

L 1–3

DIRECTIONS	**A. Be sure to use what you reviewed in this chapter, and what you know about conventions in general, to proofread the essays that you worked on in chapter 10.**

Copyright © American Book Company. DO NOT DUPLICATE. 1-888-264-5877.

> **DIRECTIONS** B. Read this passage written by a student. Look for any errors that need to be corrected, and answer the questions that follow the passage.

The Arctic Fox

1   The arctic fox lives in the Arctic region of the Northern Hemisphere. In order to protect itself from the bitter cold of the tundra, the arctic fox's fur is a thick white coat in the winter. The white coat also provides excellent camouflage to conceal it in its snowy surroundings. Blending into its surroundings helps the arctic fox catch its prey while avoiding hungry polar bears at the same time. When temperatures rise in the summer, the rocks and plants of the tundra are exposed. To maintain its camouflage, the arctic fox's coat turns a brown or gray color.

2   The arctic fox an undiscriminating eater finds food in a variety of ways. It will even eat vegetables! Foxes that live near the coast will also feed on small birds, such as puffins. Inland, the fox typically feeds on small mammals. The arctic fox listens to catch small prey such as lemmings and voles for the sound

Arctic Fox Seasonal Fur Change

of scurrying rodents. Jumping up and down on the snow to break through it, rodents are caught in the paws of the fox.

3   Despite its broad diet, the arctic fox sometimes finds food to be scarce. When that happens, the fox will eat a polar bear's leftovers. At other times, the fox finds itself with loads of food. At these times, it will bury some of it in the snow and eat it later.

4   The fox's body has adapted to its frigid environment. Its ears, nose, and legs are all small and have little surface area. This reduces heat loss because there is less skin through which heat can escape. The thick fur on its paws protects the fox's feet from the snow and keeps frost out. Its long, bushy tail helps maintain balance and also provides extra cover to help keep it warm in cold weather. The animal's lush coat is the warmest covering of any mammle and does an exceptional job of maintaining body temperature. The physical features and behavioral charateristics of the arctic fox are a striking example of how all animals adapt in order to survive in their surroundings.

Copyright © American Book Company. DO NOT DUPLICATE. 1-888-264-5877.

Read this sentence from paragraph 1.

In order to protect itself from the bitter cold of the tundra, the arctic fox's fur is a thick white coat in the winter.

1   Which adjective should have a comma after it?

   A Bitter   **B** Arctic   **C** Thick   **D** White

2   Check for wordiness and redundancy in paragraph 1. Go to that paragraph, and cross out any words and phrases that are unnecessary.

Read this sentence from paragraph 2.

The arctic fox an undiscriminating eater finds food in a variety of ways.

3   Which is the correct way to write this sentence?

   A   The arctic fox, an undiscriminating eater finds food, in a variety of ways.

   B   The arctic fox, an undiscriminating eater, finds food in a variety of ways.

   C   The arctic fox an undiscriminating eater finds food, in a variety of ways.

   D   Correct as is

Read this sentence from paragraph 2.

The arctic fox listens to catch small prey such as lemmings and voles for the sound of scurrying rodents.

4   How should this sentence be written? Why?

_____

_____

_____

_____

Read this sentence from paragraph 3.

At other times, the fox finds itself with loads of food.

5   What is the most precise word choice to replace <u>loads</u>?

   A An abundance   **C** A great capacity

   B Heaps   **D** A lot

Copyright © American Book Company. DO NOT DUPLICATE. 1-888-264-5877.

Read this sentence from paragraph 2.

Jumping up and down on the snow to break through it, rodents are caught in the paws of the fox.

6   What is the best way to revise this sentence?

    A   Jumping up and down, rodents are caught in the paws of the fox on the snow to break through it.

    B   Rodents are caught, jumping up and down on the snow to break through it, in the paws of the fox.

    C   The fox catches rodents in its paws, jumping up and down on the snow to break through it.

    D   Jumping up and down on the snow to break through it, the fox catches rodents in its paws.

Read these sentences from paragraph 4.

Its ears, nose, and legs are all small and have little surface area. This reduces heat loss because there is less skin through which heat can escape.

7   What is the best way to write this information?

    A   Its ears, nose, and legs are all small, which reduces heat loss because there is less skin through which heat can escape.

    B   Its ears, nose, and legs are all small because there is less skin through which heat can escape, so less surface area means reduced heat loss.

    C   Its ears, nose, and legs are all small, so they have little surface area, and this reduces heat loss. There is less skin through which heat can escape.

    D   Correct as is

8   Are there any misspelled words in paragraph 4? If there are, how should they be spelled?

Activity

SL 1.a–d, L 1.d, 2.a, b

Have a peer review session with a group of classmates. Exchange reports or essays that you have been working on for class. Practice finding errors in each other's writing. This will help you to read carefully for errors in the work of another student. It will also point out some of the mistakes that you may be making in your writing. Remember that other students may not always be correct or catch everything. You should still carefully proofread your own work.

Copyright © American Book Company. DO NOT DUPLICATE. 1-888-264-5877.

Chapter 12
Speaking and Listening

This chapter covers the following seventh grade strand and standards:

Speaking and Listening

Comprehension and Collaboration

1. Engage effectively in a range of collaborative discussions (one-on-one, in groups, and teacher-led) with diverse partners on grade 7 topics, texts, and issues, building on others' ideas and expressing their own clearly.

   a. Come to discussions prepared, having read or researched material under study; explicitly draw on that preparation by referring to evidence on the topic, text, or issue to probe and reflect on ideas under discussion.

   b. Follow rules for collegial discussions, track progress toward specific goals and deadlines, and define individual roles as needed.

   c. Pose questions that elicit elaboration and respond to others' questions and comments with relevant observations and ideas that bring the discussion back on topic as needed.

   d. Acknowledge new information expressed by others and, when warranted, modify their own views.

2. Analyze the main ideas and supporting details presented in diverse media and formats (e.g., visually, quantitatively, orally) and explain how the ideas clarify a topic, text, or issue under study.

3. Delineate a speaker's argument and specific claims, evaluating the soundness of the reasoning and the relevance and sufficiency of the evidence.

Presentation of Knowledge and Ideas

4. Present claims and findings, emphasizing salient points in a focused, coherent manner with pertinent descriptions, facts, details, and examples; use appropriate eye contact, adequate volume, and clear pronunciation.

5. Include multimedia components and visual displays in presentations to clarify claims and findings and emphasize salient points.

6. Adapt speech to a variety of contexts and tasks, demonstrating command of formal English when indicated or appropriate.

In school and in life, you will not only read and write. You will also need to listen carefully and speak effectively. In this chapter, you will look at some ideas about media messages. You will also review how to make presentations and how to listen to speeches effectively. Finally, you will read about working successfully in a group.

ANALYZING MEDIA

People communicate through many kinds of **media** (which is the plural of *medium*). Newspapers, magazines, pamphlets, and books are examples of print media. Blogs and web content are examples of online media. Videos, television, and pictures are examples of visual media. Radio broadcasts and podcasts are examples of audio media.

Copyright © American Book Company. DO NOT DUPLICATE. 1-888-264-5877.

Chapter 12

You might need to study a message in a speech. Media gives you many ways to see or hear that speech: on the radio, on TV, online, or in another audiovisual medium. You can also gain information from a chart or graph that accompanies a text. In all these cases, you need to know how to interpret the message. You must be able to **analyze the main ideas and supporting details presented in media**. This allows you to see how each idea can clarify something that you are studying or thinking about.

Here is an example. Say that you are studying the earth's crust, mantle, and core in science class. You learn how volcanoes are formed and sometimes erupt. Reading can provide you with the theory and the facts. Your science book will likely give you **quantitative information** (data, numbers) about where volcanoes have formed and when they have erupted. But to really "get it," you will want to see a volcano in action. A video of a volcano erupting will give you the **visual information** that will make it clear how a volcano acts. If that video has a narrator, or your teacher narrates, all the better. Now you have added **oral information** about what is happening as you watch.

Just like writing, media can be used to persuade, to inform, or to entertain. You need to figure out the message and its main idea. Try it with this example.

Number of Latchkey Kids Grows

In today's economy, more and more parents need to work longer hours outside the home. This has created more latchkey kids than ever before. "Latchkey kids" is the term used to describe children who come home after school, let themselves in, and wait alone until parents return from work. Often, families with working parents have no alternative for their children.

A recent survey in our local area found that only 4 percent of mothers stay at home with children under the age of 10, as opposed to 7 percent five years ago. Over the last decade, the number of parents with children who work more than one job has increased by 6 percent.

There are some programs in the area that serve as places where kids can go so they are not alone. Two new community centers feature tutoring, fun activities, and healthy snacks, in addition to safe places to spend time. Of course, it costs money to run these centers. Most parents with latchkey kids cannot afford to enroll their children.

Copyright © American Book Company. DO NOT DUPLICATE. 1-888-264-5877.

What is the main idea communicated by the photograph?

What does it say to you? The girl in the picture looks sad and perhaps bored. The way she is hugging her teddy bear implies that she is lonely.

How does the photo add to your understanding of the article?

The words of the article along can tell you facts. But the photograph gives you a visual image that personalizes the issue. People reading the article would be more likely to have an emotional reaction about the story when looking at the picture. They can imagine how scared and lonely the little girl might feel in this situation. Some people might even be motivated to donate to the community center to help them help those in need.

EVALUATING A SPEAKER'S ARGUMENT

As you read earlier in the chapter, one type of media message is the kind you hear. A **speech** is an oral presentation in which the speaker delivers a message to an audience. The purpose of a speech can be almost anything. However, some common situations that call for speeches might be political campaigns of any level—national, statewide, or even at your school. Speeches might also be used to provide information, such as a person giving a book report. Can you think of some other situations that call for speeches?

You need to be able to judge what a speaker is saying and decide what you think about it. In this section, you will look at how to evaluate a **speaker's argument and claims**. You will also look at how to evaluate the speaker's reasoning and evidence.

REASONING AND EVIDENCE

Sound reasoning means an argument is valid and based on a true premise. You want to make sure a speaker is using sound reasoning. A speaker may use faulty reasoning to get you to see his or her point. The argument might be framed in a way that makes some details appear to be more convincing. Looking closer at the evidence can tell you whether the speaker's argument is solid.

Inductive reasoning is the process of arriving at a conclusion based on a set of observations. First, you observe specific details. This leads to forming a general conclusion based on the evidence. Inductive reasoning is valuable because it allows us to form ideas about groups of things in real life.

Example: Observation: Kyle was not at the track meet last weekend.

What you already know: Kyle is enthusiastic about running.

Conclusion: Kyle is probably sick.

Copyright © American Book Company. DO NOT DUPLICATE. 1-888-264-5877.

Page 215

You must be careful to come to a reasonable conclusion based on what you read and know. For instance, another conclusion to the example above could be "Jana now hates school and has decided to quit." Technically, it fits with the observation and what you already know—but the conclusion is not logical.

Deductive reasoning is the process of reaching a conclusion based on known facts. In order for the conclusion to be true, the assumptions that it is based on must be true. Deductive reasoning begins with general ideas and moves to specific examples.

Example: Major premise: People who like gourmet food enjoy eating.

Minor premise: My friend likes gourmet food.

Conclusion: My friend enjoys eating.

Deductive reasoning, like inductive reasoning, can be used incorrectly.

Example: Major premise: All humans need sleep.

Minor premise: Sparky needs sleep.

Conclusion: Sparky is a human being.

Of course, a creature isn't a human just because it sleeps. The only reasonable conclusion is that Sparky may or may not be a human. Sparky may be an odd name for a human, but the premises here give no reason to conclude anything about Sparky's species.

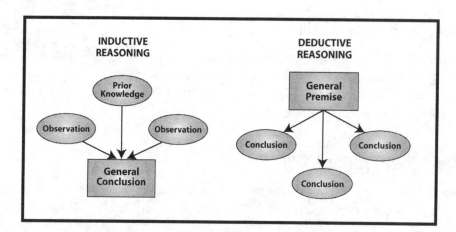

It is important to be aware of the particular reasoning a speaker uses. Double check it to make sure it is logical and not faulty.

Finally, you need to see if there is **sufficient evidence** to support the claim. As you know from other chapters about reading and writing, the strongest evidence is factual. It can be proved. It also needs to be relevant to the claim. For example, say that you are claiming that one movie was more successful than another. What facts would be sufficient evidence to support this claim? You could cite that the more successful movie earned more at the box office, more people went to see it, more copies of the DVD sold when it came out, and the film won more awards. You could also say that you liked it more because your favorite actor was in it. This final detail might be true, but it is not sufficient evidence to use in supporting your claim.

Copyright © American Book Company. DO NOT DUPLICATE. 1-888-264-5877.

Here is an example from a famous speech. Read the speech first. Then look at the explanations after it, which point out some of the ideas discussed so far in this chapter.

The Gettysburg Address (1863)

by Abraham Lincoln

Four score and seven years ago our fathers brought forth upon this continent, a new nation, conceived in liberty, and dedicated to the proposition that "all men are created equal."

Now we are engaged in a great civil war, testing whether that nation, or any nation so conceived, and so dedicated, can long endure. We are met on a great battlefield of that war. We have come to dedicate a portion of that field, as a final resting place for those who here gave their lives that that nation might live. It is altogether fitting and proper that we should do this.

But, in a larger sense, we can not dedicate, we can not consecrate, we can not hallow this ground. The brave men, living and dead, who struggled here, have consecrated it, far above our poor power to add or detract. The world will little note, nor long remember what we say here; while it can never forget what they did here. It is for us, the living, rather, to be dedicated here to the unfinished work which they who fought here have thus far so nobly advanced. It is rather for us to be here dedicated to the great task remaining before us—that from these honored dead we take increased devotion to that cause for which they gave the last full measure of devotion—that we here highly resolve that these dead shall not have died in vain—that this nation, under God, shall have a new birth of freedom—and that government of the people, by the people, for the people, shall not perish from the earth.

What is President Lincoln's argument? What main claims does he make?

The central argument of the speech is that people should remember the soldiers who have given their lives in the battle at Gettysburg and let it inspire them to work together. Lincoln starts out by reminding his listeners of the promises of the Declaration of Independence, where it states that "all men are created equal." He then makes a claim that this civil war is testing whether those promises can be kept. He also claims that those present are only commemorating what the soldiers have done, which is far more important. Finally, he claims that everyone listening needs to react with unity to thereby prevent the soldiers' sacrifice from having been in vain. With all of these claims, he is challenging listeners to learn from and be motivated by this battle that has taken place. He wants them to feel united and move forward to make the nation stronger.

Copyright © American Book Company. DO NOT DUPLICATE. 1-888-264-5877.

How sound is Lincoln's argument? Is the evidence he uses sufficient to support his claims?

To answer these questions, you need to look at the argument and each claim separately. Let's look first at the reasoning behind Lincoln's argument. The president is trying to inspire a new unity to come out of the adversity created by the civil war. He is saying it is the duty of those listening to dedicate themselves to reuniting the country after these brave soldiers have died protecting their freedoms.

On one hand, this may seem illogical, when the two opposing sides of the country have been disagreeing intensely over what those freedoms are. However, in the bigger picture, Lincoln's argument makes sense. He is saying that all of the fallen soldiers, on both sides, have died fighting for their ideals. They have shown bravery and vision no matter which side they were on. Lincoln's concluding point is that this battle marks the time to end the war, reunite the country, and fight for shared freedom.

Lincoln's claim is that the war is testing the very basis of the nation. Did Gettysburg really strain the foundation of the country more than other battles of its day? The evidence he cites is the amount of death and destruction at Gettysburg. However, he gives no statistics, and this was just one battle of many. So the evidence actually is not sufficient to support his claim. Don't worry, though—everyone in his audience knew what he meant! In this very brief speech, Lincoln does not go into detail. He is relying on those listening having some background knowledge about the war.

Sometimes speakers can rely on shared knowledge among listeners. However, you must evaluate carefully whether this strategy will work for your purposes or not.

Practice 1: Analyzing Media and Evaluating a Speaker's Argument

SL 2, 3

> **DIRECTIONS** Read this speech. Then answer the questions that follow.

School Should Not Be Year-Round

Recently, there has been much discussion about switching from the traditional school schedule to year-round school. Switching to year-round school would be a big mistake. Summer vacation serves an important purpose for students.

Aside from providing a much-needed break from school, summer vacations create a significant block of time for students to explore other interests. Summer is a time when kids can take art classes or try a new sport. The ten million kids who go away to camp each year would no longer enjoy an experience that has been proved to promote independence and self-sufficiency.

Copyright © American Book Company. DO NOT DUPLICATE. 1-888-264-5877.

Summer vacation is also a time that many students rely on being available for work. For many teens, working during the school year is not an option. There are homework demands and extracurricular activities. But in the summer, they can babysit, do yard work for neighbors, have a paper route, and so on. They depend on the money they earn from summer jobs for spending money as well as building up savings for college. It would be a serious sacrifice for many students to give up this time during which to earn money.

Despite these important and positive aspects of summer vacation, there are some people who are arguing for year-round school. The main reason these people have for moving to year-round school is their claim that much of what was learned during the school year is lost over the summer. They say that time is wasted re-teaching forgotten information in the fall. While this may be true to an extent, most teachers say that the amount of time spent re-teaching is in fact a very small portion of the school year. It is a small sacrifice to make to re-teach some material in order to preserve the benefits of having a summer vacation.

A traditional school schedule has served us well for generations. Having a summer break protects students from burnout while allowing them free time to develop new interests and maturity. Summer is also an important time for students to earn money. If an extra week or two of re-teaching is necessary to preserve the benefits of summer vacation, it is well worth it.

1 In which of the following sentences does the speaker state the main idea of this speech?

   A Switching to year-round school would be a big mistake.

   B Camp provides lessons in independence and self-sufficiency that school cannot.

   C They say that time is wasted re-teaching forgotten information in the fall.

   D A traditional school schedule has served us well for generations.

2 List two of the speaker's supporting details.

   _____

   _____

3 The speaker claims that many kids would be negatively affected by not having a break from school in the summer. What relevant evidence does the author provide as support?

   _____

   _____

Copyright © American Book Company. DO NOT DUPLICATE. 1-888-264-5877.

4 People in favor of year-round school might find that the speaker's argument lacks sound reasoning. What is a weak point of the speech?

    A It contains no statistics about how many students would be affected.

    B It gives no valid reasons for why students should have the summer off.

    C It only presents one reason for people wanting school to be year-round.

    D It overestimates the amount of homework that students are assigned.

5 What visual would best help clarify the advantages of a summer break?

_____

_____

Look at this photograph, and answer the questions that follow.

6 Which statement best communicates the main idea of this photograph?

    A This man has been a dairy farmer all of his life.

    B This man supports the healthy habit of drinking milk.

    C This man cannot eat meat and needs to find alternatives.

    D This man is promoting the local fresh produce market.

7 What type of message might this photograph accompany? Think about what it could best help to illustrate. How would it clarify the message?

_____

_____

Copyright © American Book Company. DO NOT DUPLICATE. 1-888-264-5877.

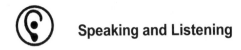

Speaking and Listening

MAKING A PRESENTATION

Sometimes instead of writing text that will be read, you will be asked to write something that will be recited out loud. You might need to make a presentation or give a speech in class. Here are some important points to keep in mind about speaking.

PURPOSE AND AUDIENCE

As with writing, the **purpose of a speech** varies. A speech can be written to inform, to describe, to explain, to persuade, or to entertain. Similarly, the **audience** of the speech also will vary. As with a written message, it is important to know your audience. This will dictate how formal the speech's language should be. It will also clarify what the audience might already know and what you need to tell them.

EFFECTIVE WAYS TO MAKE A PRESENTATION

Making presentations can be difficult. In fact, public speaking has often been referred to as the number-one fear that people have. But you can avoid feeling overwhelmed by following some guidelines for being prepared and engaging your audience.

As you prepare your presentation, be sure to make notes about or memorize your key points. Remember that you need to **state claims clearly** and **provide relevant evidence**.

Organizing speeches is similar to organizing writing. There must be a clear introduction, body, and conclusion. Make sure to state your argument early on. Emphasize the major supporting details as you speak. Be sure to present all of your information in a **focused and coherent order**.

Let's look at an example of a student preparing a presentation.

Charlie wants to make a speech about why his school should adopt a club program. Look at how he begins:

> Middle school is a time of growth. We are developing mentally and physically. During middle school, we are also learning about our individual interests. What better time than now for us to explore interests that go beyond athletics and academics? *Highland Hills Middle School needs a schoolwide club program.*

The italicized sentence is Charlie's argument. It is clear and focused. It gets directly to the point of what Charlie wants to communicate to his audience. Some relevant supporting details might include the following.

A club program would increase self-esteem among the students.

A club program would result in better behavior among the students.

A club program would be a good motivator for students to maintain academic excellence.

Page 221

Copyright © American Book Company. DO NOT DUPLICATE. 1-888-264-5877.

When you speak in front of others, some specific behaviors can help you engage the audience. For one, making **eye contact** with your audience is important. This is a way for you to connect with the people who are listening to your speech. By making eye contact, you can build a more personal connection with your audience, strengthening the impact of your words. Also, pay attention to your **speaking rate**. Be careful not to speak too quickly or too slowly. Speaking too slowly might cause listeners to tune you out, while talking too quickly might cause listeners to become confused. They might not be able to keep up with the points in your speech. In addition, be sure to use **clear pronunciation** so listeners can understand what you say.

One thing you might need to do is **adapt a speech for a variety of contexts or tasks**. An example is making a presentation in science class about a project. In this case, you would be confident about what your classmates already know about the topic. After all, the whole class has learned about it together. As you present your project in class, you do not need to explain much for your classmates to understand your point. But say that your project is later selected for presentation at a science fair, where you will be presenting to a much wider audience. Some of the people listening might not know as much about science as your classmates do. You might need to explain your project and the scientific principles behind it in simple terms so that this audience will understand you fully. You might use even more formal language than you did in your classroom presentation.

You can see speech adaptation clearly in the case of campaign speeches. You can often watch these on TV. A candidate for political office adapts his or her message. For example, say a candidate speaks to an audience of blue-collar workers. The candidate might appear with shirtsleeves rolled up and wearing a hardhat. When the candidate talks to middle-class Americans, this casual dress sends a signal that the candidate is one of them. Later, the candidate, wearing a neatly pressed suit, might address professors and students at a university. The political promises about improvements might be the same. But this time, the message might include the importance of supporting education. This is all part of knowing an audience. A speaker must think about which points are important to certain listeners and how to use these ideas to get their attention.

Copyright © American Book Company. DO NOT DUPLICATE. 1-888-264-5877.

Practice 2: Making a Presentation

SL 4–6

DIRECTIONS   **A. Answer these questions about making a presentation.**

Here is the beginning of a presentation that Justin is making in class.

> What do you see in this picture? Grasses, mud, salt water—not much else, right? These are parts of the salt marsh. There is not much variety among the plants here. That's because the plants that grow here must like both the saltiness and being at least partly in water. That spiky-looking bush over there is a glasswort. To the left, this taller clump of green foliage is cordgrass. Now look at that little patch of purple at the bottom of the picture, and I'll show you a flower that actually blooms here.

1   What are the best visuals for Justin to use in his presentation?

   A   Drawings of various plants with their parts labeled

   B   Detailed photographs of the plants in a salt marsh

   C   A map showing the salt marshes in the United States

   D   Satellite photographs of a large salt marsh

2   Why does Justin ask questions at the beginning?

   A   He is asking the listeners to answer.

   B   He does not know what is in the picture.

   C   He wants listeners to observe and pay attention.

   D   He is stalling for time until he thinks of what to say.

3   What are Justin's main points? What should he include in his presentation to support these points fully?

_____

_____

_____

_____

4   What is the purpose of Justin's speech?

_____

_____

Copyright © American Book Company. DO NOT DUPLICATE. 1-888-264-5877.

Mandy is running for a position in the student government at Kilgore Middle School. She plans to address the following topics.

1. how I will accomplish my goals

2. a little bit about me

3. what I will accomplish

4. *why I want to run*

5   In which order should she present these topics?

   A   1, 2, 3, 4   **B**   2, 3, 4, 1   **C**   2, 4, 3, 1   **D**   3, 2, 1, 4

6   What is the purpose of Mandy's speech?

_____

_____

> **DIRECTIONS**   **B. Use the instructions below to work on a presentation.**
>
> **Take out your essays that you worked on for chapters 9, 10 and 11. Choose one, and adapt it into a focused, coherent presentation. Be sure to include relevant evidence and sound reasoning. Choose a multimedia display to support your speech. Practice your presentation, and then make a video or audio recording of it, or give the presentation to a group or in class.**

PARTICIPATING IN A GROUP

Sometimes you will speak to a smaller group. It may not be to make a speech but rather to work as a team. There are some standards to follow that will help you productively contribute to the group. Let's take a look at three focus areas that can help ensure you will be a great team member.

USE YOUR TIME WISELY

If you are working with a partner or small group on a project, be sure to do your part. It is important to **prepare for discussions**. That means reading any material that you need to understand or doing research that you have been asked to do. This way, the group can focus on the task at hand without being delayed by one member who must get up to speed. Then, when you meet, take a moment to explain what information you found out. **Draw evidence from your reading and research** toward the topic you are working on.

Copyright © American Book Company. DO NOT DUPLICATE. 1-888-264-5877.

COMMUNICATE CLEARLY AND SUPPORTIVELY

Each group member needs to communicate well to make the team more effective. Be clear about your ideas, and make sure what you add to the discussion is relevant to the group's goal. **Listen to the ideas of others** and try to understand them before you respond to them. Then **ask questions to clarify**. Every question you pose should be strong, relevant, and on task. You may not agree with every idea, but keep in mind that you might be the one to change your viewpoint.

FOLLOW THE GUIDELINES FOR COLLABORATION

At the outset of your group's discussion, define specific goals. What is it that your group wants to accomplish during the discussion? If the steps to meet the goals are not clear, be sure to ask questions that help the group work toward these goals. Then **track progress toward the goals**. Keep **deadlines** in mind.

Another way to help a group run smoothly is to **define individual goals**. Of course, the group has a single goal, but how does each person help meet it? In some groups, everyone might do a bit of the same thing (such as research). In other groups, you might divide up activities so that it is clear who should be doing what. This division of roles ensures that everyone participates and that every task gets finished. Here are some typical roles for some kinds of groups.

Group Member Roles	
Role	**Description**
Leader	This student is in charge of organizing and motivating the group. He or she makes sure that the project (paper, presentation, or so on) meets the standards set out by the instructor. The leader also oversees the work of other members and helps the group reach agreements.
Information Gatherer	This student searches for useful and relevant information for the project and comes up with research data that will help the group complete its task.
Recorder	This student takes and distributes notes about group discussions so that everyone can understand what they agreed to do. He or she also keeps track of group data and sources.
Reporter	This student is responsible for summarizing the group's progress and findings to the rest of the group, the instructor, or to other groups.
Timekeeper	This student records the time spent on each portion of a meeting and ensures that the group stays on track. When there is a speech or debate, the timekeeper makes sure team members start and stop speaking in the allotted time.

Copyright © American Book Company. DO NOT DUPLICATE. 1-888-264-5877.

Practice 3: Participating in a Group

SL 1.a–d

> DIRECTIONS   **Read and answer the questions.**

1 Martin is meeting with his group to discuss each member's progress. Which of the following should Martin do in the meeting?

   A Organize his notes as other members share their progress.

   B Make sure all hear his report and think he has done the most.

   C Speak loudly so that everyone in the group will listen to him.

   D Listen carefully as others tell what they have accomplished.

2 Hannah is leading a group that is doing a research project. Which of the following is the most appropriate behavior for Hannah to use in a meeting?

   A Refuse to be distracted by other people's opinions of her work.

   B Suggest the group have a celebration after the project is finished.

   C Ask clarifying questions after the others present their information.

   D Demand to see the research sources used by others in the group.

3 Lamar is in a group that is preparing for an upcoming debate. He has been assigned the task of timekeeper as the group practices. What does he need to do?

   A He is responsible for making sure each debater starts and finishes on time.

   B He needs to organize and motivate the group to do its best in the debate.

   C He should take notes about each person's debate topic and distribute them.

   D He must summarize the meetings and progress for their faculty advisor.

4 What is the most important action to take before a meeting with a work partner or group?

   _____

   _____

5 You are in a meeting, and someone keeps talking while you have some points to add. What should you do?

   _____

   _____

Copyright © American Book Company. DO NOT DUPLICATE. 1-888-264-5877.

Activity

SL 2, 3

Attend or watch a video of an organized meeting (a city council meeting, PTA meeting, televised session of Congress, church group meeting, school board meeting, student council meeting, and so on). Note the strategies used to conduct the meeting in an orderly fashion. Then meet as a class or in small groups to answer the following questions:

Who appeared to be the leader?

What strategies did the group use to ensure orderly communication?

How did group members gain the floor?

What seemed to be the agenda of the meeting?

What consensus, if any, did the group come to?

Copyright © American Book Company. DO NOT DUPLICATE. 1-888-264-5877.

CHAPTER 12 SUMMARY

People communicate through many kinds of **media**.

You must be able to **analyze the main ideas and supporting details presented in media**.

Through media, you can gain **quantitative information**, **visual information**, and **oral information**.

A **speech** is an oral presentation in which the speaker delivers a message to an audience.

You must know how to evaluate a **speaker's argument and claims**.

Sound reasoning means an argument is valid and based on a true premise. **Inductive reasoning** is the process of arriving at a conclusion based on a set of observations. **Deductive reasoning** is the process of reaching a conclusion based on known facts.

You need to evaluate whether a speaker presents **sufficient evidence** to support a claim.

The **purpose of a speech** can be to inform, to describe, to explain, to persuade, or to entertain. The **audience** of a speech will vary but in another important consideration.

When you make a presentation, be sure to **state claims clearly** and **provide relevant evidence**.

Present all of your information in a **focused and coherent order**.

Make **eye contact** with the audience, pay attention to your **speaking rate**, and use **clear pronunciation**.

You also might need to **adapt a speech for a variety of contexts or tasks**.

When working with a partner or small group, you should do the following:

Prepare for discussions and **draw evidence from your reading and research** when presenting your findings to the group.

Communicate clearly and supportively, which means you should **listen to the ideas of others** and **ask questions to clarify**.

Follow the guidelines for collaboration by determining goals for the groups, **track progress toward the goals**, and keep **deadlines** in mind.

Be sure to **define individual goals** so that everyone in the group has clear goals. Typical roles in a group include **leader**, **information gatherer**, **recorder**, **reporter**, and **timekeeper**.

Copyright © American Book Company. DO NOT DUPLICATE. 1-888-264-5877.

CHAPTER 12 REVIEW

SL 1–6

> DIRECTIONS   **A. Read this speech, and then answer the questions that follow.**

My name is Olivia Martin, and I am a seventh grade student at Lincoln Junior-Senior High School. I have come to this school board meeting to speak to you about a financial program that I think will benefit the students at Lincoln. I have done some research into student savings programs. I hope you will listen and think about our future with this research in mind.

Last month, a representative from Center City Bank came to talk to this school board. He talked about an in-school savings-account program for students. He gave a brief overview of the bank program and the role the school would play in the program. At that time, the board voted to discuss the program at a later time. This made me wonder about the lack of financial education in our school. I think we need to change that.

Since then, I have taken time to learn more about in-school banking programs. I have studied what programs are available and which ones have had success. My research included looking at the overall financial education of students. What I learned made me certain that an in-school banking program would benefit students here. It would be a real-world application of the math we learn, give us a sense of responsibility, and emphasize the importance of saving.

To begin, let me tell you what I mean by an in-school banking program. A bank representative visits the school and works with students to set up a school branch. Some students get trained to work as tellers; they handle the deposits. Each week during homeroom, the tellers can take deposits from students and place the money in the correct accounts. The Center City Bank rep comes by each week and transfers the money to actual accounts at the bank.

The plan is flexible. Students can deposit one or two dollars, all the way up to ten dollars, per week. They don't need to deposit the same amount each time, or even make a deposit each time. All withdrawals from an account must be done in person at the bank. No one under eighteen may withdraw more than fifty dollars or close an account without a parent or guardian's signature.

Copyright © American Book Company. DO NOT DUPLICATE. 1-888-264-5877.

After learning more about this program, I looked up how many schools have this or a similar program in place. I was surprised to learn there are many thousands of schools across the country that take advantage of this opportunity. They range in size from small individual schools to large school districts. I didn't find any reported problems or negative feedback about the program. Some people said there is definitely a learning curve in the set-up of the program, but they said the bank assisted them every step of the way. For example, Mr. Thompson, the superintendent of Pine Hill Regional District, said, "The program was so successful in our middle and high schools that we expanded it to include our elementary schools. Now even our kindergarten students have an opportunity to develop their financial sense. Not only have our students benefited financially from this program, but they have also exhibited an increase in math scores."

Finally, I looked at the possible long-term effects. I read about how students eventually go to college with little or no understanding of finance. Before they even finish decorating their dorm rooms, they are flooded with credit-card offers. With little practice in managing money, they can find themselves over their heads in debt. A recent study shows that students who maintain their own savings accounts prior to college are much less likely to fall into this negative situation.

To me, this information adds up to one conclusion: In-school banking programs in middle and high schools have benefited students in the short and long run. We are a middle and high school, so our students will benefit from an in-school banking program. The program would give students here a leg up in learning about personal finances.

I thank you for allowing me to speak here tonight. I hope you will consider bringing a banking program to our school.

1   What is the speaker's argument?

    A   The idea of in-school banking is quickly spreading across the country.

    B   Students should be given a bigger role in the school's financial planning.

    C   The school should consider a banking program because it will benefit students.

    D   Students should take the time to complete thorough research before speaking in public.

2   What claims does Olivia make? Is her evidence sufficient to support each claim?

Copyright © American Book Company. DO NOT DUPLICATE. 1-888-264-5877.

3 Who is Olivia mainly addressing in the speech?

    A   Her parents   **C**   Seventh grade students

    B   The school board   **D**   The bank representative

4 List three things that can Olivia do to engage her audience most effectively.

_____

_____

_____

_____

5 Olivia wants to display a visual during her speech. Which image would support her information and viewpoint the best?

    A   A graph showing student savings over five years

    B   A poster advertising a bank's savings program

    C   A video tour of dorm rooms at a local college campus

    D   A photograph of the vault at the Center City Bank

6 Which sentences from the speech contain an example of deductive reasoning?

    A   I have done some research into student savings programs. I hope you will listen to me and think about our future with this research in mind.

    B   What I learned made me certain that an in-school banking program would benefit students here. It would be a real-world application of the math we learn, give us a sense of responsibility, and emphasize the importance of saving.

    C   Before they even finish decorating their dorm rooms, they are flooded with credit-card offers. With little practice in managing money, they can find themselves over their heads in debt.

    D   In-school banking programs in middle and high schools have benefited students in the short and long run. We are a middle and high school, so our students will benefit from an in-school banking program.

7 A group of students has been invited to meet with the school board and parents to discuss starting an in-school savings program. You will be part of the student group. You will meet ahead of time to discuss your ideas, which will be presented to the school board. What are the best steps to take at your first meeting to make sure your group is ready to meet with the school board?

_____

_____

_____

_____

Copyright © American Book Company. DO NOT DUPLICATE. 1-888-264-5877.

> **DIRECTIONS** **B. Complete the following speaking task.**

Choose one of the topics below. Do some research, and write a presentation to give in class. Review this chapter for tips about how to make your presentation more interesting and informative.

Possible Speaking Topics

Your principal is having a contest for students. You can recommend one special class that the school should add for students. Create a presentation in which you tell what kind of class should be added and why, and back up your claims with evidence.

In the last century, many helpful inventions and product innovations have appeared. Choose one of these advances that you think has most influenced people's lives. Make a presentation to explain it, and tell why you believe your choice is the most important invention of the century.

The Golden Rule states: "Treat others as you would want to be treated." Discuss why this rule is a good policy.

> **DIRECTIONS** **C. Work in a group to complete the following task.**

Six new students have just enrolled in your school. Someone has had the idea of connecting each new student with several existing students who can show the new student around, communicate all that the school has to offer, and generally make him or her feel welcome. Your principal has asked a small group of students to help organize this program over the next week. Working in a small group, use the skills of group communication mentioned in this chapter to come up with a plan of action. Work together, and use your own paper to make notes about what you will do. Then get together and share your plan with other groups. Collaborate to come up with a master plan that uses all of the best ideas.

Copyright © American Book Company. DO NOT DUPLICATE. 1-888-264-5877.